CLEP

College Level Examination Program

**History
Series**

Copyright © 2016

All rights reserved. No part of the material protected by this copyright notice may be reproduced or utilized in any form or by any means, electronic or mechanical, including photocopying or recording or by any information storage and retrievable system, without written permission from the copyright holder.

To obtain permission(s) to use the material from this work for any purpose including workshops or seminars, please submit a written request to:

XAMonline, Inc.
21 Orient Avenue
Melrose, MA 02176
Toll Free: 1-800-301-4647
Email: info@xamonline.com
Web: www.xamonline.com
Fax: 1-617-583-5552

Library of Congress Cataloging-in-Publication Data
Wynne, Sharon

CLEP History Series/ Sharon Wynne
   ISBN: 978-1-60787-578-9

1. CLEP   2. Study Guides   3. History

Disclaimer:
The opinions expressed in this publication are the sole works of XAMonline and were created independently from the College Board, or other testing affiliates. Between the time of publication and printing, specific test standards as well as testing formats and website information may change that are not included in part or in whole within this product. XAMonline develops sample test questions, and they reflect similar content as on real tests; however, they are not former tests. XAMonline assembles content that aligns with test standards but makes no claims nor guarantees candidates a passing score.

Printed in the United States of America
CLEP History Series
ISBN: 978-1-60787-578-9

TABLE OF CONTENTS

American Government 1

    Sample Test 3

    Answer Key 22

    Rationales 23

History of the United States I 75

    Sample Test 77

    Answer Key 103

    Rationales 104

History of the United States II 166

    Sample Test 167

    Answer Key 199

    Rationales 200

Western Civilization I 263

    Sample Test 265

    Answer Key 292

    Rationales 293

Western Civilization II 359

    Sample Test 361

    Answer Key 391

    Rationales 392

AMERICAN GOVERNMENT

Description of the Examination

The American Government examination covers material that is usually taught in a one-semester introductory course in American government and politics at the college level. The scope and emphasis of the exam reflect what is most commonly taught in introductory American government and politics courses in political science departments around the United States. These courses go beyond a general understanding of civics to incorporate political processes and behavior. The exam covers topics such as the institutions and policy processes of the federal government, the federal courts and civil liberties, political parties and interest groups, political beliefs and behavior, and the content and history of the Constitution.

The examination contains approximately 100 questions to be answered in 90 minutes. Some of these are pretest questions that will not be scored. Any time candidates spend on tutorials and providing personal information is in addition to the actual testing time.

Knowledge and Skills Required

Questions on the American Government examination require candidates to demonstrate one or more of the following abilities in the approximate proportions indicated.

- Knowledge of American government and politics (about 55%–60% of the exam)

- Understanding of typical patterns of political processes and behavior (including the components of the behavioral situation of a political actor), the principles used to explain or justify various governmental structures and procedures (about 30%–35% of the exam)

- Analysis and interpretation of simple data that are relevant to American government and politics (10%–15% of the exam)

The subject matter of the American Government examination is drawn from the following topics. The percentages next to the main topics indicate the approximate percentage of exam questions on that topic.

30%–35% Institutions and Policy Processes: Presidency, Bureaucracy, and Congress
- The major formal and informal institutional arrangements and powers
- Structure, policy processes, and outputs
- Relationships among these three institutions and links between them and political parties, interest groups, the media, and public opinion

15%–20% Federal Courts, Civil Liberties, and Civil Rights
- Structure and processes of the judicial system with emphasis on the role and influence of the Supreme Court
- The development of civil rights and civil liberties by judicial interpretation
- The Bill of Rights
- Incorporation of the Bill of Rights
- Equal protection and due process

AMERICAN GOVERNMENT

15%–20% **Political Parties and Interest Groups**
- Political parties (including their function, organization, mobilization, historical development, and effects on the political process)
- Interest groups (including the variety of activities they typically undertake and their effects on the political process)
- Elections (including the electoral process)

10%–15% **Political Beliefs and Behavior**
- Processes by which citizens learn about politics
- Political participation (including voting behavior)
- Public opinion
- Beliefs that citizens hold about their government and its leaders
- Political culture (the variety of factors that predispose citizens to differ from one another in terms of their political perceptions, values, attitudes, and activities)
- The influence of public opinion on political leaders

AMERICAN GOVERNMENT

SAMPLE TEST

DIRECTIONS: Read each item and select the best response.

1. **The term that best describes how the Supreme Court can block laws that may be unconstitutional from being enacted is:**

   A. Jurisprudence

   B. Judicial review

   C. Exclusionary rule

   D. Right of petition

   E. The blocking right

2. **On the spectrum of American politics, the label that most accurately describes voters "to the right of center" is:**

   A. Moderates

   B. Liberals

   C. Conservatives

   D. Socialists

   E. Independents

3. **The branch of government responsible for developing the federal budget is:**

   A. The legislative branch

   B. The judicial branch

   C. The executive branch

   D. The Congress

   E. Each of the 50 states

4. **The United States legislature is bicameral. This means:**

   A. It consists of several houses

   B. It consists of two houses

   C. It meets twice a year

   D. The vice president is in charge of the legislature when in session.

   E. It has an upper house and a lower house

AMERICAN GOVERNMENT

5. **What Supreme Court ruling established the principal of judicial review?**

    A. *Jefferson v. Madison*

    B. *Lincoln v. Douglas*

    C. *Marbury v. Madison*

    D. *Marbury v. Jefferson*

    E. *Lincoln v. Davis*

6. **To be eligible to be elected president, one must:**

    A. Be a U.S. citizen for at least five years

    B. Be a U.S. citizen for seven years

    C. Have been born a U.S. citizen

    D. Be a naturalized U.S. citizen

    E. Have been born to a U.S. citizen

7. **The international organization established to work for world peace at the end of Second World War is the:**

    A. League of Nations

    B. Union of Nations

    C. United Federation of Nations

    D. United Nations

    E. United World League

8. **In the United States, the right to declare war is a power of:**

    A. The president

    B. Congress

    C. The executive branch

    D. The Supreme Court

    E. The states

9. **Which of the following is an example of a direct democracy?**

    A. Elected representatives

    B. Greek city–states

    C. The United States Senate

    D. The United States House of Representatives

    E. State legislatures

10. **To plead the Fifth Amendment means to:**

    A. Refuse to speak so one does not incriminate oneself

    B. Plead "no contest" in court

    C. Ask for freedom of speech

    D. Ask to appear before a judge when charged with a crime

    E. Petition for self-defense

AMERICAN GOVERNMENT

11. **The political document that was the first to try to organize the newly *independent* American colonies was the:**

    A. Declaration of Independence

    B. Articles of Confederation

    C. Constitution

    D. Confederate States

    E. Magna Carta

12. **In 1792, Alexis de Tocqueville came to America to study the:**

    A. Economic system

    B. Congress

    C. Prison system

    D. Election process

    E. Constitution

13. **The first ten amendments to the Constitution are called:**

    A. Bill of petition

    B. Petition of Rights

    C. Rights of Man

    D. Constitutional rights

    E. Bill of Rights

14. **Socialists believe that the government should have a _____ role in the economy.**

    A. minimal

    B. controlling

    C. equal to business'

    D. less than the individual's

    E. nonexistent

15. **One difference between *totalitarianism* and *authoritarianism* is that totalitarianism believes in:**

    A. Total control over all aspects of society

    B. Minimum government control

    C. There is no difference

    D. The difference is unknown

    E. Authoritative control over government

16. **The constitution is called a "living document" because:**

    A. It has the ability to change with different times

    B. It was created by people

    C. It is a static document

    D. Excessive reliance on the Constitution will kill it

    E. Anyone can change it

17. **In the feudal system, who has the most power?**

    A. The peasant or serf

    B. The noble or lord

    C. The worker

    D. The merchant

    E. The soldier

18. **The idea that the European powers should stay out of the affairs of the American hemisphere is known as:**

    A. Containment policy

    B. The Eisenhower Doctrine

    C. Neo-isolationism

    D. The Truman Doctrine

    E. The Monroe Doctrine

19. **The Exclusionary Rule prevents:**

    A. Illegally seized evidence from being used in court

    B. Persons from incriminating themselves in court

    C. Police from entering a private home for any reason

    D. Evidence, however gathered, from being used in court if one side in a court case objects to it

    E. Evidence, regardless of how it is collected, from being excluded

20. **The idea that "the government is best that governs least" is most closely associated with:**

    A. The Soviet communist system

    B. The American free enterprise system

    C. British conservatism

    D. Mussolini's corporate state

    E. A dictatorship

21. **In the United States Constitution, political parties are:**

    A. Never mentioned

    B. Called "a necessary part of the political process"

    C. Most effective if there are only two major ones

    D. Called harmful to the political process

    E. Required to have at least 100 members

22. **Civil suits deal mostly, but not exclusively, with:**

    A. Money

    B. Violent crime

    C. The government

    D. Political fundraising

    E. Mental illness

AMERICAN GOVERNMENT

23. "Common law" refers mostly to:

    A. The precedents and traditions that have gone before in society and have become accepted norms

    B. The laws dealing with the "common people"

    C. Law that is written and codified

    D. The House of Commons in Great Britain

    E. Law that is common among different countries

24. Anarchists believe in:

    A. Strong government

    B. Corporate state system

    C. Weak, mild government

    D. Populist government

    E. No government

25. The U.S. government's federal system consists of:

    A. Three parts: the executive, the legislative, and the judiciary

    B. Three parts: the legislative, the Congress, and the presidency

    C. Four parts: the executive, the judiciary, the courts, and the legislative

    D. Two parts: the government, and the governed

    E. Two parts: the president and state governors

26. **One difference between a presidential and a parliamentary system is that in a parliamentary system:**

    A. The prime minister is head of government, while a president or monarch is head of state

    B. The president is head of government, and the vice president is head of state

    C. The president pro tempore of the Senate is head of state, while the prime minister is head of government

    D. The president appoints the head of state

    E. The prime minister is elected

AMERICAN GOVERNMENT

27. **The American concept of Manifest Destiny means:**

    A. America had a right to spread across the American continent from coast to coast

    B. The United States should respect the right of native peoples it encounters in its push westward

    C. The rest of the world powers should stay out of North America

    D. America should strive to be the dominant world power

    E. America belonged to the native people of the region

28. **In an indirect democracy:**

    A. All the people together decide on issues

    B. People elect representatives to act for them

    C. Democracy can never really work

    D. Government is less efficient than in a direct democracy

    E. People directly elect their representatives

29. **In a communist system, _____ controls the means of production.**

    A. A professional managerial class

    B. The owners of business and industry

    C. The workers

    D. The parliament

    E. The state

30. **Congress can override a president's veto with a _____ vote.**

    A. One-half

    B. Two-thirds

    C. Six-tenths

    D. Three-fourths

    E. Four-fifths

31. **To become a citizen, an individual generally must have lived in the United States for at least:**

    A. Six years

    B. Five years

    C. One year

    D. Ten years

    E. Fifteen years

AMERICAN GOVERNMENT

32. **Give the correct order of the following: the Constitution, the Declaration of Independence, and the Articles of Confederation.**

    A. The Constitution, the Declaration of Independence, the Articles of Confederation

    B. The Declaration of Independence, the Constitution, the Articles of Confederation

    C. The Declaration of Independence, the Articles of Confederation, the Constitution

    D. The Articles of Confederation, the Declaration of Independence, the Constitution.

    E. The Constitution, the Articles of Confederation, the Declaration of Independence

33. **The ability of the president to veto an act of Congress is an example of:**

    A. Separation of powers

    B. Checks and balances

    C. Judicial review

    D. Presidential prerogative

    E. Executive order

34. **To impeach an elected official means to:**

    A. Bring charges against the official

    B. Remove the official from office

    C. Reelect the official

    D. Override the official's veto

    E. Arrest the official

35. **An obligation identified with citizenship is:**

    A. Belonging to a political party

    B. Educating oneself

    C. Running for political office

    D. Donating to a political party

    E. Voting

36. **The doctrine that sought to keep communism from spreading was:**

    A. The Cold War

    B. Rollback

    C. Containment

    D. Détente

    E. Mutually assured destruction

AMERICAN GOVERNMENT

37. The power to declare war, establish a postal system, and coin money rests with which branch of the government?

    A. Presidential

    B. Judicial

    C. Legislative

    D. Executive

    E. State governments

38. If a president neither signs nor vetoes a bill for ten days, the bill becomes:

    A. A pocket veto

    B. A refused law

    C. Unconstitutional

    D. A presidential veto

    E. A passed law

39. What was George Washington's advice to Americans about foreign policy?

    A. America should have strong alliances

    B. America should avoid alliances

    C. Foreign policy should take precedence over domestic policy

    D. Domestic policy should take precedence over foreign policy

    E. American should build a big military

40. The belief that government should stay out of economic affairs is called:

    A. Mercantilism

    B. Laissez-faire

    C. Democratic socialism

    D. Corporatism

    E. Socialism

41. The term that describes the division of government function is:

    A. Free enterprise

    B. Constitutional prerogative

    C. Checks and balances

    D. Divisive government

    E. Separation of powers

42. Which of the following is an important idea expressed in the Declaration of Independence?

    A. People have the right to change their government

    B. People should obey the government authority

    C. A monarchy is a bad thing

    D. Indirect democracy is best

    E. People should disobey authority

AMERICAN GOVERNMENT

43. **Oligarchy refers to:**

    A. Rule of a single leader

    B. Rule of a single political party

    C. Rule by a select few

    D. Rule by many

    E. Rule by a family

44. **The Judiciary Act of 1789 established the:**

    A. Supreme Court

    B. Principle of judicial review

    C. State court system

    D. Federal and circuit court system

    E. The number of justices on the Supreme Court

45. **The international organization established to work for world peace at the end of the First World War was the:**

    A. United Earth League

    B. Confederate States

    C. United Nations

    D. League of Nations

    E. Allied Foundation

46. **Which statement closely resembles the political philosophy of John Hobbes?**

    A. Citizens should give unquestioning obedience to the state authority so long as it can maintain public order

    B. Citizens have a right to rise against the state whenever they choose

    C. All state authority is basically evil and should be eliminated

    D. People are generally good and cooperative if given a chance

    E. People should not be trusted

47. **In the United States, the right to declare war is a power of:**

    A. The president

    B. Congress

    C. The executive

    D. The states

    E. The Supreme Court

48. **A tort is:**

    A. A private or civil action brought into court

    B. A type of confection

    C. A penal offense

    D. One who solicits

    E. A case without any award

AMERICAN GOVERNMENT

49. A boycott is:

    A. The refusal to buy goods or services

    B. An imbalance of trade

    C. The refusal to speak in court

    D. A writ of assistance

    E. An agreement to trade

50. In the United States, checks and balances refers to:

    A. The ability of each branch of government to "check," or limit, the actions of the other branches

    B. Balance of payments

    C. International law

    D. The federal deficit

    E. Setting the federal budget

51. An amendment is:

    A. A change or addition to the United States Constitution

    B. The right of a state to secede from the Union

    C. The addition of a state to the Union

    D. The right of the Supreme Court to check actions of Congress and the president

    E. Changing congressional bills

52. The executive branch refers to:

    A. The Senate

    B. The legislature

    C. Congress

    D. The president and vice president

    E. The CEOs in the United States

53. An ex post facto law is:

    A. A law made against an act after it has been committed

    B. A law proclaimed unconstitutional by the Supreme Court

    C. An executive order

    D. A law relating to the postal system

    E. A law without basis

54. The judiciary refers to:

    A. The president

    B. Congress

    C. The legal system

    D. The system of states' rights

    E. A judge

AMERICAN GOVERNMENT

55. **A tariff is:**

    A. A law passed by the Congress and vetoed by the president

    B. An appointed official mandated to preserve public order

    C. A tax a government places on internationally traded goods, usually goods entering a country

    D. A tax a government places on goods produced for domestic use, also known as a sales tax

    E. A tax a government places on all exported goods

56. **In a parliamentary system, the person who becomes prime minister is usually:**

    A. The leader of the majority party in the legislature

    B. Elected by a direct national vote

    C. Chosen by the president of the country

    D. Chosen by the cabinet

    E. The leader of the minority party

57. **The Declaration of Independence owes much to the philosophy of:**

    A. Vladimir Lenin

    B. Karl Marx

    C. Thomas Hobbes

    D. Alexander Hamilton

    E. John Locke

58. **The highest appellate court in the United States is the:**

    A. Federal judiciary

    B. Circuit court

    C. Supreme Court

    D. Court of appeals

    E. District court

59. **The Bill of Rights was mostly written by:**

    A. Thomas Jefferson

    B. James Madison

    C. George Washington

    D. Alexander Hamilton

    E. John Adams

AMERICAN GOVERNMENT

60. **The U.S. Constitution was ratified by the required number of states in:**

    A. August 1861

    B. July 1776

    C. June 1788

    D. September 1848

    E. July 1864

61. **To be a naturalized citizen means:**

    A. To have been refused citizenship

    B. To have dual citizenship

    C. To be a native-born citizen

    D. To renounce one's citizenship

    E. To acquire citizenship

62. **George Washington's opinion of the United States having trade with other nations was:**

    A. Approval in only some instances

    B. Disapproval

    C. Approval

    D. Unsure

    E. Anger

63. **"Walk softly and carry a big stick" is a statement associated with:**

    A. Franklin Roosevelt

    B. Theodore Roosevelt

    C. George Washington

    D. Thomas Hobbes

    E. Ronald Reagan

64. **The Bill of Rights says that any rights it does not mention are:**

    A. Reserved to the federal government

    B. Not important

    C. Judged by the Supreme Court

    D. Not legal rights

    E. Reserved to the states or to the people

65. **The process of the state taking over industries and businesses is called:**

    A. Industrialization

    B. Nationalization

    C. Redistribution

    D. Amalgamation

    E. Reclamation

66. **The first election in which political parties played a role was in:**

    A. 1787

    B. 1776

    C. 1888

    D. 1796

    E. 1725

67. **The vast land area west of the Mississippi River that the United States bought from France was:**

    A. California and New Mexico

    B. The State of Florida

    C. The Louisiana Purchase

    D. The Gadsden Purchase

    E. The Monroe Claim

68. **The War of 1812 involved the United States and:**

    A. Russia

    B. Great Britain

    C. France

    D. Spain

    E. Germany

69. **The term *suffrage* means:**

    A. The right to vote

    B. The power of the court

    C. A Supreme Court ruling

    D. Legislative action

    E. To suffer silently

70. **What was Seward's Folly?**

    A. The purchase of Alaska

    B. The purchase of Louisiana

    C. The Mexican–American War

    D. The annexation of Texas

    E. The settlement of California

71. **Those who wanted the United States to stay out of world affairs are called:**

    A. Neo-conservatives

    B. Isolationists

    C. Non-interventionists

    D. Nationalists

    E. Independents

AMERICAN GOVERNMENT

72. **Early civilizations developed systems of government:**

    A. To provide for defense against attack

    B. To regulate trade

    C. To regulate and direct the economic activities of the people as they worked together in groups

    D. To decide on the boundaries of the different fields during planting seasons

    E. To create jobs

73. **The most common type of local government in the United States at present is:**

    A. Commission–Manager

    B. President–Legislature

    C. Council–Manager

    D. Mayor–Council

    E. Mayor–People

74. **The first political parties in the United States were:**

    A. Democratic-Republicans and Nationalists

    B. Progressives and Populists

    C. Democratic-Republicans and Federalists

    D. Democrats and Republicans

    E. Social Democrats and Populists

75. **To become a citizen, one must be at least _____ old.**

    A. 25 years

    B. 18 years

    C. 21 years

    D. 19 years

    E. 16 years

76. **The Spanish–American War started in:**

    A. 1889

    B. 1914

    C. 1927

    D. 1898

    E. 1900

77. **A major feature of many multiparty political systems is:**

    A. Separation of powers

    B. Inability to represent sectional interests

    C. Coalition government

    D. Strong centralized government

    E. Weak executive branch

AMERICAN GOVERNMENT

78. **Which of the following statements about American history is an opinion rather than a fact?**

    A. The doctrine of Manifest Destiny can be said to have been an excuse for the expansionism of the United States on the American continent

    B. America's wealth, power, and influence increased with its size

    C. America's expansion was justified by its superior political and economic system

    D. The expansion of the United States was generally detrimental to the interests of native peoples

    E. America entered the two World Wars because American interests were attacked.

79. **Which is a shared power of the federal and state governments?**

    A. The power to declare war

    B. The power to build roads

    C. The power to coin money

    D. The power to regulate interstate trade

    E. The power to educate

80. **The foreign policy known as the Good Neighbor Policy was associated with the administration of:**

    A. James Madison

    B. Franklin Roosevelt

    C. Woodrow Wilson

    D. Theodore Roosevelt

    E. John F. Kennedy

81. **Direct democracy was a feature of:**

    A. Greek city–states

    B. Ancient Rome

    C. Medieval Europe

    D. Sumerian theocracy

    E. The Indus Valley civilizations

82. **In a constitutional monarchy, like that of Great Britain, that has a parliamentary system of government, the sovereign takes the place of the:**

    A. Prime minister

    B. President

    C. Premier

    D. Speaker of Parliament

    E. Vice president

83. The type of city administration that is supposed to eliminate political patronage and fiscal waste is:

   A. Commission–Council

   B. Mayor–Council

   C. Council–Manager

   D. Metropolitan–Manager

   E. City Manager–Council

84. Which of the following statements about the Supreme Court is true?

   A. The Supreme Court has only an appellate jurisdiction in all matters

   B. The Supreme Court shall have original jurisdiction in all areas involving foreign officials, public officials, and cases in which a state is a party

   C. The Supreme Court shall exercise original jurisdiction only over those cases involving the chief executive

   D. The Supreme Court shall have original jurisdiction over appellate matters only

   E. The Supreme Court shall have jurisdiction over all matters, regardless of jurisdiction

85. What happens if the president vetoes a bill?

   A. It goes back to Congress, which can override the veto with a two-thirds vote

   B. It goes back to the congressional committees

   C. It goes back to Congress, which can override it with a three-fourths vote

   D. It still becomes a law

   E. It goes back to Congress, which can override it with a simple majority

86. The Truman Doctrine was an attempt to prevent the spread of:

   A. German expansionism

   B. Imperialism

   C. Communism

   D. Fascism

   E. Democracy

AMERICAN GOVERNMENT

87. To impeach a president:

A. The charges are brought by the House of Representatives and tried in the Senate

B. The charges are brought by the Senate and tried in the House of Representatives

C. The charges are brought by the states and tried in Congress

D. The charges are brought by Congress and tried before the Supreme Court

E. The charges are brought by the vice president and tried in the Senate

88. In the United States, the legal voting age is:

A. 19

B. 18

C. 21

D. 25

E. 16

89. In the United States' electoral system, who is allowed to vote in primary elections?

A. Generally, only registered party members are allowed to vote for their candidates in the party

B. Any registered voters may vote for candidates in either party primary

C. Only voters actively engaged in party affairs may vote in a primary

D. Generally, the United States does not engage in primary elections, though there are exceptions

E. Nonregistered individuals are allowed to vote in primary elections

90. A important *direct* consequence of the First World War was:

A. The end of European colonialism

B. The Great Depression

C. The rise of communism

D. The end of fascism

E. The socialist state

AMERICAN GOVERNMENT

91. In journalism, the term *muckraking* refers to:

A. An attempt to uncover alleged corruption of public officials

B. The attempt to cover up the alleged corruption of public officials

C. The process of buying up various media outlets

D. The investigation of government inefficiency and waste

E. Dragging a person's reputation through the mud

92. The Voting Rights Act of 1965 sought to:

A. Extend the franchise to minorities

B. Undo the last remaining features of unequal suffrage in the United States

C. Establish the party primary

D. Give women the right to vote

E. Take away the voting rights of prisoners

93. The United States is a(n):

A. Direct democracy

B. Quasi-democracy

C. Semi-democracy

D. Indirect democracy

E. Non-democracy

94. The United States is presently comprised of:

A. Fifty-two states, the District of Columbia, and various overseas territories

B. Forty-eight states, the District of Columbia, and various overseas territories

C. Fifty states, the District of Columbia, and various overseas territories

D. Fifty states and the District of Columbia

E. Fifty-six states and two territories

95. Powers concurrent to both the federal and state governments are:

A. To tax, to raise an army, to establish courts, to provide for the general welfare, and to fix the standards for weights and measures

B. To tax, to charter banks, to borrow money, to make and enforce laws, and to provide for the general welfare

C. To tax, to borrow money, to establish courts, to regulate international trade, and to make and enforce laws

D. To ratify amendments, to tax, to make and enforce laws, to provide for the general welfare, and to raise a militia

E. To tax, to regulate trade, to charter schools, and to make laws

AMERICAN GOVERNMENT

96. **The term *welfare capitalism* or *the welfare state* is used most often to describe:**

    A. The former Soviet Union

    B. The interval between mercantilism and capitalism

    C. The United States and various European countries

    D. The Chinese experiments with communism

    E. The Middle East

97. **A poll tax is associated with:**

    A. Tariffs on internationally traded goods

    B. Voting rights

    C. Government construction

    D. The income tax structure in a given state

    E. A tax imposed during an election

98. **Who of the following wrote about modern economic problems?**

    A. John Locke

    B. Thomas Hobbes

    C. John Maynard Keynes

    D. Alexander Hamilton

    E. Alexis de Tocqueville

99. ***Gerrymandering* is:**

    A. The consolidation of various voting districts into larger, more efficient entities

    B. The adjustment of voting districts to achieve some goal, usually to promote greater political representation of a given demographic of voters

    C. The removal of certain inefficient political departments

    D. The fixing of the economic infrastructure

    E. The process of endless debate in the Senate

100. **Interest groups form to influence:**

    A. Government funding

    B. State funding

    C. Government policy

    D. State policy

    E. All of the above

AMERICAN GOVERNMENT

Answer Key

Question Number	Correct Answer	Your Answer
1	B	
2	C	
3	C	
4	B	
5	C	
6	C	
7	D	
8	B	
9	B	
10	A	
11	B	
12	C	
13	E	
14	B	
15	A	
16	A	
17	B	
18	E	
19	A	
20	B	
21	A	
22	A	
23	A	
24	E	
25	A	
26	A	
27	A	
28	B	
29	E	
30	B	
31	B	
32	C	
33	B	
34	A	

Question Number	Correct Answer	Your Answer
35	E	
36	C	
37	C	
38	A	
39	B	
40	B	
41	E	
42	A	
43	C	
44	D	
45	D	
46	A	
47	B	
48	A	
49	A	
50	A	
51	A	
52	D	
53	A	
54	C	
55	C	
56	A	
57	E	
58	C	
59	B	
60	C	
61	E	
62	C	
63	B	
64	E	
65	B	
66	D	
67	C	
68	B	

Question Number	Correct Answer	Your Answer
69	A	
70	A	
71	B	
72	C	
73	D	
74	C	
75	B	
76	D	
77	C	
78	C	
79	B	
80	D	
81	A	
82	B	
83	C	
84	B	
85	A	
86	C	
87	A	
88	B	
89	A	
90	C	
91	A	
92	B	
93	D	
94	C	
95	B	
96	C	
97	B	
98	C	
99	B	
100	E	

AMERICAN GOVERNMENT

RATIONALES

1. The term that best describes how the Supreme Court can block laws that may be unconstitutional from being enacted is:

    A. Jurisprudence

    B. Judicial review

    C. Exclusionary rule

    D. Right of petition

    E. The blocking right

The answer is B
The correct answer is judicial review. Through judicial review, the Supreme Court has the power to invalidate any laws created by the legislative and executive branches which do not agree with a higher authority such as the Constitution. Jurisprudence is the philosophy of law. The exclusionary rule deals with the use of evidence in a court of law. The right to petition is a part of the First Amendment, and the blocking right is not an actual right.

2. On the spectrum of American politics, the label that most accurately describes voters "to the right of center" is:

    A. Moderates

    B. Liberals

    C. Conservatives

    D. Socialists

    E. Independents

The answer is C
The correct answer is conservatives. The spectrum of American politics ranges from Socialism on the far left to Fascism on the far right with moderates in the direct center. Conservatives are to the right of center and Liberals are to the left of center. Independents are not affiliated with any political party and can hold views that correlate with either side of the spectrum.

AMERICAN GOVERNMENT

3. **The branch of government responsible for developing the federal budget is:**

    A. The legislative branch

    B. The judicial branch

    C. The executive branch

    D. The Congress

    E. Each of the 50 states

The answer is C
The correct answer is the Executive branch. The President is required to submit a budget proposal to Congress each year. The House and the Senate create resolutions to the budget, but do not formulate the budget. Congress is the Legislative branch. The Judicial branch is in charge of interpreting the meaning of laws and the state governments are in charge of their own budgets, not the federal one.

4. **The United States legislature is bicameral. This means:**

    A. It consists of several houses

    B. It consists of two houses

    C. It meets twice a year

    D. The vice president is in charge of the legislature when in session.

    E. It has an upper house and a lower house

The answer is B
The correct answer is that it consists of two houses. Congress consists of the Senate and the House of Representatives. The two house legislature was created as a part of the system of checks and balances. The legislature does have an upper house (Senate) and a lower house (House of Representatives), but that is not the meaning of bicameral. There are elections for Congress every two years, but Congress is in session almost year round. The Vice-President is in charge of the Senate.

AMERICAN GOVERNMENT

5. **What Supreme Court ruling established the principal of judicial review?**

   A. *Jefferson v. Madison*

   B. *Lincoln v. Douglas*

   C. *Marbury v. Madison*

   D. *Marbury v. Jefferson*

   E. *Lincoln v. Davis*

The answer is C
The correct answer is Marbury vs. Madison. In 1803, William Marbury, who had been appointed Justice of the Peace, but whose commission had not been delivered, petitioned the Supreme Court to force James Madison, the new Secretary of State, to deliver the documents. The Court found Madison's refusal to be illegal and correctible, but did not force him to deliver the documents. The Court claimed Marbury petitioning was unconstitutional in the first place because it tried to extend the Court's original jurisdiction further than what was established in the Constitution, and, therefore, established judicial review. Jefferson vs. Madison was not a Supreme Court case. Madison and Jefferson were a part of the same political party, the Democratic-Republicans. Lincoln vs. Douglas was also not a Supreme Court case. Abraham Lincoln and Stephen A. Douglas had a series of famous debates when they were running for Senator of Illinois. Marbury vs. Jefferson was not a Supreme Court case. Thomas Jefferson was President during the Marbury vs. Madison case. Lincoln vs. Davis is also not a Supreme Court case. Abraham Lincoln was President of the Union and Jefferson Davis was President of the Confederacy during the Civil War.

AMERICAN GOVERNMENT

6. **To be eligible to be elected president, one must:**

   A. Be a U.S. citizen for at least five years

   B. Be a U.S. citizen for seven years

   C. Have been born a U.S. citizen

   D. Be a naturalized U.S. citizen

   E. Have been born to a U.S. citizen

The answer is C
The correct answer is have been born a citizen. Article Two Section One of the Constitution states," No person except a natural born Citizen, or a Citizen of the United States, at the time of the Adoption of this Constitution, shall be eligible to the Office of President; neither shall any person be eligible to that Office who shall not have attained the Age of thirty five years, and been fourteen Years a resident within the United States." To run for President, a candidate must have been born a U.S. citizen, be at least 35 years old, and must have lived in the United States for at least fourteen years.

7. **The international organization established to work for world peace at the end of Second World War is the:**

   A. League of Nations

   B. Union of Nations

   C. United Federation of Nations

   D. United Nations

   E. United World League

The answer is D
The correct answer is the United Nations. The United Nations was created in 1945 to promote international co-operation in order to prevent a similar conflict to World War II. The League of Nations was established in 1920 and was the predecessor to the UN. It ended up dissolving because it was ineffective in stopping the aggression of the Axis powers in the 30s. Union of Nations, United Federation of Nations, and United World League are not actual political organizations.

AMERICAN GOVERNMENT

8. **In the United States, the right to declare war is a power of:**

    A. The president

    B. Congress

    C. The executive branch

    D. The Supreme Court

    E. The states

The answer is B
The correct answer is Congress. Congress is given power to declare war in Article One Section Eight of the Constitution. The President is the commander-in-chief and in charge of the armed forces. The President is a part of the Executive branch. The Supreme Court and the 50 states have no part in declaring war.

9. **Which of the following is an example of a direct democracy?**

    A. Elected representatives

    B. Greek city–states

    C. The United States Senate

    D. The United States House of Representatives

    E. State legislatures

The answer is B
The correct answer is Greek city-states. State legislatures, the United States' Senate, and the United States' House of Representatives are all examples of indirect or representative democracy. The citizens vote elected representatives into office. The Greek city-states were a direct democracy because the citizens themselves voted on laws and policies.

AMERICAN GOVERNMENT

10. **To plead the Fifth Amendment means to:**

    A. Refuse to speak so one does not incriminate oneself

    B. Plead "no contest" in court

    C. Ask for freedom of speech

    D. Ask to appear before a judge when charged with a crime

    E. Petition for self-defense

The answer is A
The correct answer is to refuse to speak so one does not incriminate oneself. The Fifth Amendment allows a person to refuse to answer questions when acting as a witness if it means it would incriminate them. Freedom of Speech is a part of the First Amendment, and does not need to be asked for. Appearing before a judge for a crime is a part of the trial process which everyone charged of a crime has the right to be tried by a jury of their peers in the Sixth Amendment. Pleading self-defense is not an Amendment, but a justification for the crime committed. Pleading "no contest' in court is similar to a guilty plea and not part of any Amendment.

11. **The political document that was the first to try to organize the newly *independent* American colonies was the:**

    A. Declaration of Independence

    B. Articles of Confederation

    C. Constitution

    D. Confederate States

    E. Magna Carta

The answer is B
The correct answer is the Articles of Confederation. The Articles of Confederation adopted in 1777 was the predecessor to the Constitution. The Articles were too weak which led to the development of the Constitution in 1789. The Declaration of Independence did not organize the colonies. It simply stated that the colonies were no longer a part of Great Britain. The Confederate States were the group of states that seceded from the Union during the Civil War, not a political document. The Magna Carta was a political document signed by King John of England in 1215 which claimed the monarch would uphold the rights of its citizens.

AMERICAN GOVERNMENT

12. In 1792, Alexis de Tocqueville came to America to study the:

    A. Economic system

    B. Congress

    C. Prison system

    D. Election process

    E. Constitution

The answer is C

The correct answer is to study the prison system. Alexis de Tocqueville was sent to America by the French government in order to examine prisons and penitentiaries. He wrote *Democracy in America* in order to help the French people in their transition between a fading aristocratic society to a democratic society. He was not there to study the economic system, the Congress, the election process, or the Constitution.

13. The first ten amendments to the Constitution are called:

    A. Bill of petition

    B. Petition of Rights

    C. Rights of Man

    D. Constitutional rights

    E. Bill of Rights

The answer is E

The correct answer is Bill of Rights. The Bill of Rights is the first Ten Amendments to the Constitution which was drafted in 1789 to appease the Anti-Federalists because it guarantees personal freedom and limits the government. The First Amendment includes the right to petition. Petition of Rights is an English document created in 1628 which sets out liberties the king cannot infringe upon. The Rights of Man is a book written by Thomas Paine in 1791. Constitutional rights are expressed in the Constitution.

AMERICAN GOVERNMENT

14. Socialists believe that the government should have a _____ role in the economy.

    A. minimal

    B. controlling

    C. equal to business'

    D. less than the individual's

    E. nonexistent

The answer is B
The correct answer is greater. Socialism contains the belief that society as a whole should own or control property for the benefit of all people. Socialism envisions a society where the government owns and controls industry. In this way, the shared ownership would create a more equitable distribution of goods. A lesser role in the economy would be supporting free markets and capitalism.

15. One difference between *totalitarianism* and *authoritarianism* is that totalitarianism believes in:

    A. Total control over all aspects of society

    B. Minimum government control

    C. There is no difference

    D. The difference is unknown

    E. Authoritative control over government

The answer is A
The correct answer is total control over all aspects of society. True to its name, totalitarianism seeks to control the entirety of a society. Authoritarianism is when individual rights are subject to the will of a single authority. It is authoritative control over government.

AMERICAN GOVERNMENT

16. The constitution is called a "living document" because:

    A. It has the ability to change with different times

    B. It was created by people

    C. It is a static document

    D. Excessive reliance on the Constitution will kill it

    E. Anyone can change it

The answer is A

The correct answer is it has the ability to change with different times. The Amendments are an example of how it is a living document. In 1919, the Eighteenth Amendment prohibited the making and transporting of alcohol to support the Temperance movement in which people claimed alcohol was ruining society. In 1933, the Twenty-First Amendment repealed the Eighteenth Amendment. All political documents are created by people, but not all these documents are labeled as "living." It is not static since Amendments can always change the Constitution. Excessive reliance will not kill it, and it is the Supreme Law of the land which means every citizen relies on it. Not anyone can change it. There is a long process in order to pass an Amendment and a majority of the states to agree and ratify it before it will be recognized.

17. In the feudal system, who has the most power?

    A. The peasant or serf

    B. The noble or lord

    C. The worker

    D. The merchant

    E. The soldier

The answer is B

The correct answer is the noble or lord. The feudal system is a pyramid with the peasants or serfs being the most numerous and having the least rights. The merchants and workers are next as they have more rights than the serfs. Knights are the next as they are held in high regard by the lord or noble and provide military service. The noble or lord is at the top of the pyramid because they have the most power and are in control of everything,

AMERICAN GOVERNMENT

18. **The idea that the European powers should stay out of the affairs of the American hemisphere is known as:**

    A. Containment policy

    B. The Eisenhower Doctrine

    C. Neo-isolationism

    D. The Truman Doctrine

    E. The Monroe Doctrine

The answer is E
The correct answer is the Monroe Doctrine. The doctrine was created in 1823 and proclaimed the United States' dominion over America. Any interference from a European nation would have been considered an act of aggression. The containment policy was the United States' effort to contain communism during the Cold War. The Eisenhower Doctrine in 1957 was similar as it proclaimed America would come to the aid of any Middle Eastern country that was being threatened by communism. Neo-isolationism was the reluctance for America to be involved in any other commitments abroad. The Truman Doctrine in 1947 claimed to give aid to any democratic nation suffering from authoritarian forces.

19. **The Exclusionary Rule prevents:**

    A. Illegally seized evidence from being used in court

    B. Persons from incriminating themselves in court

    C. Police from entering a private home for any reason

    D. Evidence, however gathered, from being used in court if one side in a court case objects to it

    E. Evidence, regardless of how it is collected, from being excluded

The answer is A
The correct answer is illegally seized evidence from being used in court. The Exclusionary Rule upholds that evidence procured in which the defendant's constitutional rights were violated can sometimes not be used in court. The Fifth Amendment allows people to not incriminate themselves in court. The Fourth Amendment protects citizens from unlawful search and seizure which means police cannot enter your home without a warrant. Not just any evidence can be excluded from court. Without evidence, people would not be convicted.

AMERICAN GOVERNMENT

20. The idea that "the government is best that governs least" is most closely associated with:

    A. The Soviet communist system

    B. The American free enterprise system

    C. British conservatism

    D. Mussolini's corporate state

    E. A dictatorship

The answer is B
The correct answer is the American Free Enterprise system. The free enterprise system, also known as free market or capitalism, is where government puts few restrictions on the economy. The Soviet Communist System nationalized all industries and inputted a planned economy, which meant a lot of government control. British Conservatism supported the monarchy. Mussolini's Corporate State involved an economy that was jointly managed by employers, workers, and state officials. A dictatorship is when one person is in charge of the nation, and often takes this position without the acceptance of the people.

21. In the United States Constitution, political parties are:

    A. Never mentioned

    B. Called "a necessary part of the political process"

    C. Most effective if there are only two major ones

    D. Called harmful to the political process

    E. Required to have at least 100 members

The answer is A
The correct answer is never actually mentioned. Political parties are not mentioned in the Constitution. The formation of political parties happened during the ratification process when the Federalists vied for a strong national government and the Anti-Federalists opposed the ratification of the Constitution. George Washington warned against the creation of political parties because he believed it would corrupt government.

AMERICAN GOVERNMENT

22. **Civil suits deal mostly, but not exclusively, with:**

    A. Money

    B. Violent crime

    C. The government

    D. Political fundraising

    E. Mental illness

The answer is A
 The correct answer is money. Civil suits deal with money in a majority of cases such as worker's compensation claims and personal injury. Violent crime would be a criminal prosecution, not a civil lawsuit. Civil lawsuits are between two individuals, and does not deal with the federal government or have anything to do with political fundraising. Mental illness in general is not a crime or something that would be dealt with in a civil case. Mental illness would be handled by a doctor.

23. **"Common law" refers mostly to:**

    A. The precedents and traditions that have gone before in society and have become accepted norms

    B. The laws dealing with the "common people"

    C. Law that is written and codified

    D. The House of Commons in Great Britain

    E. Law that is common among different countries

The answer is A
The correct answer is the precedents and traditions that have gone before in society so that they become accepted norms. Common law is derived from precedents rather than statutes. In America, there are no laws that deal with the "common people." The law applies to everyone. All laws are written and codified. The House of Commons in Britain has nothing to do with American government. Countries can have laws in common, but there is no term for this.

AMERICAN GOVERNMENT

24. Anarchists believe in:

    A. Strong government

    B. Corporate state system

    C. Weak, mild government

    D. Populist government

    E. No government

The answer is E
The correct answer is no government. Anarchism is that belief that the state is harmful to the people, and society should be self-governed. Democrats believe in a strong government. The corporate state system is a part of Fascism. Republicans prefer a weak, mild government. Populism believes in a populist government which supports the rights of the common people.

25. The U.S. government's federal system consists of:

    A. Three parts: the executive, the legislative, and the judiciary

    B. Three parts: the legislative, the Congress, and the presidency

    C. Four parts: the executive, the judiciary, the courts, and the legislative

    D. Two parts: the government, and the governed

    E. Two parts: the president and state governors

The answer is A
The correct answer is three parts: the Executive, the Legislative, and the Judiciary. The U.S. government is split into three branches which consist of the President and Vice-President, Congress, and the Supreme Court. The government is split this way in order to create a system of checks and balances which stops one branch from becoming too powerful. Congress, the Presidency, and the courts each fall within one of the branches, but are not the official parts. The questions asked what the government consists of so, the Government and the governed is incorrect. The state governors are in charge of state governments, not federal.

AMERICAN GOVERNMENT

26. One difference between a presidential and a parliamentary system is that in a parliamentary system:

    A. The prime minister is head of government, while a president or monarch is head of state

    B. The president is head of government, and the vice president is head of state

    C. The president pro tempore of the Senate is head of state, while the prime minister is head of government

    D. The president appoints the head of state

    E. The prime minister is elected

The answer is A

The correct answer is the Prime Minister is head of government, while a president or monarch is head of state. A Prime Minister is in charge of government such as the Parliament in Britain. It is similar to the role the Speaker of the House embodies, since the Speaker is in charge of the House of Representatives. A president or a monarch is in charge of every aspect of the state. The Vice-President in America is President of the Senate, but otherwise supports the President. A President pro-tempore is someone who acts as President of the Senate when the Vice-President is absent. President of the Senate is in charge of a part of the legislative body, not the whole government. The President is the head of state, and will not appoint one. The President appoints the Secretary of State. The Prime Minister is not appointed. When a political party gains a majority in government, the leader of that party becomes the Prime Minister.

AMERICAN GOVERNMENT

27. The American concept of Manifest Destiny means:

   A. America had a right to spread across the American continent from coast to coast

   B. The United States should respect the right of native peoples it encounters in its push westward

   C. The rest of the world powers should stay out of North America

   D. America should strive to be the dominant world power

   E. America belonged to the native people of the region

The answer is A
The correct answer is America had a right to spread throughout the American continent from coast to coast. After acquiring more and more land, Americans came to a mindset that they not only could, but should, settles the entirety of the American continent. By settling the west, it meant removing Native Americans to make room for new American settlements. Moving west and removing Native Americans from their own land meant Americans did not believe the land belonged to the Indians. The belief that other world powers should stay out of the affairs in the Western Hemisphere was a part of the Monroe Doctrine. America's strive to become a dominant world power came later, after the continent had been fully settled.

28. In an <u>indirect</u> democracy:

   A. All the people together decide on issues

   B. People elect representatives to act for them

   C. Democracy can never really work

   D. Government is less efficient than in a direct democracy

   E. People directly elect their representatives

The answer is B
The correct answer is people elect representatives to act for them. America is an indirect democracy because the people vote to elect representatives in Congress to act for them. A direct democracy is where all the people together decide on issues. Democracy has been proven to work throughout the ages, starting with Ancient Athens. Direct democracy is still a type of government. People indirectly electing their representatives would not be an efficient type of government.

AMERICAN GOVERNMENT

29. In a communist system, _____ controls the means of production.

    A. A professional managerial class

    B. The owners of business and industry

    C. The workers

    D. The parliament

    E. The state

The answer is E
The correct answer is the state. The state controls the means of production in order to make sure everyone receives an equal amount. Communism does not have a class system which means there is no professional managerial class, or owners of business and industry, or workers, because everyone works for the benefit of the state as a whole. Communism also does not have a Parliament as the state is controlled by a single authority or political party.

30. Congress can override a president's veto with a _____ vote.

    A. One-half

    B. Two-thirds

    C. Six-tenths

    D. Three-fourths

    E. Four-fifths

The answer is B
The correct answer is two-thirds. Congress can override a presidential veto if a majority, two-thirds, agrees. The other answers also represent an amount that would be a majority, but a vote of two-thirds in each level is what was agreed upon when the Constitution was drafted.

AMERICAN GOVERNMENT

31. To become a citizen, an individual generally must have lived in the United States for at least:

    A. Six years

    B. Five years

    C. One year

    D. Ten years

    E. Fifteen years

The answer is B
The correct answer is five years. A person can apply to become a U.S. citizen after they have become a permanent resident for five years, or been married to a U.S. citizen for three years. Therefore, six years, one year, ten years, and fifteen years are incorrect answers.

32. Give the correct order of the following: the Constitution, the Declaration of Independence, and the Articles of Confederation.

    A. The Constitution, the Declaration of Independence, the Articles of Confederation

    B. The Declaration of Independence, the Constitution, the Articles of Confederation

    C. The Declaration of Independence, the Articles of Confederation, the Constitution

    D. The Articles of Confederation, the Declaration of Independence, the Constitution.

    E. The Constitution, the Articles of Confederation, the Declaration of Independence

The answer is C
The correct answer is the Declaration of Independence, the Articles of Confederation, the Constitution. The Declaration of Independence was signed in 1776 and separated the colonies from Britain. The Articles of Confederation was the predecessor to the Constitution and was adopted in 1777. The Constitution was ratified in 1789. Therefore, all the other answers have the wrong order.

AMERICAN GOVERNMENT

33. The ability of the president to veto an act of Congress is an example of:

    A. Separation of powers

    B. Checks and balances

    C. Judicial review

    D. Presidential prerogative

    E. Executive order

The answer is B
The correct answer is checks and balances. By vetoing laws the President does not believe to be beneficial, he is putting a check on Congress by limiting their power. The separation of powers is the purpose of the three branches of government. Judicial review is the Supreme Court's way of checking the other branches. Presidential prerogative and presidential right are not actual political terms.

34. To impeach an elected official means to:

    A. Bring charges against the official

    B. Remove the official from office

    C. Reelect the official

    D. Override the official's veto

    E. Arrest the official

The answer is A
The correct answer is bring charges against a president. The House of Representatives has the power to impeach a president for breaking the law, and the Senate as the power to try impeachment. President Nixon was impeached for obstruction of justice when he would not release some recordings during the Watergate Scandal. A president must be tried by the Senate and a majority must convict him before a president will be removed from office. A president can only be re-elected through a general election which occurs every four years. Overriding a presidential veto is a different process which requires a two-thirds majority in Congress. Impeachment is only bringing charges against a president. He is not convicted or arrested until the trial has finished and the decision has been made.

AMERICAN GOVERNMENT

35. **An obligation identified with citizenship is:**

    A. Belonging to a political party

    B. Educating oneself

    C. Running for political office

    D. Donating to a political party

    E. Voting

The answer is E
The correct answer is voting. Every U.S. citizen who is 18 years or older has the right to vote. Since the U.S. government is one based on indirect democracy, it is the duty of the citizen to vote his/her representatives into office. Belonging to a political party and donating to a political party are not obligations, but choices a citizen can make. A person can choose to be unaffiliated with a political party. Educating oneself is not an obligation of citizenship, but something that is strongly encouraged, especially when it comes to voting in elections. Running for a political office is not an obligation. People can be as much or as little involved in government as they choose to be.

36. **The doctrine that sought to keep communism from spreading was:**

    A. The Cold War

    B. Rollback

    C. Containment

    D. Détente

    E. Mutually assured destruction

The answer is C
The correct answer is containment. Containment was a part of the Truman Doctrine in 1947 by which America promised to come to the aid of countries that were being subjugated by communism. Truman's declaration is considered to start the Cold War which was a period of political and military tension between the Western Allies and the USSR and its allies. Roll-back is the process of changing a political regime, not a containment of one. Détente is the easing of strain between countries which is the opposite of what happened in this era. Mutually assured destruction is a military strategy in which both countries would annihilate each other. This is what people were afraid would happen during the Cold War.

AMERICAN GOVERNMENT

37. **The power to declare war, establish a postal system, and coin money rests with which branch of the government?**

    A. Presidential

    B. Judicial

    C. Legislative

    D. Executive

    E. State governments

The answer is C
The correct answer is Legislative. Congress has the power to declare war, establish a postal system, and coin money. Presidential and Executive branch are the same and are in charge of the state and enforces the law. The Judicial branch is in charge of interpreting the law. State governments have no power over federal concerns. When America was still the thirteen colonies, each colony had its own money which made it hard for people to travel in between colonies.

38. **If a president neither signs nor vetoes a bill for ten days, the bill becomes:**

    A. A pocket veto

    B. A refused law

    C. Unconstitutional

    D. A presidential veto

    E. A passed law

The answer is A
The correct answer is pocket veto. If the President does not accept or veto a law within ten days of it coming to his desk, it is automatically vetoed and cannot be overridden in Congress. It is not a refused law, because Congress can create a new bill for a similar law and have it pass. It is not unconstitutional as it is stated in Article One Section Seven of the Constitution: "If any Bill shall not be returned by the President within ten days (Sundays excepted) after it shall have been presented to him, the same shall be a law, in like manner as if he had signed it, unless the Congress by their Adjournment prevent its return, in which case it shall not be a Law." It is not a presidential veto because the president does not formally veto the bill. The law is also not passed because it does not receive the approval from the president.

AMERICAN GOVERNMENT

39. What was George Washington's advice to Americans about foreign policy?

    A. America should have strong alliances

    B. America should avoid alliances

    C. Foreign policy should take precedence over domestic policy

    D. Domestic policy should take precedence over foreign policy

    E. American should build a big military

The answer is B
The correct answer is America should avoid alliances. In his farewell address, Washington said America should not "entangle our peace and prosperity in the toils of European ambition." He did not want America to make alliances and create foreign entanglements that would cause America to lose its peace and prosperity. Therefore, Washington said the opposite of making strong alliances. Washington did not discuss whether foreign or domestic policy should take precedence. Washington also encouraged peace and commerce with all nations.

40. The belief that government should stay out of economic affairs is called:

    A. Mercantilism

    B. Laissez-faire

    C. Democratic socialism

    D. Corporatism

    E. Socialism

The answer is B
The correct answer is laissez-faire. Laissez-faire is a belief that things should take their own course. In economics, it means the government should not interfere in the free market; it should be hands-off. Mercantilism is a belief in the profit of trade which is supported by the protection of the government. Democratic-Socialism and Socialism believe in some form of social ownership which requires involvement of the government in the economy. Corporatism divides society into different sectors such as merchants and industries which the government controls or private organizations.

AMERICAN GOVERNMENT

41. The term that describes the division of government function is:

    A. Free enterprise

    B. Constitutional prerogative

    C. Checks and balances

    D. Divisive government

    E. Separation of powers

The answer is E
The correct answer is separation of powers. The federal government is split into three branches: the Legislative, Executive, and Judiciary. Each branch has different powers which allows for a system of checks and balances. Free enterprise is an economic system where private businesses operate free of state control. Constitutional prerogative does not separate the powers of the government. The federal government is not divisive, because they are not in disagreement.

42. Which of the following is an important idea expressed in the Declaration of Independence?

    A. People have the right to change their government

    B. People should obey the government authority

    C. A monarchy is a bad thing

    D. Indirect democracy is best

    E. People should disobey authority

The answer is A
The correct answer is people have the right to change their government. The Declaration of Independence states, "that whenever any form of government becomes destructive of these ends, it is the right of the people to alter it or to abolish it, and to institute new government." This means that the people have the right to get rid of a terrible government and create a new one. A citizen does not have to obey a government authority if it is in disagreement to their individual rights. It does not outright state that monarchy is a bad thing. It also does not claim indirect democracy is the best, but lays out the individual, natural rights of the people. It says people can abolish a destructive government, but this does not mean they can outright disobey a just authority.

AMERICAN GOVERNMENT

43. **Oligarchy refers to:**

    A. Rule of a single leader

    B. Rule of a single political party

    C. Rule by a select few

    D. Rule by many

    E. Rule by a family

The answer is C
The answer is rule by a select few. Oligarchies are when a few people, normally highly educated, rich people, are in control of the state. Autocracy is the rule by a single leader. Totalitarianism is the rule by a single political party. A polarchy or polyarchy is rule by many people. A monarchy is rule by a family.

44. **The Judiciary Act of 1789 established the:**

    A. Supreme Court

    B. Principle of judicial review

    C. State court system

    D. Federal and circuit court system

    E. The number of justices on the Supreme Court

The answer is D
The correct answer is federal and circuit court system. In the Judiciary Act of 1789, Congress decided to create the court system to make sure national laws would be enforced in all states. The Supreme Court was established in the Constitution. The principle of judiciary review was established in the court case Marbury vs. Madison. State courts are established by each individual state. The number of justices on the Supreme Court has changed throughout the years as the nation grew.

AMERICAN GOVERNMENT

45. The international organization established to work for world peace at the end of the First World War was the:

A. United Earth League

B. Confederate States

C. United Nations

D. League of Nations

E. Allied Foundation

The answer is D
The correct answer is the League of Nations. The League of Nations was created after World War I in order to maintain world peace. The League proved ineffective with the outbreak of World War II and was replaced by the United Nations in 1945. United Earth League and Allied Foundation are not actual political organizations. The Confederate states were those that seceded from the Union during the Civil War.

46. Which statement closely resembles the political philosophy of John Hobbes?

A. Citizens should give unquestioning obedience to the state authority so long as it can maintain public order

B. Citizens have a right to rise against the state whenever they choose

C. All state authority is basically evil and should be eliminated

D. People are generally good and cooperative if given a chance

E. People should not be trusted

The answer is A
The correct answer is citizens should give unquestioning obedience to the state authority so long as it can maintain public order. Thomas Hobbes was an English philosopher in the seventeenth century who supported the absolutist rule of the sovereign and created the social contract theory. Hobbes believed people gave up some individual rights in return for protection from the sovereign. This means people could not rise up against the sovereign whenever they pleased. He believed the sovereign to be good and not inherently evil. He also believed that if left without government in the state of nature, it would be chaos and all out war because people would fight each other for the things they wanted. A social contract requires trust between the people and the sovereign.

AMERICAN GOVERNMENT

47. **In the United States, the right to declare war is a power of:**

    A. The president

    B. Congress

    C. The executive

    D. The states

    E. The Supreme Court

The answer is B
The correct answer is Congress. Congress is given power to declare war in Article One Section Eight of the Constitution. The President is the commander-in-chief and in charge of the armed forces. The Executive branch is the President. The Supreme Court and the 50 states have no part in declaring war.

48. **A tort is:**

    A. A private or civil action brought into court

    B. A type of confection

    C. A penal offense

    D. One who solicits

    E. A case without any award

The answer is A
The correct answer is a private or civil action brought into court. A tort is a wrongful act which leads to legal liability. A tort is not a type of dessert, a case without any reward, nor does it refer to a person who solicits, a solicitor. A penal offense is a reason to be brought to court.

AMERICAN GOVERNMENT

49. A boycott is:

    A. The refusal to buy goods or services

    B. An imbalance of trade

    C. The refusal to speak in court

    D. A writ of assistance

    E. An agreement to trade

The answer is A
The correct answer is the refusal to buy goods or services. The Montgomery Bus Boycott was a famous boycott in which African-Americans refused to take the buses in order to fight against racial discrimination. A boycott does not deal with trade, so an imbalance of trade and an agreement to trade are incorrect. The Fifth Amendment gives people the right to refuse to speak in court if it would incriminate them. A Writ of Assistance is an order issued by the court and given to a law enforcement official to perform a task.

50. In the United States, checks and balances refers to:

    A. The ability of each branch of government to "check," or limit, the actions of the other branches

    B. Balance of payments

    C. International law

    D. The federal deficit

    E. Setting the federal budget

The answer is A
The correct answer is the ability of each branch of government to "check" or limit the actions of the others. The President can veto laws made by Congress. The Supreme Court can claim laws are unconstitutional. Congress can impeach the President for wrongful behavior. Setting the federal budget represents the separation of power because the Executive branch creates the budget, but Congress can create resolutions for it. The system of checks and balances does not refer to balance of payments, international law, or the federal deficit.

AMERICAN GOVERNMENT

51. An amendment is:

    A. A change or addition to the United States Constitution

    B. The right of a state to secede from the Union

    C. The addition of a state to the Union

    D. The right of the Supreme Court to check actions of Congress and the president

    E. Changing congressional bills

The answer is A
The correct answer is a change or addition to the United States Constitution. Amendments are created in order to change some part of the Constitution such as the Nineteenth Amendment which gave women the right to vote. Seceding from the Union is not a right since it is considered unconstitutional. Congress has the right to add states to the Union. The Supreme Court checking the actions of Congress or the President is a part of the checks and balances system. Congress is in control of changing bills; they can make amendments to the bills, but these are not Constitutional Amendments.

52. The executive branch refers to:

    A. The Senate

    B. The legislature

    C. Congress

    D. The president and vice president

    E. The CEOs in the United States

The answer is D
The correct answer is the President and Vice-President. They constitute the Executive branch which is in charge of the state. Senate is a part of Congress which is the Legislative branch. The CEO's of America do not have executive power in government.

AMERICAN GOVERNMENT

53. An ex post facto law is:

    A. A law made against an act after it has been committed

    B. A law proclaimed unconstitutional by the Supreme Court

    C. An executive order

    D. A law relating to the postal system

    E. A law without basis

The answer is A
The correct answer is a law made against an act after it has been committed. An Ex Post facto law changes the legal consequences for actions committed before the law was made. Ex post facto is Latin for after the action. Therefore, a law proclaimed unconstitutional by the Supreme Court, an Executive Act which is a presidential order that helps define the internal affairs of government, a law relating to the postal system, and a law without basis are all incorrect.

54. The judiciary refers to:

    A. The president

    B. Congress

    C. The legal system

    D. The system of states' rights

    E. A judge

The answer is C
The correct answer is the legal system. The Judiciary is the system of courts that interpret the laws, not a single judge. The President is part of the Executive branch. Senate is part of Congress and the Legislative branch. The Constitution has reserved rights for the states, but the system is not a part of the Judiciary.

AMERICAN GOVERNMENT

55. A tariff is:

    A. A law passed by the Congress and vetoed by the president

    B. An appointed official mandated to preserve public order

    C. A tax a government places on internationally traded goods, usually goods entering a country

    D. A tax a government places on goods produced for domestic use, also known as a sales tax

    E. A tax a government places on all exported goods

The answer is C
The correct answer is a tax a government places on internationally traded goods, usually goods entering a country. A tariff is meant to restrict trade as well as promote national manufacturing. There is no name for a law that is passed by Congress and then vetoed by the president. Sales tax and a tax placed on tar products are not tariffs because they do not deal with traded goods. An appointed official mandated to preserve public order is a sheriff.

56. In a parliamentary system, the person who becomes prime minister is usually:

    A. The leader of the majority party in the legislature

    B. Elected by a direct national vote

    C. Chosen by the president of the country

    D. Chosen by the cabinet

    E. The leader of the minority party

The answer is A
The correct answer is the leader of the majority party in the legislature. A Prime Minister is not elected, but takes over when his or her party becomes the majority in the Parliament. A Prime Minister is not chosen by the President or the Cabinet because the Prime Minister is in charge of the government and needs to represent the people in some capacity. He or she is not the leader of the minority party because he or she would not represent the ideals of the majority of the people.

AMERICAN GOVERNMENT

57. The Declaration of Independence owes much to the philosophy of:

    A. Vladimir Lenin

    B. Karl Marx

    C. Thomas Hobbes

    D. Alexander Hamilton

    E. John Locke

The answer is E
The correct answer is John Locke. The Declaration of Independence which states, "that all mean are created equal, that they are endowed by their Creator with certain unalienable Rights, that among these are Life, Liberty and the pursuit of Happiness." The idea of natural rights given to all men originated with John Locke. Vladimir Lenin is a famous communist and was leader of the Russian Soviet Federative Socialist Republic. Karl Marx is a German philosopher known as the father of Communism. Thomas Hobbes created the social contract theory and was in support of an absolutist sovereign. Alexander Hamilton was the founder of the Federalist Party and a major promoter of the Constitution.

58. The highest appellate court in the United States is the:

    A. Federal judiciary

    B. Circuit court

    C. Supreme Court

    D. Court of appeals

    E. District court

The answer is C
The correct answer is Supreme Court. The appellate court system is set up like this: local trial courts, state appeals court, highest state of appeals court, and then either U.S. Federal Court of Appeals or the Supreme Court. Cases from the U.S. Federal District Courts move to the U.S. Federal Court of Appeals, and then to the Supreme Court.

AMERICAN GOVERNMENT

59. The Bill of Rights was mostly written by:

   A. Thomas Jefferson

   B. James Madison

   C. George Washington

   D. Alexander Hamilton

   E. John Adams

The answer is B
The correct answer is James Madison. Madison helped write the Bill of Rights after noticing there was no clause that allowed the Constitution to be amended. The Bill of Rights led to the ratification of the Constitution. Thomas Jefferson wrote the Declaration of Independence. George Washington, Alexander Hamilton, and John Adams all helped draft the Constitution.

60. The U.S. Constitution was ratified by the required number of states in:

   A. August 1861

   B. July 1776

   C. June 1788

   D. September 1848

   E. July 1864

The answer is C
The correct answer is June, 1788. The Constitution was adopted and signed in September, 1787, but had to be ratified by at least nine of the thirteen states. Some states refused to sign until the Bill of Rights was added which secured individual rights. The required nine states ratified the Constitution in June, 1788. July, 1776 was when the Declaration of Independence was signed. All the other dates are too late. August, 1861 and July, 1864 occurred during the Civil War. September, 1848 was a year when several revolutions in Europe occurred.

AMERICAN GOVERNMENT

61. To be a naturalized citizen means:

    A. To have been refused citizenship

    B. To have dual citizenship

    C. To be a native-born citizen

    D. To renounce one's citizenship

    E. To acquire citizenship

The answer is E
The correct answer is to acquire citizenship. Naturalization is the process in which a foreigner is granted citizenship. People have the right to renounce their citizenship, but this is not a part of naturalization. Neither is being refused citizenship or to be a "natural" or native born citizen. A dual-citizenship can be granted to people who have families or ancestors in more than one country.

62. George Washington's opinion of the United States having trade with other nations was:

    A. Approval in only some instances

    B. Disapproval

    C. Approval

    D. Unsure

    E. Anger

The answer is C
The correct answer is approval. In his Farewell Address, Washington advocated free trade with all nations and the government's role in insuring this stable trade. Therefore, he approved wholeheartedly, and not only in certain cases. He also was not unsure, angry, or disapproved.

AMERICAN GOVERNMENT

63. "Walk softly and carry a big stick" is a statement associated with:

    A. Franklin Roosevelt

    B. Theodore Roosevelt

    C. George Washington

    D. Thomas Hobbes

    E. Ronald Reagan

The answer is B
The correct answer is Theodore Roosevelt. Theodore Roosevelt is the one who created the Big Stick policy in which he wanted to negotiate peacefully, while also threatening with the "big stick" or the military. Frederick Roosevelt and Theodore Roosevelt were cousins. FDR created many important policies for the economy during a depression and World War II. George Washington was the first president and preferred to stay out of foreign affairs. Thomas Hobbes was an English philosopher who believed in absolute rule by a sovereign. Ronald Reagan was president in the 80s who supported "trickle-down" economics.

64. The Bill of Rights says that any rights it does not mention are:

    A. Reserved to the federal government

    B. Not important

    C. Judged by the Supreme Court

    D. Not legal rights

    E. Reserved to the states or to the people

The answer is E
The correct answer is reserved to the states or to the people. The Tenth Amendment states, "The powers not delegated to the United States by the Constitution, nor prohibited by it to the States, are reserved to the States respectively, or to the people." Therefore, what rights are not explicitly stated become states' rights. These rights are still legal and important. They are not judged by the Supreme Court or given exclusively to the Federal Government.

AMERICAN GOVERNMENT

65. The process of the state taking over industries and businesses is called:

    A. Industrialization

    B. Nationalization

    C. Redistribution

    D. Amalgamation

    E. Reclamation

The answer is B
The correct answer is nationalization. Nationalization is when a private industry is taken ownership by the government or state. Industrialization is the process by which a state moves from an agrarian society to one based on manufacturing. Redistribution is moving one thing, such as money from the wealthy, and parceling it out to other people, such as the poor. An amalgamation is a combination of things. Reclamation is claiming something that used to be in your possession as your own. The government is not reclaiming these industries, but taking them over.

66. The first election in which political parties played a role was in:

    A. 1787

    B. 1776

    C. 1888

    D. 1796

    E. 1725

The answer is D
The correct answer is 1796. 1796 was when political parties began campaigning. The Republicans campaigned for Thomas Jefferson and the Federalists campaigned for John Adams. 1787 was the year the Constitution was adopted. 1776 was when the Declaration of Independence was signed. 1888 was during the Gilded Age. 1725 occurred before American became a nation.

AMERICAN GOVERNMENT

67. The vast land area west of the Mississippi River that the United States bought from France was:

    A. California and New Mexico

    B. The State of Florida

    C. The Louisiana Purchase

    D. The Gadsden Purchase

    E. The Monroe Claim

The answer is C
The correct answer is the Louisiana Purchase. Thomas Jefferson purchased the land from France in 1803 for $50 million which more than doubled the size of America at the time. The Treaty of Guadalupe Hidalgo in 1848 after the end of the Mexican-American War gave America the territories of California and New Mexico. Spain sold Florida to the United States in 1819 because Spain realized it could not stop the United States from taking over the territory. The Gadsden Purchase occurred in 1853 and gave America the territory of southern Arizona from Mexico. There is no Monroe Claim, but a Monroe Doctrine which claimed any interference by European powers would be considered an act of aggression.

68. The War of 1812 involved the United States and:

    A. Russia

    B. Great Britain

    C. France

    D. Spain

    E. Germany

The answer is B
The correct answer is Great Britain. America declared war against Britain in 1812 for many reasons: the impressments of American sailors and trade restrictions among others. Great Britain's war with France earlier influenced the start of the War of 1812. Spain was not officially involved in the war. Germany was not a united nation until 1871. France, led by Napoleon, invaded Russia in 1812 in order to expand its empire.

AMERICAN GOVERNMENT

69. The term *suffrage* means:

    A. The right to vote

    B. The power of the court

    C. A Supreme Court ruling

    D. Legislative action

    E. To suffer silently

The answer is A
The correct answer is the right to vote. The Women's Suffrage Movement which began in the 1840s was women's campaign for the right to vote which was granted in the Nineteenth Amendment in1919. Suffrage does not refer to the power of the court nor a Supreme Court ruling. Legislative action and suffering silently also do not have to deal with suffrage.

70. What was Seward's Folly?

    A. The purchase of Alaska

    B. The purchase of Louisiana

    C. The Mexican–American War

    D. The annexation of Texas

    E. The settlement of California

The answer is A
The correct answer is the purchase of Alaska. William Seward, the Secretary of State, signed a treaty with Russia which purchased the territory of Alaska in 1867. The reactions to it were mixed with some people calling it Seward's Folly, but it had good consequences as it weakened the British Empire. Louisiana was purchased in the Louisiana Purchase in 1803. The Treaty of Guadalupe Hidalgo is what ended the Mexican-American War. Texas was annexed by President John Tyler in 1845. The settlement of California had nothing to do with William Seward.

AMERICAN GOVERNMENT

71. Those who wanted the United States to stay out of world affairs are called:

    A. Neo-conservatives

    B. Isolationists

    C. Non-interventionists

    D. Nationalists

    E. Independents

The answer is B
The correct answer is isolationists. Isolationists believed it served America's best interests to keep all other nations out of their affairs. Neo-Conservatives believe it is the nation's best interest to get involved in international affairs. Non-Interventionists believe in not making alliances with other nations, but in continuing diplomacy. Nationalists feel pride for their nation's unique and independent culture. An Independent politician is one that is not affiliated with any political party.

72. Early civilizations developed systems of government:

    A. To provide for defense against attack

    B. To regulate trade

    C. To regulate and direct the economic activities of the people as they worked together in groups

    D. To decide on the boundaries of the different fields during planting seasons

    E. To create jobs

The answer is C
The correct answer is to regulate and direct the economic activities of the people as they worked together in groups. Ancient civilizations were concerned with trade, the boundaries of their fields, defense against attack, and having jobs, but none of this could be accomplished without first creating a stable economy which was achieved through the creation of a government.

AMERICAN GOVERNMENT

73. **The most common type of local government in the United States at present is:**

    A. Commission–Manager

    B. President–Legislature

    C. Council–Manager

    D. Mayor–Council

    E. Mayor–People

The answer is D
The correct answer is Mayor-Council. This type of local government is popular in large cities and consists of a Mayor elected by popular vote and a Council which can act as the legislature. Council-Manager is the second most common type of local government and consists of a Council that acts as the legislative branch and a Manager who provides professional management to the Council. Instead of a Council, it can also be a Commission. President-Legislature is not a type of local government and neither is Mayor-People because a Mayor requires a Council.

74. **The first political parties in the United States were:**

    A. Democratic-Republicans and Nationalists

    B. Progressives and Populists

    C. Democratic-Republicans and Federalists

    D. Democrats and Republicans

    E. Social Democrats and Populists

The answer is C
The correct answer is Democratic-Republicans and Federalists. The Democratic-Republicans were the former Anti-Federalists who had never formed an official party. Therefore, the first political parties were based on who supported the Constitution and who did not. Nationalists are not a political party. Progressives and Populists were political parties in the late nineteenth and early twentieth centuries. Democrats and Republicans are the current political parties. Answer E has only one party, Social Democrats, when the question asked for parties, not party.

AMERICAN GOVERNMENT

75. To become a citizen, one must be at least _____ old.

    A. 25 years

    B. 18 years

    C. 21 years

    D. 19 years

    E. 16 years

The answer is B
The correct answer is 18 years old. To become a citizen, a person must be at least 18 years old because that is the age when people are considered legal adults and when people can vote. At 25 years, a person can rent a car. At 21 years, a person can legally drink alcohol. At 16 years, a person can obtain a driver's license. 19 years is an incorrect answer.

76. The Spanish–American War started in:

    A. 1889

    B. 1914

    C. 1927

    D. 1898

    E. 1900

The answer is D
The correct answer is 1898. War erupted between Spain and the United States in 1898 after the U.S. became involved with the Cuban War for Independence which was a Spanish territory. In 1889, North and South Dakota, Montana, and Washington were added to the nation. World War I started in 1914. 1927 and 1900 are incorrect answers.

AMERICAN GOVERNMENT

77. **A major feature of many multiparty political systems is:**

    A. Separation of powers

    B. Inability to represent sectional interests

    C. Coalition government

    D. Strong centralized government

    E. Weak executive branch

The answer is C
The correct answer is coalition government. Many multi-party political systems create coalition governments in which several political parties cooperate in order to decrease the dominance of one party and because a single party is not large enough to create a majority. Separation of powers and the Executive branch have to deal with the branches of government, not the political parties. A strong centralized government does not depend on political parties.
Political parties are also based on ideologies, and not regions, or sections, of the country.

78. **Which of the following statements about American history is an opinion rather than a fact?**

    A. The doctrine of Manifest Destiny can be said to have been an excuse for the expansionism of the United States on the American continent

    B. America's wealth, power, and influence increased with its size

    C. America's expansion was justified by its superior political and economic system

    D. The expansion of the United States was generally detrimental to the interests of native peoples

    E. America entered the two World Wars because American interests were attacked.

The answer is C
The correct answer is America's expansion was justified by its superior political and economic system. Manifest Destiny did claim that America's destiny was to settle from coast to coast which did lead to great expansion. America was able to gain greater influence, wealth, and power when it expanded and became an international player. The expansion of the United States led to the removal of many Native Americans from their own land. America entered World War I after German submarines sank American ships and World War II after the Japanese bombed Pearl Harbor. Since all of these are factual, answer C is the only one based on opinion.

AMERICAN GOVERNMENT

79. Which is a shared power of the federal and state governments?

   A. The power to declare war

   B. The power to build roads

   C. The power to coin money

   D. The power to regulate interstate trade

   E. The power to educate

The answer is B
The correct answer is the power to build roads. Both the federal and state governments have certain powers such as building roads, collecting taxes, and enforcing the law. Congress is the only one that has the power to declare war, coin money, and regulate interstate trade. There is no power to educate, but everyone has a right to education which is why public schools are free.

80. The foreign policy known as the Good Neighbor Policy was associated with the administration of:

   A. James Madison

   B. Franklin Roosevelt

   C. Woodrow Wilson

   D. Theodore Roosevelt

   E. John F. Kennedy

The answer is D
The correct answer is Franklin Roosevelt. The Good Neighbor Policy in the 1930s meant that America would not get involved in Latin America's domestic issues. Theodore Roosevelt is noted for his Big Stick ideology. James Madison was known for drafting the Constitution and the Bill of Rights. Woodrow Wilson is connected to the Fourteen Points and John F. Kennedy was involved with the Bay of Pigs invasion in Cuba.

AMERICAN GOVERNMENT

81. Direct democracy was a feature of:

    A. Greek city–states

    B. Ancient Rome

    C. Medieval Europe

    D. Sumerian theocracy

    E. The Indus Valley civilizations

The answer is A

The correct answer is the politics of the Greek city-states. Athens was a direct democracy because everyone voted directly on policy issues and laws. Rome had consuls and a senate whose members were appointed by the consuls. Medieval Europe was a feudal state in which lords and nobles were at the top, then knights, then merchants, then peasants and serfs at the bottom. Sumer was controlled by high priests who communicated with the gods. The Indus Valley civilizations had several rulers.

82. In a constitutional monarchy, like that of Great Britain, that has a parliamentary system of government, the sovereign takes the place of the:

    A. Prime minister

    B. President

    C. Premier

    D. Speaker of Parliament

    E. Vice president

The answer is B

The correct answer is the President. The sovereign in a Constitutional Monarchy is in charge of the state, just as the President is in America. The Prime Minister is a part of a Constitutional Monarchy and is in charge of Parliament, the government. The Premier is the head of government in some countries such as China. There is no Speaker of Parliament, but there is a Speaker of the House of Commons. The Vice-President is second-in-command, while the sovereign is the sole ruler.

AMERICAN GOVERNMENT

83. The type of city administration that is supposed to eliminate political patronage and fiscal waste is:

   A. Commission–Council

   B. Mayor–Council

   C. Council–Manager

   D. Metropolitan–Manager

   E. City Manager–Council

The answer is C
The correct answer is Council-Manager. This system consists of a Council that acts as the legislative branch and a Manager who provides professional management to the Council. Since the Manager is appointed by the Council, there is no political patronage. The Manager is similar to the CEO of the city which means there should be no fiscal waste. Mayor-Council has a Mayor who is voted by the people into office; he or she needs the support of the people and could get involved in political patronage by bribing people to support him or her. Commission-Council, Metropolitan-Manager, and City-Manager-Council are not forms of city administration.

84. Which of the following statements about the Supreme Court is true?

   A. The Supreme Court has only an appellate jurisdiction in all matters

   B. The Supreme Court shall have original jurisdiction in all areas involving foreign officials, public officials, and cases in which a state is a party

   C. The Supreme Court shall exercise original jurisdiction only over those cases involving the chief executive

   D. The Supreme Court shall have original jurisdiction over appellate matters only

   E. The Supreme Court shall have jurisdiction over all matters, regardless of jurisdiction

The answer is B
The correct answer is "The Supreme Court shall have original jurisdiction in all areas involving foreign officials, public officials, and cases in which a state is a party." In Article Three Section Two Clause Two of the Constitution, the Supreme Court is given original jurisdiction in cases affecting ambassadors, ministers, and consuls, and also when a state is a party. Therefore, all the other answers are incorrect.

AMERICAN GOVERNMENT

85. What happens if the president vetoes a bill?

A. It goes back to Congress, which can override the veto with a two-thirds vote

B. It goes back to the congressional committees

C. It goes back to Congress, which can override it with a three-fourths vote

D. It still becomes a law

E. It goes back to Congress, which can override it with a simple majority

The answer is A
The correct answer is it goes back to Congress which can override the veto with a two-thirds vote. Congress needs a two-thirds vote, not three-fourths, or a majority to override the veto. If a President vetoes a bill, it means he does not want it to become a law. If the bill does not receive the two-thirds vote, then Congress can create a new, similar bill, but the bill does not go back to the Congressional committees.

86. The Truman Doctrine was an attempt to prevent the spread of:

A. German expansionism

B. Imperialism

C. Communism

D. Fascism

E. Democracy

The answer is C
The correct answer is communism. Containment was a part of the Truman Doctrine in 1947 by which America promised to come to the aid of countries that were being subjugated by communism. The Doctrine was established in 1947 after the end of World War II when Germany was devastated and in no position to expand. Imperialism had waned considerably during the twentieth century. Fascism did not present as much as a threat to the world as communism did. American wanted to come to the aid of democratic countries in order to protect democracy.

AMERICAN GOVERNMENT

87. To impeach a president:

A. The charges are brought by the House of Representatives and tried in the Senate

B. The charges are brought by the Senate and tried in the House of Representatives

C. The charges are brought by the states and tried in Congress

D. The charges are brought by Congress and tried before the Supreme Court

E. The charges are brought by the vice president and tried in the Senate

The answer is A
The correct answer is the charges are brought by the House of Representatives and tried in the Senate. The House of Representatives has the power to impeach a president while the Senate has the power to try impeachments. The House and the Senate are the two parts of Congress. The states, the Supreme Court, and the Vice-President have no power in the impeachment process.

88. In the United States, the legal voting age is:

A. 19

B. 18

C. 21

D. 25

E. 16

The answer is B
The correct answer is 18. 18 is the age in the United States when a person becomes a legal adult, and, therefore, becomes a full citizen and can vote. At 25 years, a person can rent a car. At 21 years, a person can legally drink alcohol. At 16 years, a person can obtain a driver's license. 19 years is an incorrect answer.

AMERICAN GOVERNMENT

89. **In the United States' electoral system, who is allowed to vote in primary elections?**

    A. Generally, only registered party members are allowed to vote for their candidates in the party

    B. Any registered voters may vote for candidates in either party primary

    C. Only voters actively engaged in party affairs may vote in a primary

    D. Generally, the United States does not engage in primary elections, though there are exceptions

    E. Nonregistered individuals are allowed to vote in primary elections

The answer is A
The correct answer is generally, only registered party members are allowed to vote for their candidates in the party. In some cases, an unaffiliated voter can vote in a primary election, but it is normally only registered party members that can vote. Elections are not open so a Democrat cannot vote for a Republican and vice versa. The United States always has primary elections. A voter also does not need to be active in party affairs, only to be affiliated with the party.

90. **A important *direct* consequence of the First World War was:**

    A. The end of European colonialism

    B. The Great Depression

    C. The rise of communism

    D. The end of fascism

    E. The socialist state

The answer is C
The correct answer is the rise of communism. The people of Russia were angry at their leader for involving the country in World War I. They rebelled and began reforming the state upon communist principles. European colonialism had its peak in the eighteenth and nineteenth centuries. The Great Depression was not a direct consequence as it did not occur until 1929. Fascism did not end because Mussolini created a fascist state in Italy during World War II. The USSR became a Socialist State in the 30s.

AMERICAN GOVERNMENT

91. In journalism, the term *muckraking* refers to:

   A. An attempt to uncover alleged corruption of public officials

   B. The attempt to cover up the alleged corruption of public officials

   C. The process of buying up various media outlets

   D. The investigation of government inefficiency and waste

   E. Dragging a person's reputation through the mud

The answer is A
The correct answer is an attempt to uncover alleged corruption of public officials. Muckracking is a journalistic technique to uncover corruption, not cover it up. A consequence of uncovering corruption of public officials is dragging their reputation through the mud. Muckracking has nothing to do with buying media outlets or the investigation of government inefficiency.

92. The Voting Rights Act of 1965 sought to:

   A. Extend the franchise to minorities

   B. Undo the last remaining features of unequal suffrage in the United States

   C. Establish the party primary

   D. Give women the right to vote

   E. Take away the voting rights of prisoners

The answer is B
The correct answer is undo the last remaining features of unequal suffrage in the United States. The Voting Act prohibits racial discrimination in voting. The franchise had already been given to minorities, but some states had literacy tests which excluded minorities from voting. The Nineteenth Amendment gave the right to vote to women in 1919. The Voting Act gave voting rights; it did not take them away. The Act had nothing to do with the primary elections.

AMERICAN GOVERNMENT

93. **The United States is a(n):**

    A. Direct democracy

    B. Quasi-democracy

    C. Semi-democracy

    D. Indirect democracy

    E. Non-democracy

The answer is D
The correct answer is indirect democracy. Citizens vote for other people to represent them in government. A direct democracy is when people vote directly on laws and policies. A quasi-democracy resembles a democracy and has some characteristics of it, but is not a true democracy. A semi-democracy combines principles of democracy and authoritarianism. A non-democracy is any other form of government that does not have the principles of democracy; it does not allow the people to have a say in government.

94. **The United States is presently comprised of:**

    A. Fifty-two states, the District of Columbia, and various overseas territories

    B. Forty-eight states, the District of Columbia, and various overseas territories

    C. Fifty states, the District of Columbia, and various overseas territories

    D. Fifty states and the District of Columbia

    E. Fifty-six states and two territories

The answer is C
The correct answer is 50 states, the District of Columbia, and various overseas territories. The United States consists of 50 states, Washington D.C. which is a federal district and the capital, as well as other territories overseas including Guam, Puerto Rico, and the U.S. Virgin Islands. Alaska and Hawaii were the last two additions to the states in 1959 which brought the total to 50.

95. Powers concurrent to both the federal and state governments are:

A. To tax, to raise an army, to establish courts, to provide for the general welfare, and to fix the standards for weights and measures

B. To tax, to charter banks, to borrow money, to make and enforce laws, and to provide for the general welfare

C. To tax, to borrow money, to establish courts, to regulate international trade, and to make and enforce laws

D. To ratify amendments, to tax, to make and enforce laws, to provide for the general welfare, and to raise a militia

E. To tax, to regulate trade, to charter schools, and to make laws

The answer is B
The correct answer is to tax, to charter banks, to borrow money, to make and enforce laws, and to provide for the general welfare. Concurrent powers are the ones that are shared between both the federal and the state governments. These are listed in Article One of the Constitution under Enumerated Powers. There are other powers exclusive to the federal government such as international trade and powers reserved for the state governments which were established with the Tenth Amendment.

96. The term *welfare capitalism* or *the welfare state* is used most often to describe:

A. The former Soviet Union

B. The interval between mercantilism and capitalism

C. The United States and various European countries

D. The Chinese experiments with communism

E. The Middle East

The answer is C
The correct answer is the United States and various European countries. In European countries, welfare states provide universal services for all citizens, while the American welfare state is that companies have internal welfare that benefits their employees. The Welfare State is based off of a social democratic principle which means countries that are communist like the Soviet Union and China would not be considered a Welfare State. Most governments in the Middle East are a monarchy which means they also would not be considered a Welfare State. Welfare Capitalism refers to a practice and not a time period or interval.

AMERICAN GOVERNMENT

97. A poll tax is associated with:

    A. Tariffs on internationally traded goods

    B. Voting rights

    C. Government construction

    D. The income tax structure in a given state

    E. A tax imposed during an election

The answer is B
The correct answer is voting rights. Poll means the act of voting in an election. After the passing of the Fourteenth and Fifteenth Amendments, many states that did not want people of color or people of a lower socioeconomic status to vote would institute a poll tax because they knew the people would not be able to afford it. There are no taxes for elections. Tariffs on internationally traded goods, government construction, and the income tax structure in a given state do not refer to elections at all and are, therefore, incorrect.

98. Who of the following wrote about modern economic problems?

    A. John Locke

    B. Thomas Hobbes

    C. John Maynard Keynes

    D. Alexander Hamilton

    E. Alexis de Tocqueville

The answer is C
The correct answer is John Maynard Keynes. Keynes was a British economist in the twentieth century whose ideas influenced modern-day economics. John Locke is an English philosopher from the eighteenth century who discussed the natural rights of people. Thomas Hobbes is another English philosopher from the eighteenth century who supported the absolutism of the sovereign. Alexander Hamilton supported government intervention in business. Alexis de Tocqueville was a Frenchman who wrote about democracy in America.

AMERICAN GOVERNMENT

99. *Gerrymandering* is:

    A. The consolidation of various voting districts into larger, more efficient entities

    B. The adjustment of voting districts to achieve some goal, usually to promote greater political representation of a given demographic of voters

    C. The removal of certain inefficient political departments

    D. The fixing of the economic infrastructure

    E. The process of endless debate in the Senate

The answer is B
The correct answer is the adjustment of voting districts in order to achieve some predetermined goal, usually to try to promote greater minority political representation. Gerrymandering is the change in an electoral voting district in order to bring more power to a certain political party. It has nothing to do with economic infrastructure or debate in the Senate. Consolidating voting districts does not necessarily make them more efficient and removing political departments has to do with something else.

100. Interest groups form to influence:

    A. Government funding

    B. State funding

    C. Government policy

    D. State policy

    E. All of the above

The answer is E
The correct answer is all of the above.

HISTORY OF THE UNITED STATES I

Description of the Examination

The History of the United States I: Early Colonization to 1877 examination covers material that is usually taught in the first semester of a two-semester course in United States history. The examination covers the period of United States history from early European colonization to the end of Reconstruction, with the majority of the questions on the period of 1790-1877. In the part covering the seventeenth and eighteenth centuries, emphasis is placed on the English colonies.

The examination contains approximately 120 questions to be answered in 90 minutes. Some of these are pretest questions that will not be scored. Any time candidates spend on tutorials and providing personal information is in addition to the actual testing time.

Knowledge and Skills Required

Questions on the History of the United States I examination require candidates to demonstrate one or more of the following abilities.

- Identification and description of historical phenomena
- Analysis and interpretation of historical phenomena
- Comparison and contrast of historical phenomena

The subject matter of the History of the United States I examination is drawn from the following topics. The percentages next to the main topics indicate the approximate percentage of exam questions on that topic.

Topical Specifications

35%	Political institutions, political developments, behavior, and public policy
25%	Social developments
10%	Economic developments
15%	Cultural and intellectual developments
15%	Diplomacy and international relations

Chronological Specifications

30%	1500–1789
70%	1790–1877

The following themes are reflected in a comprehensive introductory survey course:

- The impact of European discovery and colonization upon indigenous societies
- The nature of indigenous societies in North America
- The origins and nature of slavery and resistance
- Immigration and the history of ethnic minorities
- Major movements and individual figures in the history of women and the family
- The development and character of colonial societies
- British relations with the Atlantic colonies of North America
- The changing role of religion in American society
- The content of the Constitution and its amendments, and their interpretation by the Supreme Court
- The development and expansion of participatory democracy
- The growth of and changes in political parties
- The changing role of government in American life
- The intellectual and political expressions of nationalism

HISTORY OF THE UNITED STATES I

- Major movements and individual figures in the history of American literature, art, and popular culture
- Abolitionism and reform movements
- Long term democratic trends (immigration and internal migration)
- The motivations for and character of American expansionism
- The process of economic growth and development
- The causes and impacts of major wars in United States history

HISTORY OF THE UNITED STATES I

SAMPLE TEST

DIRECTIONS: Read each item and select the best response.

1. **Which of the following is a way that ancient civilizations did NOT contribute to the government of the United States?**

   A. Direct democracy

   B. Philosophy of government

   C. Indirect democracy

   D. Checks and balances

   E. Welfare

2. **The Atlantic slave trade lasted approximately how many years?**

   A. Four hundred

   B. Three hundred

   C. Two hundred

   D. One hundred

   E. Six hundred

3. **The belief that the United States should control all of North America was called:**

   A. Westward Expansion

   B. Pan Americanism

   C. Manifest Destiny

   D. Nationalism

   E. American Sovereignty

4. **Early French settlement gave the French control over which two rivers?**

   A. The Missouri and Mississippi

   B. The St. Lawrence and the Hudson

   C. The Hudson and Missouri

   D. The Mississippi and the St. Lawrence

   E. The Missouri and the St. Lawrence

5. **How did the Treaty of Paris of 1783 affect the Native Americans?**

   A. It did not

   B. It set aside areas for them to live

   C. Native American land was ceded to the United States

   D. Native American land was ceded to French Canada

   E. It ceded French Canadian land to Native Americans

6. **Geographically, how were the New England and Middle colonies different?**

   A. New England had an abundance of good soil but the Middle colonies did not

   B. New England's farms produced a large supply of food but Middle colonies imported most of their foodstuffs

   C. The Middle colonies had a rocky shoreline and the New England colonies had large seaports

   D. The Middle colonies had a less severe climate than the New England colonies

   E. The Middle colonies had shorter growing seasons than the New England colonies

7. **In what ways are the Mayflower Compact and Fundamental Orders of Connecticut similar?**

   A. They both pledged loyalty to the king of England

   B. They were joint resolutions of various communities

   C. They were expressions of views and forms of government

   D. They were both peace treaties

   E. They were created in the late 1700s before statehood

8. **In what way did spatial exchange influence the development of colonial society?**

   A. Population was diffused throughout the colonies

   B. It affected the settlement of inland colonies

   C. It was the reason colonists settled the Midwest

   D. Population focused on its importance in forming towns

   E. It caused an increased population density along the Atlantic coast

9. **What effect did the passage of acts such as the Sugar Act, the Stamp Act, and the Townshend Acts have on colonial America?**

   A. The acts polarized the colonists

   B. The acts were accepted with dignity

   C. The colonists tolerated the acts

   D. The colonists resisted the acts

   E. The acts spurred economic growth in colonial America

10. **Why did King George III repeal the Stamp Act?**

    A. He feared rebellion

    B. He no longer needed funds

    C. Parliament recommended repeal

    D. Parliament amended the act

    E. England was losing money

11. **How did England benefit from the Navigation Acts?**

    A. The acts were revenue producing

    B. The acts assured England's economic supremacy

    C. The acts required the use of English ships

    D. The acts monitored colonial commerce

    E. The acts made it easier for other nations to trade with the colonies, strengthening ties between Britain and other colonial powers

12. **All of the following are reasons why the government under the Articles of Confederation was not retained EXCEPT**

    A. It did not provide for a strong chief executive

    B. It lacked the ability to regulate finances

    C. It lacked power to enforce legislation

    D. It lacked the power to enforce treaties

    E. It allowed each state to issue its own money

13. **The Federalists:**

    A. supported states' rights

    B. desired a weak central government

    C. favored a strong central government

    D. were also called Loyalist

    E. opposed protective tariffs

14. **Generally, _____ favored low tariffs.**

    A. Democratic-Republicans

    B. the Supreme Court

    C. Federalists

    D. Congress

    E. the executive branch

15. What event sparked a great migration of people from all over the world to California during the mid-1800s?

    A. The birth of labor unions

    B. Manifest Destiny

    C. The invention of the automobile

    D. The Gold Rush

    E. The Dust Bowl

16. After the settlers inhabited _____, they believed they were destined to settle the North American continent.

    A. the Louisiana Territory

    B. the Northwest Territory

    C. the Piedmont of Virginia

    D. Texas

    E. the Florida panhandle

17. Which area was acquired last by the United States?

    A. Annexation of Texas

    B. Acquisition of Oregon

    C. The Louisiana Purchase

    D. Indian Stream Territory

    E. The Gadsden Purchase

18. Why did Northerners first oppose the admission of Texas to statehood?

    A. Texas was controlled by Mexico

    B. Texas did not have the required population

    C. Texas wanted to allow slavery

    D. Texas owed debts to the U.S. government

    E. Texas had a weak economy

19. Which was not an issue that caused sectionalism?

    A. Mechanization of farming

    B. Tariffs

    C. Slavery

    D. Land speculation

    E. Immigrant populations

20. The principle of "popular sovereignty" that allowed people in any territory to make their own decisions concerning the slavery issue was first stated by:

    A. Henry Clay

    B. Daniel Webster

    C. John C. Calhoun

    D. Stephen A. Douglas

    E. Andrew Johnson

21. **Who was a Confederate commander?**

    A. Ambrose Burnside

    B. George McClellan

    C. J. E. B. Stuart

    D. Irvin McDowell

    E. Ulysses Grant

22. **Which statement is true about the Radical Republicans?**

    A. They favored Andrew Johnson's plan of Reconstruction

    B. They favored harsh measures of Reconstruction

    C. They established the Freedmen's Bureau

    D. They opposed "black codes"

    E. They opposed the Wade-Davis Bill

23. **Why were Alfred Mahan's theories important in shaping U.S. foreign policy?**

    A. He believed America should "speak softly and carry a big stick"

    B. He believed a strong army would avoid confrontations

    C. He believed the use of the atomic bomb would end war

    D. He believed a strong navy showed a strong foreign policy

    E. He wanted the U.S. to have a stronger presence in Central America

24. **Which of the following is not an example of an advancement of transportation that took place during the post-Civil War period?**

    A. Rail passenger service

    B. Completion of the transcontinental railroad

    C. Jet planes

    D. Automobile

    E. Establishment of interstate highways

HISTORY OF THE UNITED STATES I

25. **Which political philosophy is concerned with the commonsense needs of the average person?**

    A. Popular sovereignty

    B. Populism

    C. Progressivism

    D. Protectionism

    E. Proletarianism

26. **All of the following are causes of the Industrial Revolution EXCEPT**

    A. immigrants from southeast Europe

    B. inventions

    C. machines

    D. extensive rail service

    E. The Embargo Act of 1807

27. **Which Native American tribes moved west of the Mississippi in the early nineteenth century?**

    A. The Wichitas, Comanches, and Caddoes

    B. The Coahuiltecans, Lipans, and Kiowas

    C. The Cherokee, Choctaw, and Shawnee

    D. The Tonkawas, Wichitas, and Caddoes

    E. The Cherokee, Seneca, Witchitas, and Lakota

28. **What was the cause of friction between the United States and Spain after the Louisiana Purchase in 1803?**

    A. Spain resented American involvement in the Cuban War of Independence

    B. Mexico wanted to buy the Louisiana Territory from France

    C. Spain angered the United States by sinking the American battleship The Maine

    D. Both nations disputed the boundary between Texas and Louisiana

    E. Spain still used and occupied parts of territory from the Louisiana Purchase

29. **Why did missionaries abandon east Texas in 1693?**

    A. The Mexican War of Independence forced abandonment

    B. They moved their mission into the sunny beaches of Spanish Florida

    C. American citizens began to settle in the region

    D. The climate was too harsh

    E. Tensions with Native Americans over a smallpox outbreak scared them away

30. Who was the first American allowed to obtain a colonial grant to settle in Texas?

    A. Stephen F. Austin

    B. Agustin de Iturbide

    C. Moses Austin

    D. Fray Damián Massanet

    E. Brigham Young

31. What was one of the causes of the Mexican War of Independence?

    A. Taxation of the thirteen colonies

    B. Abdication of Napoleon

    C. Debt from the War of 1812

    D. The assassination of the Catholic priest Miguel Hidalgo

    E. Confiscation of church property

32. What was the final battle of the Texas Revolution?

    A. Battle of the Alamo

    B. Battle of San Jacinto

    C. Battle of Gonzales

    D. Battle of Gettysburg

    E. Battle of Little Big Horn

33. What early Texas pioneer documented daily life during the Republic of Texas and early statehood?

    A. Sam Houston

    B. Stephen F. Austin

    C. Mary Maverick

    D. Joshua Houston

    E. Warren Dallas

34. Which event motivated Texas to hold a secessionist vote in 1861?

    A. Battle of Palmito Ridge

    B. Battle of Galveston

    C. Texas Revolution

    D. South Carolina's secession from the Union

    E. Georgia's secession from the Union

35. _____ is the fundamental law of the U.S. republic.

    A. Separation of powers

    B. Checks and balances

    C. Federalism

    D. The Constitution

    E. The Declaration of Independence

36. **Federal taxation legislation must originate in:**

    A. the House of Representatives.

    B. the Senate

    C. either the House or the Senate

    D. both the House and Senate simultaneously

    E. both the House and Supreme Court

37. **The Thirteenth, Fourteenth, and Fifteenth Amendments were called the "Civil War" amendments because they:**

    A. abolished slavery, gave voting rights to former slaves, and provided for equal protection

    B. provided due process, direct election of U.S. senators, and voting rights regardless of race, color, or previous condition of servitude

    C. provided equal protection, prohibited the poll tax, and abolished slavery

    D. prohibited the poll tax, provided for direct election of U.S. Senators, and provided due process

    E. provided due process and universal suffrage to veterans of the Civil War

38. **The American governmental system is a federal system because:**

    A. the national and state governments share powers

    B. state governments have three branches of government

    C. there are fifty states and one national government

    D. the federal government has administrative agencies

    E. each state has its own federal government

39. **How did the federal government demonstrate that education was important in the westward expansion movement?**

    A. Congress required students to attend school until the age of 15

    B. Congress provided funds for agricultural colleges

    C. Congress required each township to establish a school

    D. Congress established teacher-training colleges

    E. Congress penalized underperforming townships

40. **The temperance movement resulted in:**

    A. women gaining the right to vote

    B. the increased manufacture of alcohol

    C. enactment of the Prohibition Amendment

    D. reduction of abuses of drunkenness

    E. a decrease in birth rate

41. **The Mayflower Compact is an example of:**

    A. a resistance to illegitimate government

    B. the law of nature

    C. a divine right theory document

    D. a foreign peace treaty

    E. a social contract theory document

42. **In which type of government system are coalition parties common?**

    A. Monarchy

    B. Dictatorship

    C. Federalist

    D. Parliamentary system

    E. Oligarchy

43. **Adam Smith believed that:**

    A. labor was a value-determining factor

    B. free markets should exist without government interference

    C. aggregate spending determined the level of economic activity

    D. collective ownership and administration of goods was necessary

    E. government needed to influence free mark1ets

44. **All of the following are reasons why Europeans came to the New World EXCEPT**

    A. To provide protection for indigenous populations

    B. To increase the monarch's power

    C. To find natural resources for manufacturing

    D. To spread their nation's religious views

    E. To spread out and develop their nation's population

45. **The Department of Treasury:**

    A. handles federal investigations by making them into business activities

    B. assures fair and free competition between businesses

    C. runs the Government Accounting Office

    D. advises the president on fiscal policy

    E. monitors the development of local businesses

46. **Which publishers' newspapers included modern features such as comics, puzzles, illustrations, columnists, and sports?**

    A. William Randolph Hearst

    B. Edward W. Scripps

    C. Charles A. Dana

    D. Alfred Nobel

    E. Joseph Pulitzer

47. **All of the following are reasons why the United States went to war with Britain in 1812 EXCEPT**

    A. Spain's resentment over the sale, exploration, and settlement of the Louisiana Territory

    B. The westward expansion of settlers

    C. The agitation of Native Americans by fur traders

    D. The continued seizure of American ships on British seas

    E. The need for more land

48. There is no doubt the U.S. Constitution was a vast improvement over the weak Articles of Confederation. Which one of the five statements below is not a description of the document?

    A. The establishment of a strong central government in no way lessened or weakened the individual states.

    B. Individual rights were protected and secured.

    C. The Constitution demands unquestioned respect and subservience to the federal government by all states and citizens.

    D. Its flexibility and adaptation to change gives it a sense of timelessnesss

    E. The constitution requires ¾ of all states to agree on ratifying an amendment as opposed to requiring all states to agree.

49. From about 1870 to 1900 the settlement for America's "last frontier", in the west was made possible by:

    A. construction of major highways

    B. the building of the railroad

    C. The invention of the automobile

    D. The signing of the Treaty of Holston with the Cherokee

    E. The popularization of the steamboat

50. Who wrote the famous line "these are the times that try men's souls" in the 16 part pamphlet *The American Crisis*?

    A. Thomas Hobbes

    B. Henry Clay

    C. Thomas Paine

    D. John Locke

    E. Benjamin Franklin

51. Which country first sent explorers to the New World during the "Age of Exploration"?

    A. Portugal

    B. Denmark

    C. England

    D. Spain

    E. France

52. Which of the following is not a responsibility of U.S. political parties?

    A. Obtaining funds needed for elections

    B. Choosing candidates to run for office

    C. Raising voters' awareness of political issues

    D. Writing platforms for candidates to state their positions

    E. Holding elections

53. **Who is considered to be the father of modern economics?**

    A. John Stuart Mill

    B. John Maynard Keynes

    C. Thomas Malthus

    D. Adam Smith

    E. John Locke

54. **Immediately after the American Revolution, which nation owned the most land in the Americas?**

    A. The United States of America

    B. Great Britain

    C. France

    D. Spain

    E. Portugal

55. **Constitutionalism is a political system in which:**

    A. it is run by a head of state, the elected or self-appointed president

    B. laws and traditions put limits on the power of government

    C. a strong, centralized national government holds together the nation

    D. a group of representatives are led by a prime minister

    E. a monarch has only limited legal and ceremonial powers

56. **What was the political significance of Marbury v. Madison (1803)?**

    A. It established judicial review

    B. It made popular sovereignty possible in the U.S.

    C. It relied on the notion of supreme law of the land

    D. The elastic clause of the Constitution was a major influence on the decision

    E. It established universal suffrage

57. **Who was the first European explorer to land in Florida?**

    A. John Cabot

    B. Christopher Columbus

    C. Panfilo de Navarez

    D. Juan Marco Valdez

    E. Ponce de Leon

58. **Which Revolutionary battle was the main factor in the establishment of the Franco-American Alliance of 1777?**

    A. The Battle of Gettysburg

    B. Battle of Monmouth

    C. The Battle of Saratoga

    D. The Battle of Bunker Hill

    E. The Siege of Yorktown

HISTORY OF THE UNITED STATES I

59. **During the Treaty of Paris in 1763, Britain received _____ from Spain:**

    A. the land west of Florida (Alabama, Louisiana)

    B. Florida

    C. Texas

    D. the Great Lake States

    E. Missouri and Kansas

60. **Impeaching the President of the United States means:**

    A. removing the president from office

    B. bringing formal charges against the president

    C. reelecting the president for a second term

    D. fining the president for disagreeing with Congress

    E. overriding the president's veto

61. **_____ was established in 1789 by Article 3 of the Constitution.**

    A. The state court system

    B. The Supreme Court

    C. Judicial review

    D. The Federal circuit court system

    E. The concept of checks and balances

62. **The Bill of Rights, and most of the Constitution, were written by:**

    A. George Washington

    B. Thomas Jefferson

    C. Alexander Hamilton

    D. Andrew Jackson

    E. James Madison

63. **The United States Constitution was ratified by the required nine states on which month and year?**

    A. July, 1776

    B. August, 1861

    C. June, 1788

    D. January, 1848

    E. February, 1815

64. **Which statement is true about colonization of North America in the 1600s?**

    A. The Portuguese built a plantation society in South America

    B. The Spanish controlled much of Central America

    C. The French controlled much of the Great Lakes area

    D. The French controlled what is present-day Florida

    E. The English controlled the Mississippi River fur trade

65. **Which colonial region became known as the "breadbasket" of the New World?**

    A. New England

    B. Middle colonies

    C. Virginia

    D. The Great Lakes area

    E. West

66. **The "Trail of Tears" refers to:**

    A. Native American removal

    B. the treatment of slaves

    C. retreat of the Confederate army from Gettysburg

    D. Civil War defeats

    E. French losses in the Midwest

67. **Nullification means:**

    A. the state government had the right to decide whether a federal law was unconstitutional

    B. the state government had the right to require the state to follow federal law

    C. the federal government could nullify an act of Congress

    D. state government had the right to nullify Supreme Court decisions made in cases of a given state

    E. Congress could declare state legislation null

68. **The Compromise of 1850 did all of the following EXCEPT**

    A. addressed the issue of slavery

    B. abolished the slave trade in Washington D.C.

    C. changed the borders of Texas to its present day borders

    D. admitted California as a slave state

    E. permitted runaway slaves to be returned to their owner

69. **What was an advantage the South had as it entered the Civil War?**

    A. Confidence

    B. Population

    C. Transportation facilities

    D. Military leadership

    E. Natural resources

70. **Ulysses S. Grant was victorious at _____ and severed the western Confederacy from the eastern Confederacy.**

    A. Saratoga

    B. Chickamauga

    C. Gettysburg

    D. Bull Run

    E. Vicksburg

71. An example of a way to avoid the conditions of the Fifteenth Amendment was:

    A. Sit-ins

    B. Poll taxes

    C. Litigation

    D. Bus boycotts

    E. Freedom rides

72. Which political party first raised the women's suffrage issue?

    A. Democratic

    B. Republican

    C. Radical-Republicans

    D. Liberty

    E. Whig

73. Which of the following developments changed the lifestyles of all Native Americans in Texas?

    A. The widespread acceptance of agriculture

    B. The utilization of the mixed economy

    C. The introduction of the horse

    D. The introduction of the matrilineal society

    E. The development of a rudimentary jail system

74. What were the main causes of the Mexican-American War?

    A. Land disputes

    B. Treaty of Annexation

    C. Santa Fe Expedition

    D. Both A and B

    E. Both A and C

75. Why did the U.S. government name Quanah Parker as chief of the Comanches?

    A. He was well-respected by the Comanches

    B. He was a great military leader

    C. He transitioned quickly to reservation life

    D. He received the most votes in Congress

    E. He advocated renewing hostility with American settlers

76. What was an effect of the abolition movement?

    A. It solidified the nation

    B. It eliminated divisiveness

    C. It created unity

    D. It split the country

    E. It destroyed international trade in the Americas

HISTORY OF THE UNITED STATES I

77. **In what way was John Locke's political philosophy expressed in the Declaration of Independence?**

    A. People have the right to resist arbitrary action of a ruler

    B. Kings should not have a divine right to rule

    C. Government is a social contract

    D. Government should serve to protect the welfare of the people

    E. Government should not interfere in business

78. **Why did Federalists, such as Alexander Hamilton, want a national bank?**

    A. Because it represented states' rights

    B. Because the U.S. experienced severe inflation, surplus levels of counterfeiting, and had difficulty in financing military operations

    C. Because the U.S. population and revenue was increasing so fast that state banks could not keep up with the amount of gold species coming in

    D. Because there were to many regulations on individual state banks

    E. Because the governmental insurance was spending too much on states banks to protect deposits in case of a bank failure

79. **What did the Democrat-Republicans, such as Andrew Jackson, believe in during the early nineteenth century?**

    A. Nationalism, Centralism, Modernization, and Monetarism

    B. Pro-immigration, Pro-taxation, and Pro-trade

    C. Pro-commerce, Pro-social improvements, and Pro-manufacturing

    D. Manifest Destiny, Agriculturalism, States Rights, and Populism

    E. Anti-Masonry, Protectionism, and Social Conservatism

80. **Who drafted the Virginia Statute for Religious Freedom in 1777?**

    A. George Washington

    B. Thomas Jefferson

    C. James Madison

    D. John Dickenson

    E. Benjamin Franklin

81. **What did the Statue of Liberty symbolize for the United States in 1886?**

    A. It was a sign of friendship between France and the United States

    B. Freedom

    C. A welcoming sight for immigrants coming from boats

    D. Progress

    E. All of the above

82. **What were the men and women called who remained loyal to the British Crown in the American Revolution?**

    A. Parliament's men

    B. Tories

    C. King's army

    D. Georgenites

    E. True colonists

83. **What was one of the causes of the French and Indian War in 1754?**

    A. Land expansion conflict between the British colonists in Virginia and the French colonists east of the Great Lakes

    B. The French disagreed with how Native Americans traded

    C. France invaded Prussia

    D. The French massacred British in Uniontown, Pennsylvania near Fort Duquesne

    E. Indians raided Saratoga, New York

84. **Which Native American tribe was one of the only tribes to ally with the British during the French and Indian War?**

    A. Algonquian allies

    B. Sioux

    C. Delawares

    D. Shawnees

    E. The Iroquois League

85. **Why did Native American groups make an alliance with the British during the French and Indian War?**

    A. French animosity

    B. British colonists forced them to

    C. Strong friendship with colonists

    D. British patriotism

    E. Animosity towards other tribes and hope for British favor after the war

86. **What was the Whig parties' ideology?**

    A. The people hold popular sovereignty, rather than the people being subjects to a monarchy

    B. That one person holds sovereignty

    C. A belief that government should control the economy

    D. To maintain the existing or traditional order

    E. They believed in removing some powers from the states and giving more powers to the national government

87. **The British system of mercantilism was opposed by many American colonists because it:**

    A. discouraged the export of raw materials to England

    B. placed restrictions on trading

    C. encouraged British manufacturing

    D. benefited Native Americans

    E. placed quotas on immigration

88. **The main reason Great Britain established the Proclamation Line of 1763 was to:**

    A. avoid conflicts between American colonists and Native American Indians

    B. make a profit by selling the land west of the Appalachian Mountain

    C. prevent American industrial development in the Ohio River valley

    D. allow Canada to control the Great Lakes region

    E. to keep a monopoly on the trade market with Native Americans

89. Which act coined the famous saying "No Taxation without Representation?"

   A. Currency Act, 1764

   B. The Mayflower Compact

   C. The Tea Act, 1765

   D. The Stamp Act, 1765

   E. Boston Compromise, 1764

90. The 1494 Treaty of Tordesillas, allowed what two nations to divide the entire non-European world into two areas of exploration and colonization?

   A. England and France

   B. The Dutch Republic and Spain

   C. Spain and Portugal

   D. England and the Dutch Republic

   E. France and Portugal

91. In which battle was General Stonewall Jackson killed?

   A. The Battle of Chancellorsville

   B. The Battle of Gettysburg

   C. The Battle of Shiloh

   D. The Peninsular Campaign

   E. The First Battle of Battle Run

92. What did the Homestead Act of 1862 claim?

   A. Those of age had to enlist in the Union army

   B. Anyone who had never taken up arms against the United States could claim ownership of land, up to 160 acres, at little or no cost

   C. Anything west of the Mississippi could be claimed by white male land owners

   D. Those of age had to enlist in the Confederate army

   E. None of these

93. Which president enforced the Homestead Act of 1862?

   A. Jefferson Davis

   B. Alexander H. Stephens

   C. Abraham Lincoln

   D. Ulysses S. Grant

   E. Andrew Johnson

94. What did the Federalists, led by Alexander Hamilton in the early eighteenth and late nineteenth centuries, believe in?

    A. A fiscally sound and strong nationalistic government

    B. A weak federal government and strong states government

    C. No government

    D. Monarchy

    E. Anti-affiliation with British affairs

95. Which of the following pairings most accurately links the presidential candidate with what he advocated or embodied?

    A. John C. Calhoun-western expansion

    B. Jon Quincy Adams-opposition to an activist government

    C. Henry Clay-states' rights

    D. Andrew Jackson-nationalist pride

    E. Martin Van Buren-large government

96. In the 1830s and 1840s, the major difference between Whigs and the Democrats was that:

    A. the Democrats favored an activist role for the federal government to help the economy while the Whigs opposed such an expansion of federal power

    B. the Whigs favored the abolition of slavery while the Democrats said that it was not a federal concern

    C. the Whigs believed in an activist federal government, while the Democrats favored a federal government with conscribed powers

    D. the Democrats power stemmed from an alliance of Northern and Southern monetary interests while farmers supported the Whigs

    E. the Whigs opposed westward expansion and the Democrats favored it

97. Indian removal was an example of President Jackson's endorsement of:

    A. protectionism

    B. nullification

    C. states' rights

    D. internal improvements

    E. a strong federal judiciary

98. **Which FORMER president's wife preformed her First Lady duties for her husband and for President Thomas Jefferson?**

    A. Abigail Adams

    B. Dolley Madison

    C. Sarah York Jackson

    D. Elizabeth Monroe

    E. Martha Jefferson Randolph

99. **What was the main difference in weaponry used in the Civil War compared to wars fought earlier in the nineteenth century?**

    A. Prior wars involved rudimentary weapons which lent themselves to hand-to-hand combat and close range fighting

    B. There was no difference

    C. All of the weapons used in the Civil War were completely different

    D. Weaponry in prior wars was less accurate but more deadly

    E. Weaponry in prior wars was more accurate but not as deadly

100. **From 1790 until the early nineteenth century women were largely thought to be what characteristic?**

     A. Virtuous

     B. Courageous

     C. Intelligent

     D. Prosperous

     E. Strong

101. **Which answer describes the First Amendment?**

     A. Protection from quartering of troops

     B. Freedom of speech, press, religion, peaceable assembly, and to petition the government

     C. Right for the people to keep and bear arms, as well as to maintain a militia

     D. Civil trial by jury

     E. Due process, double jeopardy, self-incrimination, private property

102. **What was the major type of economic production in the South?**

     A. Textile

     B. Factory

     C. Transportation

     D. Agriculture

     E. Iron/Steel

103. Harriet Beecher Stowe's "Uncle Tom's Cabin" aroused northern outrage over the implications of the

   A. Missouri Compromise

   B. Virginia Run Away Slave Act

   C. Fugitive Slave Act

   D. Kansas-Nebraska Act

   E. Dred Scott decision

104. What was the main provision of the Fugitive Slave Law?

   A. Slaves were free if they got to the North

   B. The Underground Railroad was legalized

   C. Blacks found without proper litigation could be enslaved

   D. Southerners could not pursue escaped slaves

   E. Aiding runaway slaves was a crime

105. The United States refused to annex Texas in 1836 because:

   A. Most of Texas's inhabitants were native Mexicans

   B. Texans did not want to be annexed to the United States

   C. The American government was opposed to armed rebellions against established governments

   D. There weren't enough inhabitants for it to become a state

   E. Of fear that it would provoke war with Mexico

106. Which of the following people organized the first women's rights convention at Seneca Falls?

   A. Dorthea Dix and Susan B. Anthony

   B. Dorthea Dix and Lucretia Mott

   C. Lucretia Mott and Elizabeth Cady Stanton

   D. Susan B. Anthony and Elizabeth Cady Stanton

   E. Horace Mann and Noah Webster

107. **What did the Neutrality Proclamation on 1793 mean for the United States?**

    A. That Congress could declare war and neutrality

    B. That the President could declare war and neutrality

    C. That the President could declare neutrality but not war

    D. That Congress could not declare war or neutrality

    E. None of the above

108. **What effect did railroads play in westward expansion?**

    A. Quicker transportation and it increased national revenue

    B. Allowed slaves to escape easier

    C. Decreased the overall population

    D. Increased the national debt

    E. Decreased agricultural economy and implanted it with manufacturers

109. **The Indian Removal Act of 1830 removed southeastern tribes to Indian Territory. In what present day state was this territory located?**

    A. Nebraska

    B. Oklahoma

    C. Kansas

    D. Texas

    E. Indiana

110. **What was one factor that influenced the creation of the National Market Economy?**

    A. Revolution in transportation

    B. Public policy at state and national levels to promote enterprise

    C. Nationalism of the Republican Party (aka Jefferson Party)

    D. Judicial nationalism, creation of legal requirements for a national market

    E. All of the above

111. Why was the "penny press" or the Daily News Papers (1835) a technological advancement in mass media?

   A. Only the rich could afford it, therefore, they held common knowledge over citizens of less income, Native Americans, or slaves

   B. It was an affordable and economically savvy way to spread information, political views and agendas

   C. It was the first newspaper

   D. It was the first time the nation could become unified over any mass media advancement

   E. None of the above

112. What was the fastest growing social class during the Antebellum Era?

   A. Low-class

   B. Slave

   C. Middle-class

   D. Upper-class

   E. Immigrants

113. The second Great Awakening of the first half of the nineteenth century had what effect on life in America?

   A. It increased concern over slavery

   B. Promoted a greater focus on democratic ideals that coincided with the Age of Jacksonian ideology- "the common man"

   C. Created a desire for control and order

   D. Bars, brothels, and jails closed down

   E. All of the above

114. Mormonism in the Antebellum Period reflected:

   A. a strong antislavery bias

   B. a celebration of individual liberty

   C. a desire to improve the status of women

   D. a strong desire to isolate believers from general society

   E. a belief in human perfectibility

115. **The creation of "asylums" for social deviants was an effort to:**

    A. punish the inmates

    B. get the deviants out of society

    C. reform and rehabilitate the inmates

    D. cut down the cost of crime and punishment

    E. All answers are correct

116. **What group of people had the largest population in the South during the early to mid-nineteenth century:**

    A. yeoman farmers

    B. merchants

    C. slaves

    D. planters

    E. seafaring merchants

117. **What effect did the Slave Trade Act of 1807 have on the United States?**

    A. That slavery was abolished

    B. That one could buy slaves in all states, despite state laws

    C. That no one could import international slaves

    D. That 1/3 of every slave bought internationally would be taxed higher than slaves bought within the nation

    E. That only white landowners could buy international slaves

118. **A major difference between Northern and Southern societies prior to the Civil War is illustrated by the role women played in the:**

    A. establishment of educational institutions in the South

    B. growth of the Northern factory system

    C. emergence of a Southern literary tradition

    D. explosion of religious revivalism in the North

    E. political spheres

119. **The U.S. Naturalization Law of March 26, 1790 included only:**

    A. free white persons

    B. Asians

    C. Native Americans

    D. free blacks

    E. indentured whites

120. **What document contains a list of individual rights and liberties that limit the United States federal government?**

    A. The Declaration of Independence

    B. Magna Carta

    C. Liberty Bill

    D. Bill of Rights

    E. Petition of Rights

HISTORY OF THE UNITED STATES I

ANSWER KEY

Question Number	Correct Answer	Your Answer	Question Number	Correct Answer	Your Answer	Question Number	Correct Answer	Your Answer
1	D		41	E		81	E	
2	A		42	D		82	B	
3	C		43	B		83	A	
4	D		44	A		84	E	
5	C		45	D		85	E	
6	D		46	E		86	A	
7	E		47	A		87	B	
8	B		48	C		88	A	
9	D		49	B		89	D	
10	A		50	C		90	C	
11	D		51	A		91	A	
12	C		52	E		92	B	
13	C		53	D		93	C	
14	A		54	D		94	A	
15	D		55	B		95	D	
16	A		56	A		96	C	
17	E		57	E		97	C	
18	C		58	C		98	B	
19	A		59	A		99	A	
20	D		60	B		100	A	
21	C		61	B		101	B	
22	B		62	E		102	D	
23	D		63	C		103	C	
24	B		64	B		104	E	
25	B		65	B		105	E	
26	A		66	A		106	C	
27	C		67	A		107	C	
28	D		68	D		108	A	
29	E		69	A		109	B	
30	C		70	E		110	E	
31	E		71	B		111	B	
32	B		72	D		112	C	
33	C		73	C		113	E	
34	D		74	D		114	E	
35	D		75	C		115	C	
36	C		76	D		116	C	
37	A		77	A		117	C	
38	C		78	B		118	B	
39	B		79	D		119	A	
40	C		80	B		120	D	

HISTORY OF THE UNITED STATES I

RATIONALES

1. **Which of the following is a way that ancient civilizations did NOT contribute to the government of the United States?**

    A. Direct democracy

    B. Philosophy of government

    C. Indirect democracy

    D. Checks and balances

    E. Welfare

The answer is D
Checks and balances is a system where one branch of government limits the other branch of government so one branch does not get too big or powerful. The idea came from the French philosopher Montesquieu in 1689. Therefore, it was relatively new compared to direct democracy, indirect government, philosophy of government, and welfare which all found their origins in ancient Athens.

2. **The Atlantic slave trade lasted approximately how many years?**

    A. Four hundred

    B. Three hundred

    C. Two hundred

    D. One hundred

    E. Six hundred

The answer is A
The first African slave that was brought over was in 1502. Brazil became the last nation in the Western Hemisphere to outlaw the Atlantic slave trade in 1888.

HISTORY OF THE UNITED STATES I

3. The belief that the United States should control all of North America was called:

    A. Westward Expansion

    B. Pan Americanism

    C. Manifest Destiny

    D. Nationalism

    E. American Sovereignty

The answer is C
Manifest Destiny was the idea that American settlers were destined to spread throughout the entire continent. A, B, D, and E all attributed to this, but were not the main cause.

4. Early French settlement gave the French control over which two rivers?

    A. The Missouri and Mississippi

    B. The St. Lawrence and the Hudson

    C. The Hudson and Missouri

    D. The Mississippi and the St. Lawrence

    E. The Missouri and the St. Lawrence

The answer is D
The United States acquired both rivers after the Louisiana Purchase in 1803. The Missouri (parts of it) and the Hudson had already been obtained earlier by the United States.

5. How did the Treaty of Paris of 1783 affect the Native Americans?

   A. It did not

   B. It set aside areas for them to live

   C. Native American land was ceded to the United States

   D. Native American land was ceded to French Canada

   E. It ceded French Canadian land to Native Americans

The answer is C
After the loss of the French and Indian War, France gave up land that was formerly owned by France and Native American tribes. American colonists slowly made their way over the Appalachian Mountains. Therefore, all other answers are incorrect.

6. Geographically, how were the New England and Middle colonies different?

   A. New England had an abundance of good soil but the Middle colonies did not

   B. New England's farms produced a large supply of food but Middle colonies imported most of their foodstuffs

   C. The Middle colonies had a rocky shoreline and the New England colonies had large seaports

   D. The Middle colonies had a less severe climate than the New England colonies

   E. The Middle colonies had shorter growing seasons than the New England colonies

The answer is D
The Middle colonies' lands were more fertile and the weather was less harsh. C and E describe New England lands. A and B describe the Middle colonies' landscape.

HISTORY OF THE UNITED STATES I

7. **In what ways are the Mayflower Compact and Fundamental Orders of Connecticut similar?**

    A. They both pledged loyalty to the king of England

    B. They were joint resolutions of various communities

    C. They were expressions of views and forms of government

    D. They were both peace treaties

    E. They were created in the late 1700s before statehood

The answer is E
The Mayflower Compact was created in 1620 and the Fundamental Orders of Connecticut was created in 1639. The Mayflower was created to give a framework for the government once the Mayflower had landed at Plymouth. The Fundamental Orders of Connecticut was the same thing, but it was a little more complex.

8. **In what way did spatial exchange influence the development of colonial society?**

    A. Population was diffused throughout the colonies

    B. It affected the settlement of inland colonies

    C. It was the reason colonists settled the Midwest

    D. Population focused on its importance in forming towns

    E. It caused an increased population density along the Atlantic coast

The answer is B
Due to the increase of people coming from Britain, the colonists had to continue to move inland where there was more land to be settled and farmed.

9. **What effect did the passage of acts such as the Sugar Act, the Stamp Act, and the Townshend Acts have on colonial America?**

    A. The acts polarized the colonists

    B. The acts were accepted with dignity

    C. The colonists tolerated the acts

    D. The colonists resisted the acts

    E. The acts spurred economic growth in colonial America

The answer is D
Colonists felt that they were not being represented in Parliament, and, therefore, should not be taxed. The events set off larger events (such as the Boston Tea party), assimilating into the American Revolution. Thus, A, B, and C, are incorrect. E is incorrect because the taxes took money away from the colonists and acts of disobedience caused Britain to enforce stricter control, particularly on ports.

10. **Why did King George III repeal the Stamp Act?**

    A. He feared rebellion

    B. He no longer needed funds

    C. Parliament recommended repeal

    D. Parliament amended the act

    E. England was losing money

The answer is A
The colonists acted with violence and economic retaliation against the taxations. A general boycott of British goods began, and the Sons of Liberty staged attacks on the customhouses and homes of tax collectors in Boston. It was after months of protest and economic turmoil, and an appeal by Benjamin Franklin, before the British House of Commons, Parliament, voted to repeal the Stamp Act in March 1766.

HISTORY OF THE UNITED STATES I

11. **How did England benefit from the Navigation Acts?**

    A. The acts were revenue producing

    B. The acts assured England's economic supremacy

    C. The acts required the use of English ships

    D. The acts monitored colonial commerce

    E. The acts made it easier for other nations to trade with the colonies, strengthening ties between Britain and other colonial powers

The answer is D
The Navigation acts were a series of laws that restricted the use of foreign ships for trade between Britain and its colonies. Many of the laws created by the act restricted colonists from trading with other sovereign nations. These acts did not necessarily mean that England remained economically superior, and in many ways it made it harder for both countries. Britain had to use its navy while the colonists had to go out of their way at times to make or sell goods that could have been bought or made for cheaper. Therefore, A, B, C, and E are all wrong.

12. **All of the following are reasons why the government under the Articles of Confederation was not retained EXCEPT**

    A. It did not provide for a strong chief executive

    B. It lacked the ability to regulate finances

    C. It lacked power to enforce legislation

    D. It lacked the power to enforce treaties

    E. It allowed each state to issue its own money

The answer is C
Article II of the Articles of Confederation state, "Each state retains its sovereignty, freedom, and independence, and every power, jurisdiction, and right, which is not by this Confederation expressly delegated to the United States, in Congress assembled." Therefore, Congress has weak powers, whereas, states have the most power (E). The Articles lacked the power to enforce laws. However, the Articles acted like a federal government by having an executive power (A), Congress, and state representatives to deal with national and international problems (B and D).

13. **The Federalists:**

    A. supported states' rights

    B. desired a weak central government

    C. favored a strong central government

    D. were also called Loyalist

    E. opposed protective tariffs

The answer is C
Federalists, led by such politicians as Alexander Hamilton, believed in a fiscally sound and nationalistic government. It existed from the early 1790s to 1816. A, B, and E describe Republicans. D and E describe colonists (before the political shift, i.e. Loyalists were colonists who were in favor of the Crown).

14. **Generally, _____ favored low tariffs.**

    A. Democratic-Republicans

    B. the Supreme Court

    C. Federalists

    D. Congress

    E. the executive branch

The answer is A
Democrat-Republicans, such as Thomas Jefferson, disliked large governments. High tariffs gave money to large governments so they could do what they felt was needed. B, D, and E were all in favor of high tariffs because it brought them revenue. C, Federalists, believed the opposite of Republicans. They wanted a large government.

HISTORY OF THE UNITED STATES I

15. **What event sparked a great migration of people from all over the world to California during the mid-1800s?**

    A. The birth of labor unions

    B. Manifest Destiny

    C. The invention of the automobile

    D. The Gold Rush

    E. The Dust Bowl

The answer is D
Numerous gold rushes happened across the world throughout the nineteenth century. The California Gold rush started in 1848. People testified that they could pick gold nuggets up right off the ground. Eventually, gold became harder to find, as mining took place. The gold-seekers, called "forty-niners" traveled by sailing ship and in covered wagons, and often faced substantial hardships on the trip. While most of the newly arrived were Americans, the Gold Rush attracted tens of thousands from Latin America, Europe, Australia, and Asia.

16. **After the settlers inhabited _____, they believed they were destined to settle the North American continent.**

    A. the Louisiana Territory

    B. the Northwest Territory

    C. the Piedmont of Virginia

    D. Texas

    E. the Florida panhandle

The answer is A
Before the Louisiana Purchase, the United States' west border was the Mississippi River. The Louisiana Purchase doubled the size of the nation. After a few explorations, United States citizens slowly made their way west. No other treaty/occupation gave the United Sates that much land.

17. **Which area was acquired last by the United States?**

    A. Annexation of Texas

    B. Acquisition of Oregon

    C. The Louisiana Purchase

    D. Indian Stream Territory

    E. The Gadsden Purchase

The answer is E
The United States purchased it on December 30, 1853. A is incorrect because Texas was annexed in 1845. B is incorrect because Oregon became a U.S. territory in 1848. C is incorrect because it was purchased in 1803. D is incorrect because the land dispute was settled by 1842.

18. **Why did Northerners first oppose the admission of Texas to statehood?**

    A. Texas was controlled by Mexico

    B. Texas did not have the required population

    C. Texas wanted to allow slavery

    D. Texas owed debts to the U.S. government

    E. Texas had a weak economy

The answer is C
Texas wanted to enter the Union as a slave state which would greatly add to the slaveholding size of America which the northerners, who were mostly against slavery, opposed. Texas was not controlled by Mexico as it became its own Republic in 1837. Texas owed debts, but not to the Union. It also had a good economy since there were rich fields of cotton which attracted immigrants and meant Texas had a decent sized population.

HISTORY OF THE UNITED STATES I

19. **Which was not an issue that caused sectionalism?**

    A. Mechanization of farming

    B. Tariffs

    C. Slavery

    D. Land speculation

    E. Immigrant populations

The answer is A
Tariffs, slavery, land speculation, and immigrant populations all caused rifts throughout the American political landscape. Examples range from Loyalists liking tariffs, Southerners being more prompt to like slavery, rich colonists liking land speculation, and Irish immigrants being not allowed to work certain jobs. Not many people were complaining about the mechanization of farming, if anything, everyone was applauding.

20. **The principle of "popular sovereignty" that allowed people in any territory to make their own decisions concerning the slavery issue was first stated by:**

    A. Henry Clay

    B. Daniel Webster

    C. John C. Calhoun

    D. Stephen A. Douglas

    E. Andrew Johnson

The answer is D
Popular sovereignty was a thought that came from the Revolution. It is the principle that the authority of the government is created and sustained by the consent of its people through their elected representatives. It stems from liberalism.

HISTORY OF THE UNITED STATES I

21. Who was a Confederate commander?

A. Ambrose Burnside

B. George McClellan

C. J. E. B. Stuart

D. Irvin McDowell

E. Ulysses Grant

The answer is C
Stuart was a Confederate officer from the state of Virginia. He became known as Robert E. Lee's "eyes and ears." Burnside, McClellan, McDowell, and Grant fought for the Union.

22. Which statement is true about the Radical Republicans?

A. They favored Andrew Johnson's plan of Reconstruction

B. They favored harsh measures of Reconstruction

C. They established the Freedmen's Bureau

D. They opposed "black codes"

E. They opposed the Wade-Davis Bill

The answer is B
Radical Republicans feared the South might rise again. They also felt the North had no business helping the South. Thus, A, E, and C are incorrect. The radical Republicans opposed the "black codes." Therefore, D is incorrect.

23. **Why were Alfred Mahan's theories important in shaping U.S. foreign policy?**

    A. He believed America should "speak softly and carry a big stick"

    B. He believed a strong army would avoid confrontations

    C. He believed the use of the atomic bomb would end war

    D. He believed a strong navy showed a strong foreign policy

    E. He wanted the U.S. to have a stronger presence in Central America

The answer is D
Alfred Mahon believed in having a strong navy presence to show that the United States had a strong foreign policy. Therefore, A, C and E are all incorrect because they are the opposite. B is incorrect because Mahan spoke of the navy, not the army.

24. **Which of the following is not an example of an advancement of transportation that took place during the post-Civil War period?**

    A. Rail passenger service

    B. Completion of the transcontinental railroad

    C. Jet planes

    D. Automobile

    E. Establishment of interstate highways

The answer is B
The transcontinental railroad was completed in 1869 which was during the Civil War era. A, C, D, and E are all advancements post-Civil War.

HISTORY OF THE UNITED STATES I

25. Which political philosophy is concerned with the commonsense needs of the average person?

    A. Popular sovereignty

    B. Populism

    C. Progressivism

    D. Protectionism

    E. Proletarianism

The answer is B

Populism is a political ideology that appeals to the interest of the people. A is wrong because it acts on the consent of the people, through representatives voted into office. Progressivism is the political ideology that asserts that advancement in science, technology, economic development, and social organization are vital to improve the human condition, thus incorrect. Protectionism is incorrect because it refers to restraining trade between two countries. Proletarianism has to do with downward movement in a social society (Marxist theory). It does not apply here.

26. All of the following are causes of the Industrial Revolution EXCEPT

    A. immigrants from southeast Europe

    B. inventions

    C. machines

    D. extensive rail service

    E. The Embargo Act of 1807

The answer is A

Large immigration from Southeast Asia came in the early twentieth century. Thus, it did no attribute to the Industrial Revolution.

HISTORY OF THE UNITED STATES I

27. **Which Native American tribes moved west of the Mississippi in the early nineteenth century?**

    A. The Wichitas, Comanches, and Caddoes

    B. The Coahuiltecans, Lipans, and Kiowas

    C. The Cherokee, Choctaw, and Shawnee

    D. The Tonkawas, Wichitas, and Caddoes

    E. The Cherokee, Seneca, Witchitas, and Lakota

The answer is C
The Indian Removal Act of 1830 removed all Native Americans and relocated them to Indian Territory (Oklahoma). The Cherokee, Choctaw, and the Shawnee were all eastern tribes.

28. **What was the cause of friction between the United States and Spain after the Louisiana Purchase in 1803?**

    A. Spain resented American involvement in the Cuban War of Independence

    B. Mexico wanted to buy the Louisiana Territory from France

    C. Spain angered the United States by sinking the American battleship The Maine

    D. Both nations disputed the boundary between Texas and Louisiana

    E. Spain still used and occupied parts of territory from the Louisiana Purchase

The answer is D
Neutral Grounds was an area Spain and the United Sates disputed over after the Louisiana Purchase. Neutral Ground, as it was called, remained neutral from 1806 to 1821 when the United States eventually took it over.

29. Why did missionaries abandon east Texas in 1693?

    A. The Mexican War of Independence forced abandonment

    B. They moved their mission into the sunny beaches of Spanish Florida

    C. American citizens began to settle in the region

    D. The climate was too harsh

    E. Tensions with Native Americans over a smallpox outbreak scared them away

The answer is E
Missionaries believed that it was "God's holy will" that the east Texas Native Americans (Tejas) got small pox. Tejas told them to get out or be killed.

30. Who was the first American allowed to obtain a colonial grant to settle in Texas?

    A. Stephen F. Austin

    B. Agustin de Iturbide

    C. Moses Austin

    D. Fray Damián Massanet

    E. Brigham Young

The answer is C
Moses Austen received a land grant from Spain and planned to make an English settlement in Spanish Texas (1820). He eventually died and his son became his successor. His son saw the formation of the Republic of Texas.

31. What was one of the causes of the Mexican War of Independence?

    A. Taxation of the thirteen colonies

    B. Abdication of Napoleon

    C. Debt from the War of 1812

    D. The assassination of the Catholic priest Miguel Hidalgo

    E. Confiscation of church property

The answer is E
The Bourbon reforms took power from the Catholic Church in Mexico. Parish priests and other secular clergy experienced not only loss of status, but loss of income. At times, Bourbon representatives, not being religious, would cause unruly protests during church events and on Church property. A, B, and C are nonfactual. D is correct, but the war was caused due to the confiscation of Church property.

32. What was the final battle of the Texas Revolution?

    A. Battle of the Alamo

    B. Battle of San Jacinto

    C. Battle of Gonzales

    D. Battle of Gettysburg

    E. Battle of Little Big Horn

The answer is B
After an 18-minute battle, Texans routed Santa Anna's forces, eventually taking Santa Anna prisoner. This was the last battle of the Texas Revolution. 630 Mexicans killed, 208 wounded, 730 captured, and nine Texans killed, 30 wounded. A, D, and E, are all battles from different wars. C was the first battle of the Texas Revolution.

HISTORY OF THE UNITED STATES I

33. What early Texas pioneer documented daily life during the Republic of Texas and early statehood?

    A. Sam Houston

    B. Stephen F. Austin

    C. Mary Maverick

    D. Joshua Houston

    E. Warren Dallas

The answer is C
Mary Maverick was an early Texan pioneer and author of memoirs which form an important source of information about daily life in and around San Antonio during the Republic of Texas period through the American Civil War. Sam Houston was an important politician that brought Texas into the United States. B, D, and E are all made-up.

34. Which event motivated Texas to hold a secessionist vote in 1861?

    A. Battle of Palmito Ridge

    B. Battle of Galveston

    C. Texas Revolution

    D. South Carolina's secession from the Union

    E. Georgia's secession from the Union

The answer is D
On February 1, 1861, Texas declared secession from the Union. South Carolina led the way after Abraham Lincoln was elected in 1860. A, B, and C had little to nothing to do with the secession. Georgia seceded after Texas, therefore, E is incorrect.

HISTORY OF THE UNITED STATES I

35. _____ **is the fundamental law of the U.S. republic.**

   A. Separation of powers

   B. Checks and balances

   C. Federalism

   D. The Constitution

   E. The Declaration of Independence

The answer is D
Created in 1787, the Constitution is the supreme law of the United States of America. A, B, and C are all methods and ideologies of government, therefore, incorrect. E declares separation from Great Britain, but it does not create the foundational laws for a new nation.

36. Federal taxation legislation must originate in:

   A. the House of Representatives.

   B. the Senate

   C. either the House or the Senate

   D. both the House and Senate simultaneously

   E. both the House and Supreme Court

The answer is C
Federal taxation laws must originate in the House or Senate as notified in the Origination Clause (1789) written in the Constitution. Therefore, E is incorrect. It must start in the House or Senate and then the other has a chance to turn it down if it wants to. Therefore, A, B, and D are all incorrect.

HISTORY OF THE UNITED STATES I

37. The Thirteenth, Fourteenth, and Fifteenth Amendments were called the "Civil War" amendments because they:

A. abolished slavery, gave voting rights to former slaves, and provided for equal protection

B. provided due process, direct election of U.S. senators, and voting rights regardless of race, color, or previous condition of servitude

C. provided equal protection, prohibited the poll tax, and abolished slavery

D. prohibited the poll tax, provided for direct election of U.S. Senators, and provided due process

E. provided due process and universal suffrage to veterans of the Civil War

The answer is A
The Reconstruction Amendments, the Thirteenth, Fourteenth, and Fifteenth Amendments, were all established within five years after the Civil War. The Thirteenth Amendment abolished slavery. The Fourteenth Amendment included the privileges and immunities clause, applicable to all citizens, and the due process and equal protection clauses applicable to all persons. The Fifteenth Amendment prohibits discrimination in voting rights of citizens on the basis of "race, color, or previous condition of servitude."

38. The American governmental system is a federal system because:

A. the national and state governments share powers

B. state governments have three branches of government

C. there are fifty states and one national government

D. the federal government has administrative agencies

E. each state has its own federal government

The answer is C
The American government is a federal system because it has a group of members (states) that are bound together by a covenant with a governing representative head (national government). A is incorrect because national and state governments have different powers. B is wrong because the national government has three branches, not the state. D is wrong because it doesn't matter if it has different agencies. E is wrong because each state has its own state government.

HISTORY OF THE UNITED STATES I

39. How did the federal government demonstrate that education was important in the westward expansion movement?

    A. Congress required students to attend school until the age of 15

    B. Congress provided funds for agricultural colleges

    C. Congress required each township to establish a school

    D. Congress established teacher-training colleges

    E. Congress penalized underperforming townships

The answer is B
Morrill Land-Grant Acts, which started in 1862, was proposed because a large political movement was calling for agricultural schools in the west. Michigan State University serves as one example. A, C, D, and E are all incorrect.

40. The temperance movement resulted in:

    A. women gaining the right to vote

    B. the increased manufacture of alcohol

    C. enactment of the Prohibition Amendment

    D. reduction of abuses of drunkenness

    E. a decrease in birth rate

The answer is C
The Temperance movement was a movement in the 1820s that was against alcohol consumption. It eventually gained so much support that alcohol was outlawed in the 1920s with the Eighteenth Amendment.

41. The Mayflower Compact is an example of:

    A. a resistance to illegitimate government

    B. the law of nature

    C. a divine right theory document

    D. a foreign peace treaty

    E. a social contract theory document

The answer is E
A social contract addresses the questions of the origin of society and the legitimacy of the authority of the state over the individual. A, B, C, and D all fail to do so.

42. In which type of government system are coalition parties common?

    A. Monarchy

    B. Dictatorship

    C. Federalist

    D. Parliamentary system

    E. Oligarchy

The answer is D
A coalition government is a cabinet of a parliamentary government in which several political parties cooperate, reducing the dominance of any one party within that coalition. The usual reason given for this arrangement is that no party on its own can achieve a majority in the parliament. A and B are incorrect because there is only one head of government. Federalist is part of a republican government, so incorrect. E is incorrect because it states that power should rest with a small amount of people, such as royalty.

HISTORY OF THE UNITED STATES I

43. Adam Smith believed that:

    A. labor was a value-determining factor

    B. free markets should exist without government interference

    C. aggregate spending determined the level of economic activity

    D. collective ownership and administration of goods was necessary

    E. government needed to influence free mark1ets

The answer is B
Adam Smith believed in the concept of laissez-faire. He believed free markets should exist without government interference. A, D, and E were Marxist thoughts, thus incorrect. C was more Keynesian theory, also incorrect.

44. All of the following are reasons why Europeans came to the New World EXCEPT

    A. To provide protection for indigenous populations

    B. To increase the monarch's power

    C. To find natural resources for manufacturing

    D. To spread their nation's religious views

    E. To spread out and develop their nation's population

The answer is A
They did the opposite. Some historians say up to 99% of Native Americans in North America died because of European settlers.

45. **The Department of Treasury:**

    A. handles federal investigations by making them into business activities

    B. assures fair and free competition between businesses

    C. runs the Government Accounting Office

    D. advises the president on fiscal policy

    E. monitors the development of local businesses

The answer is D
The Department of Treasury is an executive department and the treasury of the United States' federal government. It was established by an Act of Congress in 1789 to manage government revenue. A, B, C, and E are all run by other facets of the United States government

46. **Which publishers' newspapers included modern features such as comics, puzzles, illustrations, columnists, and sports?**

    A. William Randolph Hearst

    B. Edward W. Scripps

    C. Charles A. Dana

    D. Alfred Nobel

    E. Joseph Pulitzer

The answer is E
Joseph Pulitzer was a Hungarian-born American newspaper publisher of the St. Louis Post Dispatch and the New York World. Pulitzer introduced the techniques of "new journalism" to the newspapers he acquired in the 1880s. He became a leading national figure in the Democratic Party and was elected Congressman from New York. He is also known for "yellow journalism" and the Pulitzer Prize is named after him. A, B, C, and D are all people who have prizes named after them and all are incorrect.

HISTORY OF THE UNITED STATES I

47. **All of the following are reasons why the United States went to war with Britain in 1812 EXCEPT**

    A. Spain's resentment over the sale, exploration, and settlement of the Louisiana Territory

    B. The westward expansion of settlers

    C. The agitation of Native Americans by fur traders

    D. The continued seizure of American ships on British seas

    E. The need for more land

The answer is A
The War of 1812 was between Britain and America, not Spain and America. Therefore, Spain had nothing to do with the War of 1812.

48. **There is no doubt the U.S. Constitution was a vast improvement over the weak Articles of Confederation. Which one of the five statements below is not a description of the document?**

    A. The establishment of a strong central government in no way lessened or weakened the individual states.

    B. Individual rights were protected and secured.

    C. The Constitution demands unquestioned respect and subservience to the federal government by all states and citizens.

    D. Its flexibility and adaptation to change gives it a sense of timelessnesss

    E. The constitution requires ¾ of all states to agree on ratifying an amendment as opposed to requiring all states to agree.

The answer is C
The one purpose of the Articles of Confederation was to fight against monarchy and large governments. C represents both and is, therefore, the correct answer.

49. **From about 1870 to 1900 the settlement for America's "last frontier", in the west was made possible by:**

    A. construction of major highways

    B. the building of the railroad

    C. The invention of the automobile

    D. The signing of the Treaty of Holston with the Cherokee

    E. The popularization of the steamboat

The answer is B
The beginning of the Gilded Age saw a lot of industrialization, particularly in the North. The first transcontinental railroad that reached the Pacific was built in 1869. D and E happened before 1870 and only influenced the east coast, so incorrect. A and C came after the invention of the railroad.

50. **Who wrote the famous line "these are the times that try men's souls" in the 16 part pamphlet *The American Crisis*?**

    A. Thomas Hobbes

    B. Henry Clay

    C. Thomas Paine

    D. John Locke

    E. Benjamin Franklin

The answer is C
Thomas Paine was an English-American political activist, philosopher, political theorist, and revolutionary. His work *The American Crisis* was written during the American Revolution. The pamphlets were contemporaneous with early parts of the American Revolution and during a time when colonists needed inspiring works. They were written in a language that the common man could understand, and represented Paine's liberal philosophy.

HISTORY OF THE UNITED STATES I

51. Which country first sent explorers to the New World during the "Age of Exploration"?

    A. Portugal

    B. Denmark

    C. England

    D. Spain

    E. France

The answer is A

The Age of Discovery is a loosely defined European historical period from the fifteenth century to the eighteenth century. It was the period in which global exploration started with the Portuguese discovery of the Atlantic archipelago of the Azores, the western coast of Africa, and discovery of the ocean route to the East in 1498.

52. Which of the following is not a responsibility of U.S. political parties?

    A. Obtaining funds needed for elections

    B. Choosing candidates to run for office

    C. Raising voters' awareness of political issues

    D. Writing platforms for candidates to state their positions

    E. Holding elections

The answer is E

If U.S. political parties held the elections, then they could hypothetically be altered. This goes against democratic-republic principles. Therefore, E is the correct answer.

HISTORY OF THE UNITED STATES I

53. Who is considered to be the father of modern economics?

A. John Stuart Mill

B. John Maynard Keynes

C. Thomas Malthus

D. Adam Smith

E. John Locke

The answer is D

Adam Smith is often thought to be the world's first free-market capitalist. Although not entirely precise, Smith is considered the father of modern economics and a major proponent of laissez-faire economic policies. The Scottish philosopher argued against mercantilism, for open markets, and relatively barrier-free domestic and international trade. Therefore, D is the correct answer.

54. **Immediately after the American Revolution, which nation owned the most land in the Americas?**

   A. The United States of America

   B. Great Britain

   C. France

   D. Spain

   E. Portugal

The answer is D
Up until the American Revolution, Spain had dominion over half of North and South American land. A map reveals this:

Map taken from
https://en.wikipedia.org/wiki/Spanish_colonization_of_the_Americas#/media/File:Spanish_America_XVIII_Century_(Most_Expansion).png

HISTORY OF THE UNITED STATES I

55. Constitutionalism is a political system in which:

    A. it is run by a head of state, the elected or self-appointed president

    B. laws and traditions put limits on the power of government

    C. a strong, centralized national government holds together the nation

    D. a group of representatives are led by a prime minister

    E. a monarch has only limited legal and ceremonial powers

The answer is B
Constitutionalism is a set of laws that are set into place in order to restrict government. They are made up of a mix of ideas, attitudes, and patterns. Therefore, A and C are incorrect because they represent a large government. D and E are incorrect because they represent a parliament.

56. What was the political significance of Marbury v. Madison (1803)?

    A. It established judicial review

    B. It made popular sovereignty possible in the U.S.

    C. It relied on the notion of supreme law of the land

    D. The elastic clause of the Constitution was a major influence on the decision

    E. It established universal suffrage

The answer is A
The decision helped define the boundary between the constitutionally separate executive and judicial branches of the American form of government. Justice of the Peace, William Marbury of Washington DC, petitioned the Supreme Court to force the new Secretary of State, James Madison, to deliver the documents. The Court found that Madison's refusal to deliver the commission was both illegal and correctible. Nonetheless, the Court did not order Madison to hand over Marbury's commission. They insisted that Marbury bringing his case to the Supreme Court was itself unconstitutional, since it purported to extend the Court's original jurisdiction beyond that which Article III established. The petition was therefore denied.

HISTORY OF THE UNITED STATES I

57. Who was the first European explorer to land in Florida?

    A. John Cabot

    B. Christopher Columbus

    C. Panfilo de Navarez

    D. Juan Marco Valdez

    E. Ponce de Leon

The answer is E
Ponce de Leon spotted Florida on April 2, 1513. John Cabot is thought to have been the first European to explore the Newfoundland area, not Florida.

58. Which Revolutionary battle was the main factor in the establishment of the Franco-American Alliance of 1777?

    A. The Battle of Gettysburg

    B. Battle of Monmouth

    C. The Battle of Saratoga

    D. The Battle of Bunker Hill

    E. The Siege of Yorktown

The answer is C
The Battle of Saratoga was decisive for the Americans. The Battle of Saratoga and the Battle of York were the only big battles that they won. The battle was so decisive that the French felt the Americans had a shot at winning. Thus, France entered the war and turned the Revolutionary War into a global war. Britain had to remove many resources from the colonies in order to fight a more powerful enemy; France.

HISTORY OF THE UNITED STATES I

59. During the Treaty of Paris in 1763, Britain received _____ from Spain:

   A. the land west of Florida (Alabama, Louisiana)

   B. Florida

   C. Texas

   D. the Great Lake States

   E. Missouri and Kansas

The answer is A
Great Britain won the Seven Years' War against France, Spain, and Portugal. It became the world leader in dominance outside of Europe. Spain ceded Florida and lands to the west of Florida to Britain. France ceded the area west of the Appalachian mountain to the Mississippi as well as half of French Canada. Therefore, D, and E are wrong. Texas came after the Texas Revolution, thus C is incorrect. B is only half true, thus incorrect.

60. Impeaching the President of the United States means:

   A. removing the president from office

   B. bringing formal charges against the president

   C. reelecting the president for a second term

   D. fining the president for disagreeing with Congress

   E. overriding the president's veto

The answer is B
Article I of the United States Constitution gives the House of Representatives the sole power of impeachment and the Senate the sole power to try impeachments. Impeachment is the equivalent of a grand jury indictment. All it means is that there is enough evidence to bring the president to court (i.e. Bill Clinton was impeached and then cleared by the Senate). Therefore, A, C, D, and E are all wrong.

HISTORY OF THE UNITED STATES I

61. _____ was established in 1789 by Article 3 of the Constitution.

    A. The state court system

    B. The Supreme Court

    C. Judicial review

    D. The Federal circuit court system

    E. The concept of checks and balances

The answer is B
Article III of the Constitution establishes the Supreme Court and the lower courts that are set up by Congress. Therefore, C, D, and E are all wrong. A is wrong because the state court has nothing to do with the judicial federal court.

62. The Bill of Rights, and most of the Constitution, were written by:

    A. George Washington

    B. Thomas Jefferson

    C. Alexander Hamilton

    D. Andrew Jackson

    E. James Madison

The answer is E
The Bill of Rights and the Constitution were mostly written by James Madison. Washington was there, but did not attribute to the writing. Jefferson wrote most of the Declaration of Independence. Hamilton and Jackson came into the political picture a little later, so they did not write them either.

HISTORY OF THE UNITED STATES I

63. **The United States Constitution was ratified by the required nine states on which month and year?**

    A. July, 1776

    B. August, 1861

    C. June, 1788

    D. January, 1848

    E. February, 1815

The answer is C
Georgia, Massachusetts, Connecticut, New York, South Carolina, Virginia, Rhode Island, Maryland, and New Hampshire all ratified the Constitution on June 21, 1788 which was after the establishment of the Constitution.

64. **Which statement is true about colonization of North America in the 1600s?**

    A. The Portuguese built a plantation society in South America

    B. The Spanish controlled much of Central America

    C. The French controlled much of the Great Lakes area

    D. The French controlled what is present-day Florida

    E. The English controlled the Mississippi River fur trade

The answer is B
Spain had claimed most of Central America in the 1600s. A is wrong because the British had done so. C is wrong because that was Native American territory. D is wrong because Spain controlled Florida. E is wrong because the French controlled the Mississippi (although the British dominated the fur trading industry in North America at this point).

65. Which colonial region became known as the "breadbasket" of the New World?

    A. New England

    B. Middle colonies

    C. Virginia

    D. The Great Lakes area

    E. West

The answer is B
The Middle colonies had less harsh landscape than the North and South which meant more could be produced. C could be correct, but the Middle colonies consisted of more than Virginia. E is wrong because the West was not yet colonized at this point.

66. The "Trail of Tears" refers to:

    A. Native American removal

    B. the treatment of slaves

    C. retreat of the Confederate army from Gettysburg

    D. Civil War defeats

    E. French losses in the Midwest

The answer is A
The Trail of Tears was the process of removing Native Americans from southeastern United States in the Removal Act of 1830.

67. **Nullification means:**

    A. the state government had the right to decide whether a federal law was unconstitutional

    B. the state government had the right to require the state to follow federal law

    C. the federal government could nullify an act of Congress

    D. state government had the right to nullify Supreme Court decisions made in cases of a given state

    E. Congress could declare state legislation null

The answer is A
Nullification is a legal theory that a state has the right to nullify, or invalidate, any federal law which that state has deemed unconstitutional.

68. **The Compromise of 1850 did all of the following EXCEPT**

    A. addressed the issue of slavery

    B. abolished the slave trade in Washington D.C.

    C. changed the borders of Texas to its present day borders

    D. admitted California as a slave state

    E. permitted runaway slaves to be returned to their owner

The answer is D
Henry Clay drafted the Compromise of 1850. It was passed by the United States Congress in September 1850, which defused confrontation between slave and free states regarding the status of territories acquired during the Mexican-American War (1846–1848). D mistakenly claims California was admitted as a slave state, when it was actually admitted as a free state.

69. What was an advantage the South had as it entered the Civil War?

    A. Confidence

    B. Population

    C. Transportation facilities

    D. Military leadership

    E. Natural resources

The answer is A
The South had higher morale. The war was a defensive one for the South, which meant they had more of a home field advantage. Also, their military leaders were a bit more superior to the Northern ones who lacked experience.

70. Ulysses S. Grant was victorious at _____ and severed the western Confederacy from the eastern Confederacy.

    A. Saratoga

    B. Chickamauga

    C. Gettysburg

    D. Bull Run

    E. Vicksburg

The answer is E
The Battle or Siege of Vicksburg (May 18 – July 4, 1863) was the final major military action in the Vicksburg Campaign of the American Civil War. Union Major General Ulysses S. Grant and his army crossed the Mississippi River and drove the Confederate Army of Mississippi led by Lieutenant General John C. Pemberton into the fortress city of Vicksburg, Mississippi. Vicksburg was the last major Confederate stronghold on the Mississippi River. With the loss of Pemberton's army and this vital stronghold on the Mississippi, the Confederacy was effectively split in half.

71. An example of a way to avoid the conditions of the Fifteenth Amendment was:

    A. Sit-ins

    B. Poll taxes

    C. Litigation

    D. Bus boycotts

    E. Freedom rides

The answer is B
The Fifteenth Amendment allowed black men to vote. It was put into the U.S. Constitution on March 30, 1870. It states, "the right of citizens of the United States to vote shall not be denied or abridged by the United States or by any State on account of race, color, or previous condition of servitude." Therefore, the states that did not support the Amendment created poll taxes so many of the black men who had previously been slaves, Native Americans, and poor whites could not afford to vote. A, C, D, and E were all used in the twentieth century civil rights era.

72. Which political party first raised the women's suffrage issue?

    A. Democratic

    B. Republican

    C. Radical-Republicans

    D. Liberty

    E. Whig

The answer is D
In May, 1848 the Liberty Party approved a resolution calling for "universal suffrage" in its broadest sense, including women as well as men.

HISTORY OF THE UNITED STATES I

73. Which of the following developments changed the lifestyles of all Native Americans in Texas?

   A. The widespread acceptance of agriculture

   B. The utilization of the mixed economy

   C. The introduction of the horse

   D. The introduction of the matrilineal society

   E. The development of a rudimentary jail system

The answer is C
Horses were introduced to North America from Spain. Native American culture was changed forever. Trading, food, clothing, and even warfare transformed drastically. Native American tribes that were once much weaker, with the addition of horses, became much stronger than former enemy tribes.

74. What were the main causes of the Mexican-American War?

   A. Land disputes

   B. Treaty of Annexation

   C. Santa Fe Expedition

   D. Both A and B

   E. Both A and C

The answer is D
After the Texas Revolution, Mexico told the United States not to let Texas enter as a state or it would declare war. President John Tyler wanted Texas, but he could not get enough support in Congress to allow Texas into the Union. Tyler then began to allow (and setup) skirmishes over land disputes to gain support. Eventually, the U.S. declared war on Mexico. C was an expedition by Texas when it was its own nation. Therefore, C and E are wrong.

HISTORY OF THE UNITED STATES I

75. Why did the U.S. government name Quanah Parker as chief of the Comanches?

    A. He was well-respected by the Comanches

    B. He was a great military leader

    C. He transitioned quickly to reservation life

    D. He received the most votes in Congress

    E. He advocated renewing hostility with American settlers

The answer is C
Quanah Parker was one of the last chiefs of the Comanche tribe. The Comanche had lost some decisive battles to the United States. Parker, Comanche/English-American, assimilated well into American society. He was chosen to assimilate the tribe. He led the Comanche tribe to its government selected reservation and became a wealthy rancher.

76. What was an effect of the abolition movement?

    A. It solidified the nation

    B. It eliminated divisiveness

    C. It created unity

    D. It split the country

    E. It destroyed international trade in the Americas

The answer is D
The abolition movement was against slavery. The movement pushed Americans apart, particularly the southern planters and northern mercantilists. A, B, and C, are obviously wrong then. The abolition movement helped end the slave trade, not trade in general, therefore, E is incorrect.

HISTORY OF THE UNITED STATES I

77. **In what way was John Locke's political philosophy expressed in the Declaration of Independence?**

   A. People have the right to resist arbitrary action of a ruler

   B. Kings should not have a divine right to rule

   C. Government is a social contract

   D. Government should serve to protect the welfare of the people

   E. Government should not interfere in business

The answer is A
John Locke believed in natural rights. Therefore, the less control government has on people the better. B, C, and D are all incorrect then. E is too vague, so incorrect.

78. **Why did Federalists, such as Alexander Hamilton, want a national bank?**

   A. Because it represented states' rights

   B. Because the U.S. experienced severe inflation, surplus levels of counterfeiting, and had difficulty in financing military operations

   C. Because the U.S. population and revenue was increasing so fast that state banks could not keep up with the amount of gold species coming in

   D. Because there were to many regulations on individual state banks

   E. Because the governmental insurance was spending too much on states banks to protect deposits in case of a bank failure

The answer is B
Federalists believed in a fiscally strong federal government. A national bank would come in conjunction with this. A is incorrect because it didn't represent states' rights. C is incorrect because it is not factual. D and E are incorrect because the government at the time was much smaller.

HISTORY OF THE UNITED STATES I

79. **What did the Democrat-Republicans, such as Andrew Jackson, believe in during the early nineteenth century?**

   A. Nationalism, Centralism, Modernization, and Monetarism

   B. Pro-immigration, Pro-taxation, and Pro-trade

   C. Pro-commerce, Pro-social improvements, and Pro- manufacturing

   D. Manifest Destiny, Agriculturalism, States Rights, and Populism

   E. Anti-Masonry, Protectionism, and Social Conservatism

The answer is D
Democrat-Republicans believed they were for the middle class. The lesser the government intervened the better. The only time they did intervene was to protect or serve the white populous (such as the Trail of Tears). A, B, and C are all pro-large government, thus incorrect. E is incorrect because they were not social conservative or anti-masonry.

80. **Who drafted the Virginia Statute for Religious Freedom in 1777?**

   A. George Washington

   B. Thomas Jefferson

   C. James Madison

   D. John Dickenson

   E. Benjamin Franklin

The answer is B
Thomas Jefferson drafted the Virginia Statute for Religious Freedom in 1777. The statute disestablished the Church of England in Virginia and guaranteed freedom of religion to people of all religious faiths.

HISTORY OF THE UNITED STATES I

81. What did the Statue of Liberty symbolize for the United States in 1886?

    A. It was a sign of friendship between France and the United States

    B. Freedom

    C. A welcoming sight for immigrants coming from boats

    D. Progress

    E. All of the above

The answer is E
The Statue of Liberty was dedicated on October 28, 1886. It was a gift from the French indicating friendship between the two countries, freedom, and liberty to all; a welcoming sign to immigrants that crossed the Atlantic.

82. What were the men and women called who remained loyal to the British Crown in the American Revolution?

    A. Parliament's men

    B. Tories

    C. King's army

    D. Georgenites

    E. True colonists

The answer is B
Tories or Loyalists in England were traditionally more conservative. They favored the monarch over the Parliament. In the American Revolution, they favored the British Crown over the colonies. All other answers are nonfactual.

HISTORY OF THE UNITED STATES I

83. What was one of the causes of the French and Indian War in 1754?

    A. Land expansion conflict between the British colonists in Virginia and the French colonists east of the Great Lakes

    B. The French disagreed with how Native Americans traded

    C. France invaded Prussia

    D. The French massacred British in Uniontown, Pennsylvania near Fort Duquesne

    E. Indians raided Saratoga, New York

The answer is A
As land became scarcer and colonists became greedier for better lands, they moved west over the Appalachian Mountains and west of the Great Lakes. This created a number of disputes amongst Native Americans, colonists, and French and British governments. B, E, and D are all true, but it was not one of these events that started the war as much as it was the continual invasion of Native American property. C had nothing to with the war.

84. Which Native American tribe was one of the only tribes to ally with the British during the French and Indian War?

    A. Algonquian allies

    B. Sioux

    C. Delawares

    D. Shawnees

    E. The Iroquois League

The answer is E
The Shawnees were the Iroquois' ancestral rival. As much as most Native American tribes disliked colonists, many chose different sides of the political spheres in order to gain advantages for their tribe. A, B, C, and D were all allies with the French.

HISTORY OF THE UNITED STATES I

85. Why did Native American groups make an alliance with the British during the French and Indian War?

   A. French animosity

   B. British colonists forced them to

   C. Strong friendship with colonists

   D. British patriotism

   E. Animosity towards other tribes and hope for British favor after the war

The answer is E
Native American tribes were more for their own self-interest than actually supporting Britain and its colonists. In some cases, such as the Iroquois, it was more beneficial to ally with one of the powers.

86. What was the Whig parties' ideology?

   A. The people hold popular sovereignty, rather than the people being subjects to a monarchy

   B. That one person holds sovereignty

   C. A belief that government should control the economy

   D. To maintain the existing or traditional order

   E. They believed in removing some powers from the states and giving more powers to the national government

The answer is A
Opponents of Andrew Jackson and the Democrat-Republican party, the Whig party believed in Liberalism, protectionism, and modernization. Therefore, B, C, D, and E are all wrong.

HISTORY OF THE UNITED STATES I

87. The British system of mercantilism was opposed by many American colonists because it:

   A. discouraged the export of raw materials to England

   B. placed restrictions on trading

   C. encouraged British manufacturing

   D. benefited Native Americans

   E. placed quotas on immigration

The answer is B

Britain required the colonies to send raw materials to Britain in order to support manufacturing. Therefore, B is correct because Britain wanted to restrict the trade in the colonies in order to support its own mercantilism. E is incorrect because immigration quotas were set in place much later.

88. The main reason Great Britain established the Proclamation Line of 1763 was to:

   A. avoid conflicts between American colonists and Native American Indians

   B. make a profit by selling the land west of the Appalachian Mountain

   C. prevent American industrial development in the Ohio River valley

   D. allow Canada to control the Great Lakes region

   E. to keep a monopoly on the trade market with Native Americans

The answer is A

The Proclamation Line created a line along the Appalachian Mountains in which colonists were not allowed to settle anywhere to the west of the line. This was to avoid further conflicts with Native Americans as colonists could not take away more land from the Native Americans.

89. **Which act coined the famous saying "No Taxation without Representation?"**

    A. Currency Act, 1764

    B. The Mayflower Compact

    C. The Tea Act, 1765

    D. The Stamp Act, 1765

    E. Boston Compromise, 1764

The answer is D
Colonists believed that, as they were not directly represented in the distant British Parliament, any laws it passed affecting the colonists (such as the Sugar Act and the Stamp Act) were illegal under the Bill of Rights of 1689, and denied them their rights as Englishmen.

90. **The 1494 Treaty of Tordesillas, allowed what two nations to divide the entire non-European world into two areas of exploration and colonization?**

    A. England and France

    B. The Dutch Republic and Spain

    C. Spain and Portugal

    D. England and the Dutch Republic

    E. France and Portugal

The answer is C
On June 7, 1494, Spain and Portugal split newly discovered lands outside Europe. At this point Britain, the Dutch Republic, and
France had not discovered or claimed anything in the New World.

HISTORY OF THE UNITED STATES I

91. In which battle was General Stonewall Jackson killed?

    A. The Battle of Chancellorsville

    B. The Battle of Gettysburg

    C. The Battle of Shiloh

    D. The Peninsular Campaign

    E. The First Battle of Battle Run

The answer is A
General Stonewall Jackson is the second most famous Confederate soldier (second to General Robert E. Lee). Confederate pickets accidentally shot him (friendly fire) at the Battle of Chancellorsville on May 2, 1863. The General survived with the loss of an arm to amputation, but died from pneumonia eight days later. Therefore, B, C, D, and E are incorrect.

92. What did the Homestead Act of 1862 claim?

    A. Those of age had to enlist in the Union army

    B. Anyone who had never taken up arms against the United States could claim ownership of land, up to 160 acres, at little or no cost

    C. Anything west of the Mississippi could be claimed by white male land owners

    D. Those of age had to enlist in the Confederate army

    E. None of these

The answer is B
The Act made lands out west free for those willing to move. The first of the acts, the Homestead Act of 1862, was signed into law by President Abraham Lincoln on May 20, 1862. It eventually became known as the "Free Soil" policy. It benefited slaves and northerners. It was an attempt for people to operate their own farm. A and D are both incorrect because anyone as long as they were older than 21 and had never lifted arms against the United States could benefit from this policy. Obviously not all lands could be given, but large sections were given to the people.

HISTORY OF THE UNITED STATES I

93. **Which president enforced the Homestead Act of 1862?**

    A. Jefferson Davis

    B. Alexander H. Stephens

    C. Abraham Lincoln

    D. Ulysses S. Grant

    E. Andrew Johnson

The answer is C
The Homestead Act of 1862 was signed into law by President Abraham Lincoln on May 20, 1862.

94. **What did the Federalists, led by Alexander Hamilton in the early eighteenth and late nineteenth centuries, believe in?**

    A. A fiscally sound and strong nationalistic government

    B. A weak federal government and strong states government

    C. No government

    D. Monarchy

    E. Anti-affiliation with British affairs

The answer is A
Many Federalists supported or admired Britain. The reason they did not want affiliation with Britain is because they did not want to go to war with them (War of 1812).

95. **Which of the following pairings most accurately links the presidential candidate with what he advocated or embodied?**

    A. John C. Calhoun-western expansion

    B. Jon Quincy Adams-opposition to an activist government

    C. Henry Clay-states' rights

    D. Andrew Jackson-nationalist pride

    E. Martin Van Buren-large government

The answer is D
Andrew Jackson is infamous for his devotion to the white, average American. He caused the ending of the first National Bank, supported the Trail of Tears, and was a military enthusiast. A, B, C, and E are all incorrect because they state the opposite of each presidential candidates' beliefs.

96. **In the 1830s and 1840s, the major difference between Whigs and the Democrats was that:**

    A. the Democrats favored an activist role for the federal government to help the economy while the Whigs opposed such an expansion of federal power

    B. the Whigs favored the abolition of slavery while the Democrats said that it was not a federal concern

    C. the Whigs believed in an activist federal government, while the Democrats favored a federal government with conscribed powers

    D. the Democrats power stemmed from an alliance of Northern and Southern monetary interests while farmers supported the Whigs

    E. the Whigs opposed westward expansion and the Democrats favored it

The answer is C
The Whigs believed the government should be active, such as in protecting the nation. The Democrats believed that the government should have limited powers.

HISTORY OF THE UNITED STATES I

97. **Indian removal was an example of President Jackson's endorsement of:**

    A. protectionism

    B. nullification

    C. states' rights

    D. internal improvements

    E. a strong federal judiciary

The answer is C
Many southeastern states wanted Native American lands. The states' government seized lands before the federal government enacted the removal. There were several skirmishes.

98. **Which FORMER president's wife preformed her First Lady duties for her husband and for President Thomas Jefferson?**

    A. Abigail Adams

    B. Dolley Madison

    C. Sarah York Jackson

    D. Elizabeth Monroe

    E. Martha Jefferson Randolph

The answer is B
Thomas Jefferson did not have a wife. Dolly Madison (James Madison's wife) took the honor of First Lady. Jefferson's daughter, Martha Washington Jefferson Randolph, took the office at times as well.

99. What was the main difference in weaponry used in the Civil War compared to wars fought earlier in the nineteenth century?

    A. Prior wars involved rudimentary weapons which lent themselves to hand-to-hand combat and close range fighting

    B. There was no difference

    C. All of the weapons used in the Civil War were completely different

    D. Weaponry in prior wars was less accurate but more deadly

    E. Weaponry in prior wars was more accurate but not as deadly

The answer is A
The Civil War introduced new weaponry that revolutionized American warfare. One example, rifles, allowed soldiers to fire from longer distances as well as be more accurate. Therefore, B, D, and E are all incorrect. C is incorrect because many weapons used in prior wars were still used, such as muskets, swords, machetes, etc.

100. From 1790 until the early nineteenth century women were largely thought to be what characteristic?

    A. Virtuous

    B. Courageous

    C. Intelligent

    D. Prosperous

    E. Strong

The answer is A
Women in the nineteenth century were thought to be more morale, virtuous, and overall "good" than their counterparts, men, who was looked at as intelligent, rough, and more decadent.

HISTORY OF THE UNITED STATES I

101. Which answer describes the First Amendment?

    A. Protection from quartering of troops

    B. Freedom of speech, press, religion, peaceable assembly, and to petition the government

    C. Right for the people to keep and bear arms, as well as to maintain a militia

    D. Civil trial by jury

    E. Due process, double jeopardy, self-incrimination, private property

The answer is B
The First Amendment states, "Congress shall make no law respecting an establishment of religion, or prohibiting the free exercise thereof; or abridging the freedom of speech, or of the press; or the right of the people peaceably to assemble, and to petition the Government for a redress of grievances."

102. What was the major type of economic production in the South?

    A. Textile

    B. Factory

    C. Transportation

    D. Agriculture

    E. Iron/Steel

The answer is D
The South had eighty-three percent of all large farms in the United States. The fertile soil and warm climate of the South made it ideal for large-scale farms and crops like tobacco and cotton. Because agriculture was so profitable, few Southerners saw a need for industrial development. Eighty percent of the labor force worked on the farm.

103. Harriet Beecher Stowe's "Uncle Tom's Cabin" aroused northern outrage over the implications of the

    A. Missouri Compromise

    B. Virginia Run Away Slave Act

    C. Fugitive Slave Act

    D. Kansas-Nebraska Act

    E. Dred Scott decision

The answer is C
The law allowed slave holders (and slave hunters) to enter Free states and retrieve slaves that were thought to be runaways. *Uncle Tom's Cabin* is a story of a slave who runs away in order to try to stop her owner from selling her son.

104. What was the main provision of the Fugitive Slave Law?

    A. Slaves were free if they got to the North

    B. The Underground Railroad was legalized

    C. Blacks found without proper litigation could be enslaved

    D. Southerners could not pursue escaped slaves

    E. Aiding runaway slaves was a crime

The answer is E
The Fugitive Slave Act required all escaped slaves to be returned to their masters and that Free states had to cooperate in this law.

HISTORY OF THE UNITED STATES I

105. The United States refused to annex Texas in 1836 because:

    A. Most of Texas's inhabitants were native Mexicans

    B. Texans did not want to be annexed to the United States

    C. The American government was opposed to armed rebellions against established governments

    D. There weren't enough inhabitants for it to become a state

    E. Of fear that it would provoke war with Mexico

The answer is E
After the Texas Revolution, Mexico told the United States that if it allowed Texas into the nation, then they would declare war on them. A, B, C, and D are all nonfactual.

106. Which of the following people organized the first women's rights convention at Seneca Falls?

    A. Dorthea Dix and Susan B. Anthony

    B. Dorthea Dix and Lucretia Mott

    C. Lucretia Mott and Elizabeth Cady Stanton

    D. Susan B. Anthony and Elizabeth Cady Stanton

    E. Horace Mann and Noah Webster

The answer is C
The Seneca Falls Convention on July 18-19, 1848 was the first women's rights convention. It advertised itself as "a convention to discuss the social, civil, and religious condition and rights of woman." Lucretia Mott and Elizabeth Cady Stanton were both abolitionists, Quakers, and women's rights activists. Mott is notable for attending this conference while on her honeymoon. Stanton was president of the National Woman Suffrage Association from 1892 until 1900.

107. What did the Neutrality Proclamation on 1793 mean for the United States?

   A. That Congress could declare war and neutrality

   B. That the President could declare war and neutrality

   C. That the President could declare neutrality but not war

   D. That Congress could not declare war or neutrality

   E. None of the above

The answer is C
The Neutrality Proclamation of 1793 was authorized by George Washington on April 22, 1793. It stated that the U.S. would take no part in a war between two or more other powers, specifically France and Great Britain. The Neutrality Proclamation of 1793 also threatened legal proceedings against any American citizen giving assistance to any country at war. This is important because it still limits the federal power. Though the president can declare neutrality, only Congress can declare war which is an example of a balance of power Therefore, A, B, D, and E are all incorrect.

108. What effect did railroads play in westward expansion?

   A. Quicker transportation and it increased national revenue

   B. Allowed slaves to escape easier

   C. Decreased the overall population

   D. Increased the national debt

   E. Decreased agricultural economy and implanted it with manufacturers

The answer is A
The railroad system created quicker transportation and it increased national revenue. States could grow enormous amounts of crops that actually gave yield in their climate and trade them for profit with states that couldn't usually grow those crops. Blacks, most times, were not allowed on trains, therefore, B is incorrect. The railroad system actually did the opposite of C, D, and E which are incorrect.

HISTORY OF THE UNITED STATES I

109. The Indian Removal Act of 1830 removed southeastern tribes to Indian Territory. In what present day state was this territory located?

    A. Nebraska

    B. Oklahoma

    C. Kansas

    D. Texas

    E. Indiana

The answer is B
Indian Territory was an evolving land area set aside by the United States government for the relocation of the indigenous peoples of the Americas who held aboriginal title to their land. The 1907 Oklahoma Enabling Act created the single state of Oklahoma by combining Oklahoma Territory and Indian Territory, ending the existence of an Indian Territory.

110. What was one factor that influenced the creation of the National Market Economy?

    A. Revolution in transportation

    B. Public policy at state and national levels to promote enterprise

    C. Nationalism of the Republican Party (aka Jefferson Party)

    D. Judicial nationalism, creation of legal requirements for a national market

    E. All of the above

The answer is E
Factors include: High profits from the War of 1812, internal expansion, development of commercial agriculture, revolution in transportation creating cheaper and faster modes, public policy decisions at the state and national levels to foster enterprise, Nationalism of the Republican (Jefferson) Party, judicial nationalism which created the legal requirements for a national market.

111. **Why was the "penny press" or the Daily News Papers (1835) a technological advancement in mass media?**

    A. Only the rich could afford it, therefore, they held common knowledge over citizens of less income, Native Americans, or slaves

    B. It was an affordable and economically savvy way to spread information, political views and agendas

    C. It was the first newspaper

    D. It was the first time the nation could become unified over any mass media advancement

    E. None of the above

The answer is B
It allowed everyone to read the news for a cheap price. Before this, newspapers were strictly for businesses. The Penny Press made this obsolete.

112. **What was the fastest growing social class during the Antebellum Era?**

    A. Low-class

    B. Slave

    C. Middle-class

    D. Upper-class

    E. Immigrants

The answer is C
Because of the Industrial Revolution and the influx of railroads, canals, turnpikes and steam boats, jobs and traveling became accessible to more people. Therefore, a middle class emerged.

HISTORY OF THE UNITED STATES I

113. The second Great Awakening of the first half of the nineteenth century had what effect on life in America?

    A. It increased concern over slavery

    B. Promoted a greater focus on democratic ideals that coincided with the Age of Jacksonian ideology- "the common man"

    C. Created a desire for control and order

    D. Bars, brothels, and jails closed down

    E. All of the above

The answer is E
The Second Great Awakening sought to remedy the evils of society before the Second Coming of Christ which caused a lot of reform movements. Therefore, all of the answers are true.

114. Mormonism in the Antebellum Period reflected:

    A. a strong antislavery bias

    B. a celebration of individual liberty

    C. a desire to improve the status of women

    D. a strong desire to isolate believers from general society

    E. a belief in human perfectibility

The answer is E
Reformers, including those who embraced transcendentalism, promoted the divinity of the individual and sought to perfect human society. Though A, B, C, and D all happened and were shared beliefs amongst certain factions in the Second Great Awakening, the belief in human perfectibility was a shared concept by the majority.

HISTORY OF THE UNITED STATES I

115. The creation of "asylums" for social deviants was an effort to:

   A. punish the inmates

   B. get the deviants out of society

   C. reform and rehabilitate the inmates

   D. cut down the cost of crime and punishment

   E. All answers are correct

The answer is C
Starting in the mid to late nineteenth century, many of these mental institutions were created so that inmates could be rehabilitated and reformed. Sometimes that meant being able to function in society, or it meant being a Christian, or it meant quitting drinking alcohol. Thus E is incorrect. A, B, and D are partially correct.

116. What group of people had the largest population in the South during the early to mid-nineteenth century:

   A. yeoman farmers

   B. merchants

   C. slaves

   D. planters

   E. seafaring merchants

The answer is C
In 1960 there were over 3,950,546 slaves in the United States.

HISTORY OF THE UNITED STATES I

117. What effect did the Slave Trade Act of 1807 have on the United States?

    A. That slavery was abolished

    B. That one could buy slaves in all states, despite state laws

    C. That no one could import international slaves

    D. That 1/3 of every slave bought internationally would be taxed higher than slaves bought within the nation

    E. That only white landowners could buy international slaves

The answer is C
The Atlantic slave trade was abolished in 1807, but Americans still found ways to bring slaves in from international waters illegally for another two decades. Most planters did not need international slaves. They "bred" their female slaves to make new slaves. Thus the population of slavery skyrocketed in the United States. A is wrong because slavery did not end until the Civil War. B is incorrect because one could not buy or sell slaves in many northern states. D is incorrect because that refers to the 1/3 Compromise. E is incorrect because anyone could buy slaves up until the 1807 law.

118. A major difference between Northern and Southern societies prior to the Civil War is illustrated by the role women played in the:

    A. establishment of educational institutions in the South

    B. growth of the Northern factory system

    C. emergence of a Southern literary tradition

    D. explosion of religious revivalism in the North

    E. political spheres

The answer is B
The growth of factories in the North gave women (and even children) an avenue to work, particularly in textile factories. Unlike the North, the South was an agriculture based society, which meant women stayed home and were thought of as more virtuous. A, C, D, and E all are partially correct, but most were not the majority.

HISTORY OF THE UNITED STATES I

119. The U.S. Naturalization Law of March 26, 1790 included only:

    A. free white persons

    B. Asians

    C. Native Americans

    D. free blacks

    E. indentured whites

The answer is A
The U.S. Naturalization Law provided the first rules in the granting of national citizenship. However, immigrants, blacks, indentured whites, and Native Americans all were not included.

120. What document contains a list of individual rights and liberties that limit the United States federal government?

    A. The Declaration of Independence

    B. Magna Carta

    C. Liberty Bill

    D. Bill of Rights

    E. Petition of Rights

The answer is D
The Bill of Rights is the name for the first ten Amendments in the Constitution. The Amendments limit judicial and presidential powers as well as give individual rights, and reserve power for the states.

HISTORY OF THE UNITED STATES II

Description of the Examination

The History of the United States II: 1865 to the Present examination covers material that is usually taught in the second semester of what is often a two-semester course in United States history. The examination covers the period of United States history from the end of the Civil War to the present, with the majority of the questions being on the twentieth century.

The examination contains approximately 120 questions to be answered in 90 minutes. Some of these are pretest questions that will not be scored. Any time candidates spend on tutorials and providing personal information is in addition to the actual testing time.

Knowledge and Skills Required

Questions on the History of the United States II examination require candidates to demonstrate one or more of the following abilities.
- Identification and description of historical phenomena
- Analysis and interpretation of historical phenomena
- Comparison and contrast of historical phenomena

The subject matter of the History of the United States II examination is drawn from the following topics. The percentages next to the main topics indicate the approximate percentage of exam questions on that topic.

Topical Specifications

35% Political institutions, behavior, and public policy
25% Social developments
10% Economic developments
15% Cultural and intellectual developments
15% Diplomacy and international relations

Chronological Specifications

30% 1865–1914
70% 1915–present

The following are among the specific topics tested:
- The impact of the Civil War and Reconstruction upon the South
- The motivations and character of American expansionism
- The content of constitutional amendments and their interpretations by the Supreme Court
- The changing nature of agricultural life
- The development of American political parties
- The emergence of regulatory and welfare-state legislation
- The intellectual and political expressions of liberalism, conservatism, and other such movements
- Long-term demographic trends
- The process of economic growth and development
- The changing occupational structure, nature of work, and labor organization
- Immigration and the history of racial and ethnic minorities
- Urbanization and industrialization
- The causes and impacts of major wars in American history
- Major movements and individual figures in the history of American arts and letters
- Trends in the history of women and the family

HISTORY OF THE UNITED STATES II

SAMPLE TEST

DIRECTIONS: Read each item and select the best response.

1. What law was passed that finally abolished slavery in December of 1865?
   (Political Institutions, Behavior, and Public Policy) (1865-1914)

   A. The Appomattox Treaty

   B. The Thirteenth Amendment

   C. The Fourteenth Amendment

   D. Emancipation Proclamation

   E. Black Codes

2. What treaty ended the Civil War on April 9, 1865?
   (Political Institutions, Behavior, and Public Policy) (1865-1914)

   A. The Appomattox Treaty

   B. The Thirteenth Amendment

   C. Reconstruction Treaty

   D. Force Act

   E. There was no treaty

3. Which era, started in 1863 and ended in 1877, covers the complete history of the entire country following the Civil War and focuses on the transformation of the Southern United States?
   (Political Institutions, Behavior, and Public Policy) (1865-1914)

   A. Civil Rights

   B. Civil War era

   C. Reconstruction era

   D. Antebellum era

   E. Gilded Age

4. What is a practice that was defended by Ulysses S. Grant in 1872 in which a political party, after winning an election, gives government jobs to its supporters, friends and relatives as a reward for working toward victory, and as an incentive to keep working for the party?
   (Political Institutions, Behavior, and Public Policy) (1865-1914)

   A. The Spoil System

   B. Enfranchisement

   C. Merit System

   D. The Jacksonian System

   E. Republicanism

5. The _____ Act of 1887 allowed the United States to divide Indian Territories for Native Americans who wanted their own land, individually. Those that did were allowed American citizenship.
(Political Institutions, Behavior, and Public Policy) (1865-1914)

   A. Dawes

   B. Medill

   C. Roosevelt

   D. Separation

   E. Indian

6. What organization in the United States encouraged families to band together to promote the economic and political well-being of the community and agriculture? This organization was responsible for implementing the Granger Laws, which helped raise fare prices of railroad and grain elevator companies.
(Political Institutions, Behavior, and Public Policy) (1865-1914)

   A. Agrarian party

   B. Agricultural movement

   C. The Green party

   D. The Grange movement

   E. Kelly's agrarian movement

7. As modernism and the industrial revolution swept over America what movement advocated for social justice and environmentalism?
(Political Institutions, Behavior, and Public Policy) (1865-1914)

   A. Suffragette movement

   B. Conservationist movement

   C. Anti-Communist movement

   D. The Democratic movement

   E. The Progressive movement

8. Which event symbolizes the idea of the "Wild West" in 1890?
(Political Institutions, Behavior, and Public Policy) (1865-1914)

   A. Johnson County War

   B. Dead Man's Tree

   C. Castellammaarese War

   D. Oxnard Strike

   E. Hay–Bunau-Varilla Treaty

9. What did the landmark case Lochner vs New York ensue?
(Political Institutions, Behavior, and Public Policy) (1865-1914)

   A. New York could regulate the hours of bakers (They were not permitted to work above 60 hours a week).

   B. New York's regulation of the working hours of bakers was not a justifiable restriction (they could work over 60 hours a week) on the right to contract freely under the 14th Amendment's guarantee of liberty.

   C. Facilities for blacks and whites are constitutional under the doctrine of separate but equal, which holds for close to 60 years.

   D. With only a few narrow exceptions, every person born in the United States acquires United States citizenship at birth via the Citizenship Clause of the Fourteenth Amendment.

   E. The Constitution grants to the states the power to prosecute individuals for wrongful interference with the right to travel.

10. What was the informal agreement between the United States and the Empire of Japan in which the United States of America would not impose restriction on Japanese immigration, and Japan would not allow further emigration to the U.S. called?
(Political Institutions, Behavior, and Public Policy) (1865-1914)

   A. Gentlemen's Agreement of 1907

   B. Japanese-American Agreement

   C. The Immigration Act

   D. The Emigration Act

   E. Treaty of Mutual Cooperation and Security

11. What was the name of an union that formed an international, radical labor union, consisting of anarchist and socialist movements, 1905? The union combines general unionism with industrial unionism.
(Political Institutions, Behavior, and Public Policy) (1865-1914)

   A. Communist Party

   B. International Association of Bridge and Structural Iron Workers

   C. Amalgamated Clothing Workers

   D. Industrial Workers of the World

   E. Teamsters

12. **What act sought to prevent anticompetitive practices in their incipiency?**
    (Political Institutions, Behavior, and Public Policy) (1865-1914)

    A. Congressional Review Act

    B. Clayton Antitrust Act

    C. Federal Reserve Act

    D. Pure food and Drug Act

    E. Dawes Severely Act

13. **How did the American public feel about entering World War One in 1914?**
    (Political Institutions, Behavior, and Public Policy) (1865-1914)

    A. They wanted to remain neutral

    B. They wanted to remain Neutral, even though they supported Germany.

    C. They immediately entered the war on the side of the Allies.

    D. They immediately entered the war on the side of the Central powers.

    E. After the sinking of sinking of the passenger liner RMS Lusitania, the US entered the conflict.

14. **What opened in 1914 that opened trade to the Far East?**
    (Political Institutions, Behavior, and Public Policy) (1865-1914)

    A. Panama Canal

    B. American Frontier

    C. Cuba

    D. Bohemian Canal

    E. Mexican Straight

15. **In the 1920s what was prohibited to manufacture and sell by an amendment by the constitution, but later ratified?**
    (Political Institutions, Behavior, and Public Policy) (1915-present)

    A. Marijuana

    B. Firearms

    C. Cocaine

    D. Alcohol

    E. Coke a cola

HISTORY OF THE UNITED STATES II

16. The United States (as well as other Allie nations) imposed what treaty on Germany, which demanded unrealistic demands and became a key factor in the rise of the Nazi party?
    (Political Institutions, Behavior, and Public Policy) (1915-present)

    A. Versailles

    B. Grenoble

    C. Berlin

    D. Normandy

    E. Allies

17. What era was named after the great economic prosperity, festive (namely jazz) music, excessive style, and embrace of modernity?
    (Political Institutions, Behavior, and Public Policy) (1915-present)

    A. Prosperity Years

    B. The Modern Era

    C. Roaring Twenties

    D. Gilded Age

    E. Counter Culture

18. What hate organization reached up to four million members in the 1920s, claiming membership of President Harding, and sympathies of President Wilson?
    (Political Institutions, Behavior, and Public Policy) (1915-present)

    A. Aryan Nation

    B. The KKK

    C. American Nazi Party

    D. Communist Party

    E. Extreme Democrats

19. What event officially ended the Great Depression?
    (Political Institutions, Behavior, and Public Policy) (1915-present)

    A. The New Deal

    B. Keynesian Theory

    C. The election of Franklin Roosevelt

    D. Social Security

    E. The admission into War World II

HISTORY OF THE UNITED STATES II

20. **What is the New Deal?**
    (Political Institutions, Behavior, and Public Policy) (1915-present)

    A. President Franklin D. Roosevelt and Democrats different efforts to end the Great Depression and reform the American economy, principally by enlarging the United States government and its spending.

    B. A time period when President Harry S. Truman enlarged local governments and minimalized the federal government in order to bring more power back to the states.

    C. A series of events which eventually caused the Great Depression.

    D. President Harry S.Truman and Republican different efforts to end the Great Depression and reform the American economy, principally by enlarging the United States government and its spending.

    E. A time period when President Franklin D. Roosevelt enlarged local governments and minimalized the federal government in order to bring more power back to the states.

21. **What event caused the United States of America to enter World War II?**
    (Political Institutions, Behavior, and Public Policy) (1915-present)

    A. Zimmerman Note

    B. The bombing of Pearl Harbor

    C. The invasion of France

    D. The invasion of Poland

    E. The Holocaust

22. **What is the line called that separated the US, Britain, and France from the Soviet Union?**
    (Political Institutions, Behavior, and Public Policy) (1915-present)

    A. The Berlin Wall

    B. Soviet Union Border

    C. Satellite Border

    D. The Iron Curtain

    E. The Bronze Wall

23. **What was the fundamental theoretical problem that divided the US and the Soviet Union that caused the Cold War?**
    (Political Institutions, Behavior, and Public Policy) (1915-present)

    A. capitalism with liberal democracy vs totalitarian communism

    B. capitalism with conservative democracy vs totalitarian communism

    C. liberal democracy vs communism

    D. capitalism with liberal democracy vs mass communism

    E. capitalism with liberal democracy vs Trotskyite communism

24. **What general successfully won at the Battle of Inchon, turning the Korean War around; eventually leading to an invasion of North Korea?**
    (Political Institutions, Behavior, and Public Policy) (1915-present)

    A. Robert A. Parson

    B. Dwight D. Eisenhower

    C. Douglas MacArthur

    D. Colin Powell

    E. Daniel McDaniel

25. **What was the policy in which Americans fought communist expansion where ever it occurred?**
    (Political Institutions, Behavior, and Public Policy) (1915-present)

    A. Control Policy

    B. Anti-Communist Strategy

    C. Increase Liberty

    D. Containment Policy

    E. Pro- Capitalism Strategy

26. **What did the outcome of the court case Roe v. Wade legalize in 1973?**
    (Political Institutions, Behavior, and Public Policy) (1915-present)

    A. Abortion

    B. Communism

    C. Alcohol consumption

    D. Women's right to vote

    E. Integrated school systems

27. What was the Civil Rights Act of 1964?
(Political Institutions, Behavior, and Public Policy) (1915-present)

   A. Prohibited individual citizens from carrying firearms

   B. A civil rights act that provided private solutions.

   C. Prohibited individuals to purchase or loiter in private sectors (super markets, bars, etc.) if unwanted.

   D. Outlawed discrimination based on race, color, religion, and national origin, but not sex.

   E. Outlawed discrimination based on race, color, religion, sex, or national origin.

28. Which three were famous African American Civil Rights activists that were assonated in the 1960s?
(Political Institutions, Behavior, and Public Policy) (1915-present)

   A. Bull Connor, Nathan B. Forest, and Medgar Evans

   B. Bull Connor, Martin Luther King, and Medgar Evers

   C. Rev. George Lee, Martin Luther King, and Medgar Evers

   D. William Lewis Moore, Martin Luther King, and Medgar Evers

   E. Nathan B. Forest, Martin Luther King, and Medgar Evers

29. What program was a result of Lyndon B Johnson's "Great Societies" War on Poverty"?
(Political Institutions, Behavior, and Public Policy) (1915-present)

   A. Medicare

   B. Obama Care

   C. Johnson care

   D. Social Security

   E. Department of Education

30. What was the multi-billion dollar research project for a missile defense system that could shoot down incoming Soviet missiles and eliminate the need for mutually assured destruction?
(Political Institutions, Behavior, and Public Policy) (1915-present)

   A. Missile Defense Program

   B. Star Wars (Strategic Defense Initiative)

   C. US Nuclear Program

   D. US Missile Security

   E. None of the above

HISTORY OF THE UNITED STATES II

31. What Landmark Supreme Court decision declared that racial segregation in schools is unconstitutional?
    (Political Institutions, Behavior, and Public Policy) (1915-present)

    A. Black v. Department of Education

    B. Rice v. Board of Education

    C. Sweatt v. Painter

    D. Brown v. Board of Education

    E. Roe v. Wade

32. The Twenty-Sixth Amendment lowered the voting age from ___ to ____ in 1971?
    (Political Institutions, Behavior, and Public Policy) (1915-present)

    A. 21 to 18

    B. 24 to 21

    C. 20 to 18

    D. 30 to 18

    E. The Twenty-Sixth Amendment had nothing to do with the voting age.

33. McCarthyism in the 1950's was similar to the Palmer Raids (Red Scare) in the 1920s in what way?
    (Political Institutions, Behavior, and Public Policy) (1915-present)

    A. American citizen's liberties were breached

    B. Immigrants were suspicious of white communists

    C. Anarchists were the biggest conspirators

    D. The Ku Klux Klan led the assault against "Anti-Americans"

    E. No immigrants entered the country during these time periods.

34. How did president Nixon Presidency end?
    (Political Institutions, Behavior, and Public Policy) (1915-present)

    A. Impeachment

    B. Resignation

    C. Death

    D. Illness

    E. Like every other president, he was president for four years. However, he was not voted in again because of the Watergate scandal.

HISTORY OF THE UNITED STATES II

35. What hurt economic growth the most during the 1970s through the 1980s?
   (Political Institutions, Behavior, and Public Policy) (1915-present)

   A. Decrease in manual labor

   B. Inflation on unique metals

   C. Increase in oil prices

   D. Lack of technology innovation

   E. Increase in water prices

36. What island(s) in the Caribbean did the US invade in 1983 in order to stop a small Marxist faction with holding power?
   (Political Institutions, Behavior, and Public Policy) (1915-present)

   A. Cuba

   B. Grenada

   C. Portugal

   D. Bermuda

   E. Virgin Islands

37. Who was sworn in as the first woman Supreme court Justice?
   (Political Institutions, Behavior, and Public Policy) (1915-present)

   A. Sandra Day O'Connor

   B. Ruth Bader Ginsberg

   C. Sonia Sotomayor

   D. Elena Kagan

   E. Condoleezza Rice

38. What were the economic policies of the former US president Ronald Reagan called that associated especially with the reduction of taxes and the promotion of unrestricted free-market activity?
   (Political Institutions, Behavior, and Public Policy) (1915-present)

   A. Reaganomics

   B. Keynesian Economics

   C. Command Economics

   D. Traditional Economics

   E. Conservative Economics

HISTORY OF THE UNITED STATES II

39. **Under what era did the United States have its longest time frame of economic prosperity?**
    (Political Institutions, Behavior, and Public Policy) (1915-present)

    A. Roaring Twenties

    B. Progressive Years

    C. Antebellum

    D. Reconstruction

    E. 1990s (Information Age)

40. **What was Truman Doctrine?**
    (Political Institutions, Behavior, and Public Policy) (1915-present)

    A. It was an American foreign policy during President Harry S. Truman's term to stop Soviet imperialism during the Cold War.

    B. President Harry S. Truman plan to give American citizens universal healthcare.

    C. President Franklin D. Roosevelts great depression bailout plan, though up by vice president Harry S. Truman.

    D. A set of rules brought to the U.N. by President Harry S. Truman to hinder fascist leaders from gaining power in former axis powers lands.

    E. A set of pro-Soviet laws enforced during President Harry S. Truman's candidacy.

41. **What landmark piece of federal legislation was in 1964 in the United States lead by Lyndon B. Johnson prohibits racial discrimination in voting such as requiring some states (mostly in the south) that want to change its districts have to go through the department of justice?**
    (Political Institutions, Behavior, and Public Policy) (1915-present)

    A. Public Law

    B. Help America Vote Act

    C. Voting Rights Act

    D. Patriot Act

    E. 15th Amendment

42. **What was the initial reason of the First Persian Gulf War?**
    (Political Institutions, Behavior, and Public Policy) (1915-present)

    A. U.N. need for oil

    B. American need for oil

    C. Saddam Hussein's genocide of northern Iraqis

    D. Iran's invasion of Iran

    E. Iraq's invasion of Kuwait

43. Which administration used the term "War on Terrorism" first when referring to terrorist?
    (Political Institutions, Behavior, and Public Policy) (1915-present)

    A. George H. W. Bush

    B. George W. Bush

    C. Ronald Reagan

    D. Bill Clinton

    E. Lyndon B. Johnson

44. What agreement in 1994 tried to eliminate barriers to trade and investment between the U.S., Canada and Mexico?
    (Political Institutions, Behavior, and Public Policy) (1915-present)

    A. North American Nationality Organization (NANO)

    B. Western Alliance, Sect II

    C. The North American Triple Alliance (NTATA)

    D. North American Free Trade Agreement (NAFTA)

    E. Canada–United States Free Trade Agreement

45. What is the traditional view of why the United States "won" the Cold War?
    (Political Institutions, Behavior, and Public Policy) (1915-present)

    A. During the Carter and Reagan Administrations the United States upped military spending. The USSR tried to keep up, however, could not afford it and eventually collapsed.

    B. During the Bush and Clinton Administrations the United States upped military spending. The USSR tried to keep up, however, could not afford it and eventually collapsed.

    C. The Soviet Union eastern satellite nations won independence, severing the USSR economy.

    D. The USSR could not evoke desire in its citizens to work, therefore the economy eventually collapsed.

    E. Covert successful CIA mission missions in Afghanistan against Soviets led to a total breakdown of Soviet military and then later economy.

46. What was the label President John F Kennedy's give the 1960s with its unknown opportunities and perils such as uncharted areas of science and space, unsolved problems of peace and war, unconquered problems of ignorance and prejudice, unanswered questions of poverty and surplus?
(Political Institutions, Behavior, and Public Policy) (1915-present)

    A. The Beat Generation

    B. The Lost Generation

    C. The New Age

    D. The Peace Age

    E. The New Frontier

47. The New Left in the 1960s and 70s sympathized with what school of thought?
(Political Institutions, Behavior, and Public Policy) (1915-present)

    A. Frankfurt School of Critical Theory

    B. Taoism

    C. Functionalism

    D. Classic Liberalism

    E. Republicanism

48. What was the plans that was enacted in 1947 that goals were to rebuild war-devastated regions, remove trade barriers, modernize industry, make Europe prosperous again, and prevent the spread of communism called?
(Political Institutions, Behavior, and Public Policy) (1915-present)

    A. Dawes Plan

    B. Marshall Plan

    C. Truman Plan

    D. Morganthau Plan

    E. Versailles Compromise

49. **What was the difference between First New Deal and Second New Deal?**
(Political Institutions, Behavior, and Public Policy) (1915-present)

   A. The First New Deal regulated the private sector of society, however, the Second New Deal focused on regulating the corporate sector.

   B. The First New Deal focused more or the war effort, whereas the Second New Deal was more about poverty.

   C. The First New Deal was an effort to reshape the American electoral. landscape whereas the Second New Deal focused on ending poverty.

   D. At first it was just trying to find an immediate stop the depression. Relief, Recovery and Reform. The second was to have government regulate labor, housing, and farms.

   E. There really was no difference except Franklin D. Roosevelt changed the name in order to invoke more votes because of the popularity of the first deal.

50. **Before ratification of the 22nd amendment in 1951, most presidents served no more than two terms because of**
(Political Institutions, Behavior, and Public Policy) (1915-present)

   A. Tradition

   B. Federal law

   C. Supreme Court Decision

   D. The Eight Year Clause

   E. Anti-tyranny laws

51. **The 15th Amendment allowed former African American slaves to _____.**
(Social developments) (1865-1914)

   A. buy land

   B. vote

   C. acquire ownership of a public facility

   D. return back to Africa for free

   E. be compensated for free labor

HISTORY OF THE UNITED STATES II

52. **What were Jim Crow Laws?**
    (Social developments)(1865-1914)

    A. State and local laws enforcing racial segregation predominantly in the South. Enacted after the Reconstruction period, these laws continued in force until 1965.

    B. Racist laws enforced by Alabama Governor Jim Crow. Northerner politicians coined the universal racist laws in the South after him.

    C. Laws that supported black rights during the Reconstruction period.

    D. Laws enforced by the national government to restrict African. Americans directly after the Civil War.

    E. Racist laws enforced by South Carolina Governor Jim Crow. Northerner politicians coined the universal racist laws in the South after him.

53. **What was a key device for the removal of ex-Confederates from the political arena during the Reconstruction of the United States in the 1860s, requiring every white male to swear they had never borne arms against the Union or supported the Confederacy (in the Wade–Davis Bill)?**
    (Social developments)(1865-1914)

    A. Reconstruction Plan

    B. Fourteenth Amendment

    C. Ten-Percent Plan

    D. Ironclad Oath

    E. Republican Circle

54. **What was the series of acts of Congress that promoted the construction of a "transcontinental railroad" through authorizing the issuance of government bonds and granting Native American, private, and government lands to railroad companies?**
    (Social developments) (1865-1914)

    A. Pacific Railroad Acts

    B. Transcendental Acts

    C. Johnson Acts

    D. West Acts

    E. The Gilead Acts

55. Congress passed ten-year restrictions on _____ immigration in 1882 and 1892 and a permanent exclusion act in 1902.
(Social developments) (1865-1914)

    A. German

    B. Irish

    C. Japanese

    D. Italian

    E. Chinese

56. What was the idea called, led by William Graham Sumner, that argued the best equipped to win the struggle for survival was the American businessman, and concluded that taxes and regulations serve as dangers to his survival?
(Social developments) (1865-1914)

    A. Marxism

    B. Social Darwinism

    C. Capitalism

    D. Laissez Faire

    E. Imperialism

57. What was the name given to the cultural, social, and artistic explosion that took place in Harlem between the end of World War I and the middle of the 1930s?
(Social developments) (1865-1914)

    A. Civil Rights Movement

    B. Black Lives Matter

    C. Reconstruction Era

    D. African American Rights

    E. Harlem Renaissance

58. What genre of dancing was famous from 1900 to 1918, beginning in African American communities?
(Social developments) (1865-1914)

    A. The Waltz

    B. Swing Dance

    C. Ragtime

    D. Modern Dance

    E. Balboa

HISTORY OF THE UNITED STATES II

59. What was the process in which people moved (or migrated) toward the city in the early twentieth century in order to work in the booming industrial era?
(Social developments) (1865-1914)

   A. Urbanization

   B. Modernization

   C. Counterurbanization

   D. Reconstruction

   E. City Overhaul

60. During the Progressive era what was supported in order to bring about a more "purer" vote to the American elections?
(Social developments) (1865-1914)

   A. Prohibition laws

   B. African American rights

   C. Woman Suffrage

   D. Anti-Immigration laws

   E. Immigration laws

61. What did President Wilson's "New Freedom" campaign seek to reform?
(Social developments) (1915-present)

   A. Tariff, Business, and Banking

   B. Tariff, Race, and State Rights

   C. Business, Race, and Banking

   D. Race, Tariff, and Banking

   E. Federal Rights, State Rights, and Tariff

62. Before World War I, what was the general reaction towards external conflicts by American citizens?
(Social developments) (1915-present)

   A. Interventionism

   B. Indirect Interference

   C. Interference

   D. Isolationism

   E. Reactionary

63. What was one reason the US entered World War I?
(Social developments) (1915-present)

   A. Invasion of Poland

   B. The sinking of the Lusitania

   C. Pearl Harbor

   D. Invasion of Austria

   E. Attacks on Britain

64. Two Senators and fifty Representatives voted against the war resolution, including the first female ever to sit in Congress, _____ of Montana.
(Social developments) (1915-present)

   A. Joni Ernst

   B. Hattie Caraway

   C. Rebecca Felton

   D. Jeannette Rankin

   E. Ruth Elandor

65. What authorized the federal government to raise a national army for the American entry into World War I through the compulsory enlistment of people?
(Social developments) (1915-present)

   A. Draft

   B. Selective Service Act

   C. Draft Lottery

   D. Conscription Act

   E. There was no draft during WWI

66. The widespread use of what technological advancement in the 1920s revolutionized dating, education, change in work patters as well as an increase in recreational time?
(Social developments) (1915-present)

   A. Radio

   B. Train

   C. Automobile

   D. Airplane

   E. Bicycle

67. The American Mafia, an Italian-American organized-crime network with operations in cities across the United States, particularly New York and Chicago, rose to power through its success in the illicit _____ during the 1920s Prohibition era.
(Social developments) (1915-present)

   A. Illicit narcotic drug trade

   B. Alcohol trade

   C. Firearms trade

   D. Assignations of corporate leaders

   E. Burglary

68. **What was the series of raids in 1919-1920 called that focused on eastern Europeans and sympathizers of communist and anarchist ideology?**
    (Social developments) (1915-present)

    A. Second Red Scare

    B. McCarthyism

    C. Anti-Communism

    D. Swift Raids

    E. Palmer Raids

69. **What was one result of the Great depression?**
    (Social developments) (1915-present)

    A. Increase in divorce rates

    B. Crime rates dropped

    C. Recreations activities dropped such as watching movies in a cinema.

    D. Migration from rural areas to urban

    E. Individuals in rural areas stayed stationary (cities were expensive and the transportation procedure was too expensive)

70. **Prodded by Eleanor Roosevelt, FDR created women's auxiliary forces for?**
    (Social developments) (1915-present)

    A. Transportation system

    B. Conservation

    C. Agriculture

    D. Universities

    E. Military

71. **What attributed to the rise in suburbia in the 1950s?**
    (Social developments) (1915-present)

    A. Increase in revenue

    B. Outburst of population from rural areas

    C. Overpopulation

    D. Racial fears, affordable living, avoidance of the "dirtiness" of the city

    E. Growth of conservative citizens that could not stand the normally progressive stance held by cities

72. What groups of individuals, led by writers such as Jack Kerouac and Alan Ginsberg, were specifically known for their refusal to conform to social norms?
    (Social developments) (1915-present)

    A. Renaissance Era

    B. Post-Moderns

    C. Baby Boomers

    D. Beat Generation

    E. Lost Generation

73. What Supreme Court decision overruled the Plessy v. Ferguson case and declared that in the field of public education the doctrine of separate but equal' has no place. Separate educational facilities are inherently unequal.
    (Social developments) (1915-present)

    A. Plessy v. Ferguson II

    B. Brown v. Board of Education

    C. Shelley v. Kraemer

    D. Powell v. Anderson

    E. Powell v. Alabama

74. The Maoist tenet "Political power comes through the barrel of a gun" was adopted by which group?
    (Social developments) (1915-present)

    A. Nation of Yahweh

    B. Black Back To Africa

    C. Black Panther

    D. NAACP

    E. United Nuwaubian Nation of Moors

75. What war started because France was determined to reclaim all its territories after World War II? This war was unique because American tradition dictated sympathy for the revolutionaries over any colonial power. However, supporting the Marxist in this given circumstance was unthinkable, given the new strategy of containing communism.
    (Social developments) (1915-present)

    A. Korean War

    B. Afghanistan

    C. Vietnam War

    D. Geneva Island

    E. Chile Civil War

HISTORY OF THE UNITED STATES II

76. Who was the first US President to visit China after the communist takeover?
    (Social developments) (1915-present)

    A. Franklin D. Roosevelt

    B. Dwight D. Eisenhower

    C. Harry Truman

    D. Lyndon B. Johnson

    E. Richard Nixon

77. What was one aspect that feminists such as Margret Sanger fought for in the early 1960s?
    (Social developments) (1915-present)

    A. The use of contraceptives

    B. The right to vote

    C. The enforcement of prohibition laws

    D. Improved childcare laws

    E. Free Trade

78. What did the New Right consist of?
    (Social developments) (1915-present)

    A. Extremist immigrants groups

    B. Extremist political groups, conservative Christians, and CEO's of corporations

    C. Fringe political groups, Christian evangelicals, and higher ups of corporations

    D. Extreme Libertarians

    E. Followers of Reagan

79. With the growing economy, many middle-class Americans rushed to invest in the stock market and to flaunt their newly acquired wealth. What group of people supplanted the hippies of the former generation?
    (Social developments) (1915-present)

    A. Young Urban Professionals

    B. Rockers

    C. Punk rockers

    D. Society of X's

    E. Baby Boomers

80. What was the historic time called throughout 1997–2000 during which stock markets in industrialized nations saw their equity value rise rapidly from growth in the Internet sector and related fields (especially with the invention of the World Wide Web)?
    (Social developments) (1915-present)

    A. The Information Age

    B. Dot-Com Bubble

    C. Great Moderation

    D. Golden Age of Capitalism

    E. World Wide Consumerism

HISTORY OF THE UNITED STATES II

81. The rapid expansion of _____ led to real wage growth of 60% between 1860 and 1890.
(Economic Developments) (1865-1914)

   A. Agriculture

   B. Racial equality

   C. Industrialization

   D. Emigration

   E. Progressive ideals

82. In 1869, the First Transcontinental Railroad opened new areas of opportunity in _____.
(Economic Developments) (1865-1914)

   A. Far-west mining and ranching regions

   B. South American mining

   C. African American mobility

   D. Oil Revenue

   E. Exotic fur trade

83. The Reconstruction era brought many changes to the very poor and broken South such as _____.
(Economic Developments) (1865-1914)

   A. Higher Education

   B. Equality

   C. Republicanism

   D. Mercantilism

   E. Sharecropping

84. What was the US financial crisis called that took place over a three-week period starting in mid-October, when the New York Stock Exchange fell almost 50% from its peak the previous year? Panic occurred, and eventually spread throughout the nation when many state and local banks and businesses entered bankruptcy.
(Economic Developments) (1865-1914)

   A. Depression of 1910

   B. Great Depression

   C. Panic of 1907

   D. The End of the Industrial Age

   E. The Second Great Depression

85. The Federal road building program ended in 1818, 98 year gap, leaving states to build roads until the _____.
    (Economic Developments) (1865-1914)

    A. Car and Road Act 1916

    B. Autobahn

    C. Dwight D. Eisenhower National System of Interstate and Defense Highways

    D. Federal Road Act of 1916

    E. Highway act of 1916

86. In order to deal with the crisis in banking at the time of his inauguration, President Franklin D Roosevelt.
    (Economic Developments) (1915-present)

    A. Closed the banking system for four days giving them a "banking holiday."

    B. Enlarged the Federal Bank.

    C. Prohibited for more than 1000 USD to be taking from any accounts that were to be used for recreational purposes.

    D. Fired all the Federal Bank board members and replaced them with Keynesian theorists

    E. President Roosevelt did nothing, he thought the bank would come out of its cycle if left alone.

87. What was the policy adopted by the United States in 1939 to preserve neutrality while aiding the Allies? Britain and France could buy goods from the United States if they paid in full and transported them.
    (Economic Developments) (1915-present)

    A. Isolation act

    B. Cash and Carry

    C. Prohibition Act

    D. Debt Default Act

    E. New Deal

88. What is one reason the US has had a dramatic increase in economic since the 1950s?
    (Economic Developments) (1915-present)

    A. The end of the Korean War

    B. The end of the Vietnam War

    C. Oil prices have decreased

    D. More of a focus is agriculture

    E. Baby Boomers

89. **What policy did the Office of Economic Opportunity originate from?**
(Economic Developments) (1915-present)

   A. Personal Responsibility and Work Opportunity Act

   B. War on Poverty

   C. VISTA

   D. New Deal

   E. None of the Above

90. **The 1973 Oil Crisis began when**
(Economic Developments) (1915-present)

   A. OAPEC proclaimed an oil embargo- raising the price of oil to four times as much.

   B. OPEC proclaimed and oil embargo- raising the price of oil to four times as much.

   C. large Oil fields caught on fire in Saudi Arabia, causing global oil prices to rise.

   D. the United States congress voted against drilling in Alaska and Texas, raising oil prices to three times as much.

   E. There was no Oil crisis in 1973.

91. **What was one term used to define President Reagan's economic policy to cut both federal spending and taxes to release private revenue for future investments?**
(Economic Developments) (1915-present)

   A. Supply-side

   B. Reagan Conservatism

   C. Laissez-faire

   D. New Conservative Economics

   E. Capitalism

92. **What was reason for the longest and largest economic boom in the 1990s?**
(Economic Developments) (1915-present)

   A. Cost of living decreased

   B. Lower taxes

   C. The ending of the food tax

   D. The creation of the World Wide Web

   E. Invasion of Iraq

93. What organization formed after the ending of the Civil War in 1865, later became known as the largest hate organization known in the United States?
(Cultural and intellectual developments 1865-1914)

   A. White Aryan Resistance

   B. Southern Democrats

   C. Ku Klux Klan

   D. Anti-Defense League

   E. White Supremists

94. The idea (that originated in the 1880s by farmers and their associates) that the government was being made up of industrialists and bankers was called?
(Cultural and intellectual developments 1865-1914)

   A. Progressivism

   B. Populism

   C. Conservatism

   D. True Liberalism

   E. Free Republicanism

95. Many of the middle class in the beginning of the 20th century believed that unfair election systems, exploitation of workers, women and children, corruption in the business class and the legal system all meant that there was an unfair political system. These people were called?
(Cultural and intellectual developments 1865-1914)

   A. Progressivism

   B. Populism

   C. Conservatism

   D. True Liberalism

   E. Free Republicanism

96. What was the genre of writing called that appeared after the Civil War and had great effect on the American populist all the wat into the Twentieth Century? The style of writing derived from the presentation of the features and peculiarities of a particular locality and its inhabitants.
(Cultural and intellectual developments 1865-1914)

   A. Beat Generation

   B. Transcendentalism

   C. Realism

   D. Local Colour

   E. Expressionism

HISTORY OF THE UNITED STATES II

97. What did Jeffries V. Johnson boxing fright prove to the United States populace?
(Cultural and intellectual developments 1865-1914)

    A. The United States was the strongest nation

    B. Anyone can fulfil the American dream

    C. Whites were more intelligent

    D. Blacks were equals

    E. That blacks were not meant to live in cities

98. The NAACP was developed in order to?
(Cultural and intellectual developments) (1915-present)

    A. Fight radical black activism.

    B. Defend Jim Crow laws.

    C. To fight for equality on a national front.

    D. Support Ku Klux Klan

    E. Support Progressive politicians

99. Conscription policies in the First and Second World Wars differed significantly in that in the First World War
(Cultural and intellectual developments) (1915-present)

    A. The draft began before the US entered

    B. Blacks were enlisted

    C. German skepticism

    D. Airplanes were not used

    E. Automatic weapons were not used

100. What were the northern, urban, single, young, middle-class women from the 1920s called who enjoyed dancing to jazz music, wearing dresses at their knees, wearing short hair, and participating in night life?
(Cultural and intellectual developments) (1915-present)

    A. Revolutionists

    B. Hippies

    C. Valley girls

    D. Flappers

    E. Victorians

101. **What was the third largest political party in 1920?**
(Cultural and intellectual developments) (1915-present)

   A. Republicans

   B. Democrats

   C. Socialist

   D. Communists

   E. Whig

102. **In 1925 Tennessee passed what law that prohibited the teaching of Darwin's theory of evolution in schools?**
(Cultural and intellectual developments) (1915-present)

   A. Bryan Laws

   B. Religious Freedom Law

   C. Creationism act

   D. Separate but Equal act

   E. Butler Law

103. **What is the term for the practice of making accusations of subversion or treason without proper regard for evidence originating from the Second Red Scare, characterized by heightened political repression against communists?**
(Cultural and intellectual developments) (1915-present)

   A. Anti-Soviet

   B. McCarthyism

   C. Palmerizing

   D. False allegations

   E. Anti-American

HISTORY OF THE UNITED STATES II

104. What was the Indian Termination Policy?
(Cultural and intellectual developments) (1915-present)

A. President Franklin Roosevelts plan to destroy all Native American ancestry in the US

B. President Dwight Eisenhower's policy to shape a series of laws and policies with the intent of assimilating Native Americans into mainstream American society fairly quickly (ending reservations and Native American sovereignty)

C. President Franklin Roosevelts policy to shape a series of laws and policies with the intent of assimilating Native Americans into mainstream American society fairly quickly (ending reservations and Native American sovereignty)

D. President Franklin Roosevelts plant to end Americans plans to destroy Native American plans by creating suburbs on Native American reservations.

E. President Harry Truman's plan to end Native American ancestry in the US

105. What was the anti-establishment cultural phenomenon in the 1950s and 1960s called?
(Cultural and intellectual developments) (1915-present)

A. The Counter-Culture

B. Brights Movement

C. Ecofeminism

D. Cultural Movement

E. Human Rights Movement

106. What is one difference in first and second wave feminism?
(Cultural and intellectual developments) (1915-present)

A. First wave feminism pursued the right to vote while second wave feminism sought equality in the workforce

B. First wave feminism was much more radical than its counterparts

C. Second wave feminism was more focused on woman outside the United States

D. First wave feminism pursued the equality in the work place, second wave feminism focused on solely education

E. Second wave feminism was more ideological

HISTORY OF THE UNITED STATES II

107. Why did (/do) the majority of African American women not participate in all three feminist movements?
(Cultural and intellectual developments) (1915-present)

   A. They did not like white people

   B. The majority of the movement was made up of middle class white women. Blacks felt they could not relate with the white experience.

   C. All three movements did not admit African Americans.

   D. Black women were not educated enough.

   E. Question is incorrect, the majority of the feminist movement was black.

108. What started the Montgomery Bus Boycott and was one reason that sparked the Civil Rights movement?
(Cultural and intellectual developments) (1915-present)

   A. Rosa Parks refusal to move on a Montgomery bus.

   B. Martin Luther King's organization of the Montgomery Bus riots.

   C. The assignation of Rosa Parks.

   D. Ralph Abernathy, King formed the Southern Christian Leadership Conference (SCLC), which invoked African Americans to riot, including bus riots.

   E. Malcom X refusal to get off a Montgomery all white bus

109. From the beginning of the decade until the end of the 90s, new forms of entertainment, commerce, research, work, and communication became commonplace in the United States. The driving force behind much of this change was an innovation popularly known as the Internet. This age is known as the _____?
(Cultural and intellectual developments) (1915-present)

   A. Information age

   B. Modernity

   C. Education age

   D. Consumer age

   E. Baby Boomers

110. What was the term for the 1970s decade when many young people were focused on themselves, rather than the world at large?
(Cultural and intellectual developments) (1915-present)

   A. Me Decade

   B. The Counter Culture

   C. Hippies

   D. Civil Rights

   E. Rockers

195

111. _____ was one of the most significant restrictions on free immigration in US history, prohibiting all immigration of Chinese laborers.
(Diplomacy and international relations) (1865-1914)

   A. Anti-Chinese Act

   B. Chinese Exclusion Act

   C. Civil Rights Act

   D. Magnuson Act

   E. Immigration and Nationality Act

112. What was the policy proposed in 1899 to keep China open to trade with all countries on an equal basis?
(Diplomacy and international relations) (1865-1914)

   A. Immigration Act

   B. Mutual Security Act

   C. Foreign Assistance Act

   D. Open Door Policy

   E. Act for International Development

113. What did the Roosevelt Corollary mean for the US international position?
(Diplomacy and international relations) (1865-1914)

   A. It allowed the United States to intervene in Russian affairs.

   B. It allowed the United States to intervene in the Middle East.

   C. Being an addition to the Monroe doctrine, it allowed the United States to interfere in Europe and South American countries.

   D. It ended a hundred year suppression on Native American lands.

   E. It allowed the ending of colonization in South America.

114. **Why is the Alaska Purchase sometimes called "Seward folly"?**
(Diplomacy and international relations) (1865-1914)

   A. Because he had to pay Russia and then he had to pay Siberia for it.

   B. Secretary of State William Seward bought Alaska on behalf of the US and died in Alaska when trying to relocate the territories capital.

   C. The purchase threatened British colonies in the Pacific west, causing Britain to put tariffs on Western United States goods.

   D. People were critical of the deal and thought Secretary State William Seward payed too much for a piece of land that was mostly unexplored.

   E. Secretary of State William Seward killed thousands of local tribes trying to inhabit the newly purchased land.

115. **What did the United States Congress in the 1930s, do in response to the growing turmoil in Europe and Asia that eventually led to World War II?**
(Diplomacy and international relations) (1915-present)

   A. Ludlow Amendments

   B. McGovern–Hatfield Amendment

   C. World War II Acts

   D. Spot Resolutions

   E. Neutrality Acts of the 1930s

116. **What was the first international difficulty the U.S. had with the U.S.S.R.?**
(Diplomacy and international relations) (1915-present)

   A. Yugoslavia revolt

   B. Cuban Missile Crisis

   C. Bay of Pigs

   D. Berlin Blockade

   E. War in Vietnam

117. **How did the U.S. help stop communism in Afghanistan form 1979-1989?**
(Diplomacy and international relations) (1915-present)

   A. Created sanctions against the Soviet Union.

   B. Fought Soviet Union directly in Afghanistan.

   C. Assonated rebel leader Zulfikar Ali Bhutto

   D. Practiced the doctrine of containment by giving military aid to Afghanistan rebels.

   E. All are incorrect. The U.S. stayed neutral in this particular situation.

118. **What example would best describe Reagan doctrine?**
(Diplomacy and international relations) (1915-present)

A. Giving covert aid to anti-communist militia

B. Creating an isolationist society

C. Creating open trade diplomacy with the USSR

D. Creating open trade with every country except the USSR

E. Fight the Soviet Union with a direct military offensive.

119. **What was the largest military operation after Vietnam War in the United States?**
(Diplomacy and international relations) (1915-present)

A. Persian Gulf war

B. Somalia

C. Yugoslavia

D. Grenada

E. India-Pakistan War

120. **Journalist organization, WikiLeaks, released a United States cable leak describing**
(Diplomacy and international relations) (1915-present)

A. classified receipts of illegal transactions of military weapons sent from the U.S. government.

B. classified information about the Iraq War

C. classified cables that had been sent to the U.S. State Department by 274 of its consulates, embassies, and diplomatic missions around the world.

D. classified information about the U.S military presence in eastern European countries.

E. falsified information that supposedly exposed U.S. senate members of embezzling money.

HISTORY OF THE UNITED STATES II

ANSWER KEY

Question Number	Correct Answer	Your Answer	Question Number	Correct Answer	Your Answer	Question Number	Correct Answer	Your Answer
1	B		41	C		81	C	
2	E		42	E		82	A	
3	C		43	C		83	E	
4	A		44	D		84	C	
5	A		45	A		85	D	
6	D		46	E		86	A	
7	E		47	A		87	B	
8	A		48	B		88	E	
9	B		49	D		89	B	
10	A		50	A		90	A	
11	D		51	B		91	A	
12	B		52	A		92	D	
13	A		53	D		93	C	
14	A		54	A		94	B	
15	D		55	E		95	A	
16	A		56	B		96	D	
17	C		57	E		97	D	
18	B		58	C		98	C	
19	E		59	A		99	A	
20	A		60	C		100	D	
21	B		61	A		101	C	
22	D		62	D		102	E	
23	A		63	B		103	B	
24	C		64	D		104	B	
25	D		65	B		105	A	
26	A		66	C		106	A	
27	E		67	B		107	B	
28	C		68	E		108	A	
29	A		69	D		109	A	
30	B		70	E		110	A	
31	D		71	D		111	B	
32	A		72	D		112	D	
33	A		73	B		113	C	
34	B		74	C		114	D	
35	C		75	C		115	E	
36	B		76	E		116	D	
37	A		77	A		117	D	
38	A		78	C		118	A	
39	E		79	A		119	A	
40	A		80	B		120	C	

HISTORY OF THE UNITED STATES II

RATIONALES

1. **What law was passed that finally abolished slavery in December of 1865?**
   (Political Institutions, Behavior, and Public Policy) (1865-1914)

   A. The Appomattox Treaty

   B. The Thirteenth Amendment

   C. The Fourteenth Amendment

   D. Emancipation Proclamation

   E. Black Codes

The answer is B.
Many have thought that the Emancipation Proclamation was the law that freed all slaves, however, though northerners accepted this law, obviously, southerners did not. It was not until April 8, 1964 that the Senate actually passed a law stating all slaves were free and it was not until January 31, 1865 that the House followed suit. On December 18, 1865, Secretary of State William H. Seward proclaimed its adoption after the United States achieved enough votes to ratify the amendment. However, Black codes were still enforced in many of these areas, therefore, E is false. A is nonfactual and the Fourteenth Amendment was a response to the Thirteenth Amendment, addresses citizenship rights and equal protection of the laws, thus, both are false.

2. **What treaty ended the Civil War on April 9, 1865?**
   (Political Institutions, Behavior, and Public Policy) (1865-1914)

   A. The Appomattox Treaty

   B. The Thirteenth Amendment

   C. Reconstruction Treaty

   D. Force Act

   E. There was no treaty

The answer is E.
There was no treaty signed to end the Civil War. The surrender at Appomattox Court House was a military surrender of an army which was surrounded. The Confederate government never surrendered and even had it wanted to the United States government would likely not have accepted.

HISTORY OF THE UNITED STATES II

3. Which era, started in 1863 and ended in 1877, covers the complete history of the entire country following the Civil War and focuses on the transformation of the Southern United States?
   (Political Institutions, Behavior, and Public Policy) (1865-1914)

   A. Civil Rights

   B. Civil War era

   C. Reconstruction era

   D. Antebellum era

   E. Gilded Age

The answer is C.
The Reconstruction period stated from the Emancipation Proclamation until 1877. It tells the complete history of the entire country and focuses on the transformation of the Southern United States. A and E are incorrect because they happened after the Reconstruction Period. The Antebellum period happened before, therefore, incorrect. The Civil War was an event, not a era, in the Reconstruction period, thus incorrect.

4. What is a practice that was defended by Ulysses S. Grant in 1872 in which a political party, after winning an election, gives government jobs to its supporters, friends and relatives as a reward for working toward victory, and as an incentive to keep working for the party?
   (Political Institutions, Behavior, and Public Policy) (1865-1914)

   A. The Spoil System

   B. Enfranchisement

   C. Merit System

   D. The Jacksonian System

   E. Republicanism

The answer is A.
The Spoil System originated in America when Andrew Jackson released a ten percent of all government positions and gave them to supporters, friends, and family. American citizens demanded social reforms on the spoil system near the end of the reconstruction era. C is wrong because it is the opposite. B, D, and E are all irrelevant.

HISTORY OF THE UNITED STATES II

5. The _____ Act of 1887 allowed the United States to divide Indian Territories for Native Americans who wanted their own land, individually. Those that did were allowed American citizenship.
   (Political Institutions, Behavior, and Public Policy) (1865-1914)

   A. Dawes

   B. Medill

   C. Roosevelt

   D. Separation

   E. Indian

The answer is A.
The Dawes Act allowed the United States further jurisdiction within Indian territories and further assimilate Native American groups. The Act was named for its creator,

6. What organization in the United States encouraged families to band together to promote the economic and political well-being of the community and agriculture? This organization was responsible for implementing the Granger Laws, which helped raise fare prices of railroad and grain elevator companies.
   (Political Institutions, Behavior, and Public Policy) (1865-1914)

   A. Agrarian party

   B. Agricultural movement

   C. The Green party

   D. The Grange movement

   E. Kelly's agrarian movement

The answer is D.
The Grange movement was the first fraternal organization to advocate for agricultural. All other answers are nonfactual.

HISTORY OF THE UNITED STATES II

7. **As modernism and the industrial revolution swept over America what movement advocated for social justice and environmentalism?**
   (Political Institutions, Behavior, and Public Policy) (1865-1914)

   A. Suffragette movement

   B. Conservationist movement

   C. Anti-Communist movement

   D. The Democratic movement

   E. The Progressive movement

The answer is E.
The progressive movement started in the 1890s as a turn-of-the-century political movement interested in furthering social and political reform, curbing political corruption caused by political machines, and limiting the political influence of large corporations. A is incorrect because it was primarily about women's rights and B is incorrect because it was essential for only environmental issues. C and D are nonfactual.

8. **Which event symbolizes the idea of the "Wild West" in 1890?**
   (Political Institutions, Behavior, and Public Policy) (1865-1914)

   A. Johnson County War

   B. Dead Man's Tree

   C. Castellammaarese War

   D. Oxnard Strike

   E. Hay–Bunau-Varilla Treaty

The answer is A.
In Johnson, Wyoming, between 1889 and 1893, conflicts started between two cattle companies. Both companies would harass supposed rustlers throughout the grazing lands of Wyoming. As tensions swell between the large established ranchers and the smaller settlers in the state, violence finally culminated in Powder River Country, when one company hired armed gunmen to invade the county and wipe out the competition. When word came out of the gunmen's initial incursion in the territory, the small-time farmers and ranchers, as well as the state lawmen, formed a posse of 200 men to fight them back which led to a grueling stand-off. The war ended when the United States Cavalry, on the orders of President Benjamin Harrison, relieved the two forces, and the failure to convict the invaders of the murders they had committed. This event has allowed for the creation of many stories pertaining to the "Wild West". All other answers are

incorrect. B and C have to do with the Mafia. D has to do with strikes and E pertains to the Panama Canal.

9. **What did the landmark case Lochner vs New York ensue?**
   (Political Institutions, Behavior, and Public Policy) (1865-1914)

   A. New York could regulate the hours of bakers (They were not permitted to work above 60 hours a week).

   B. New York's regulation of the working hours of bakers was not a justifiable restriction (they could work over 60 hours a week) on the right to contract freely under the 14th Amendment's guarantee of liberty.

   C. Facilities for blacks and whites are constitutional under the doctrine of separate but equal, which holds for close to 60 years.

   D. With only a few narrow exceptions, every person born in the United States acquires United States citizenship at birth via the Citizenship Clause of the Fourteenth Amendment.

   E. The Constitution grants to the states the power to prosecute individuals for wrongful interference with the right to travel.

The answer is B.
A is non-factual. Al other answers are different court cases: C is Plessy vs Ferguson, D is United States vs Wong Kim Ark, and E is United States vs Wheeler.

HISTORY OF THE UNITED STATES II

10. What was the informal agreement between the United States and the Empire of Japan in which the United States of America would not impose restriction on Japanese immigration, and Japan would not allow further emigration to the U.S. called?
    (Political Institutions, Behavior, and Public Policy) (1865-1914)

    A. Gentlemen's Agreement of 1907

    B. Japanese-American Agreement

    C. The Immigration Act

    D. The Emigration Act

    E. Treaty of Mutual Cooperation and Security

The answer is A.
The Gentleman's Act was an informal agreement between the United States and the Empire of Japan. The agreement was never ratified by Congress and eventually terminated by the Immigration Act of 1924. All other answers are nonfactual.

11. What was the name of an union that formed an international, radical labor union, consisting of anarchist and socialist movements, 1905? The union combines general unionism with industrial unionism.
    (Political Institutions, Behavior, and Public Policy) (1865-1914)

    A. Communist Party

    B. International Association of Bridge and Structural Iron Workers

    C. Amalgamated Clothing Workers

    D. Industrial Workers of the World

    E. Teamsters

The answer is D.
Industrial Workers of the World (IWW) promotes the concept of "One Big Union", and contends that all workers should be united as a social class to supplant capitalism and wage labor with industrial democracy. All other answers (except A) are legitimate Labor Unions, however, not as radical as the IWW.

12. **What act sought to prevent anticompetitive practices in their incipiency?**
    (Political Institutions, Behavior, and Public Policy) (1865-1914)

    A. Congressional Review Act

    B. Clayton Antitrust Act

    C. Federal Reserve Act

    D. Pure food and Drug Act

    E. Dawes Severely Act

The answer is B.
The Clayton Antitrust Act (1914) was a continuation of the Sherman Antitrust Act in 1890. Its main focus was to stop monopolies. However, it was primarily manipulated into agitating and maltreating unions. C is incorrect because it was used to solidify central banking. D is incorrect because it was used to ban falsely labeled food. E is wrong because it was used to dismantle Native American tribes. And A is incorrect because it pertains to congress law procedures.

13. **How did the American public feel about entering World War One in 1914?**
    (Political Institutions, Behavior, and Public Policy) (1865-1914)

    A. They wanted to remain neutral

    B. They wanted to remain Neutral, even though they supported Germany.

    C. They immediately entered the war on the side of the Allies.

    D. They immediately entered the war on the side of the Central powers.

    E. After the sinking of sinking of the passenger liner RMS Lusitania, the US entered the conflict.

The answer is A.
At the onslaught of World War One the mass majority was taken by surprise. Woodrow Wilson called for neutrality. It was not until the German navy called for an all-out war on commercial ships as well as the Zimmerman note did the US really decide to enter into the Great War.

HISTORY OF THE UNITED STATES II

14. **What opened in 1914 that opened trade to the Far East?**
    (Political Institutions, Behavior, and Public Policy) (1865-1914)

    A. Panama Canal

    B. American Frontier

    C. Cuba

    D. Bohemian Canal

    E. Mexican Straight

The answer is A.
Before the Panama Canal was built in August 15, 1914 the western powers had to travel over a thousand miles by sea and land in order to trade. For Americans that meant sailing around the dangerous southern tip of South America, Cape Horn. The Panama Canal split the mileage in half and made trips extraordinarily safer. D and E are non-factual, B (Cuba) is not connected to the Pacific, and though the frontier west did make the Far East easier to trade with, the eastern side of the United States struggled moving goods by land. Because most manufacturing came from the North East, this made trade difficult.

15. **In the 1920s what was prohibited to manufacture and sell by an amendment by the constitution, but later ratified?**
    (Political Institutions, Behavior, and Public Policy) (1915-present)

    A. Marijuana

    B. Firearms

    C. Cocaine

    D. Alcohol

    E. Coke a cola

The answer is D.
In January of 1920 alcohol was prohibited in the United States for thirteen years. A and C were not widely used as in the present time (cocaine did not get large recognition in the United States until the 70 and 80s). Coke a cola and fire arms have never banned in the United States.

16. The United States (as well as other Allie nations) imposed what treaty on Germany, which demanded unrealistic demands and became a key factor in the rise of the Nazi party?
    (Political Institutions, Behavior, and Public Policy) (1915-present)

    A. Versailles

    B. Grenoble

    C. Berlin

    D. Normandy

    E. Allies

The answer is A.
After World War one, Germany faced harsh punishments. With a weak political structure, pressure from the east and west, weak economic, and rules put on them from Versailles, Germany was bound to fascism.

17. What era was named after the great economic prosperity, festive (namely jazz) music, excessive style, and embrace of modernity?
    (Political Institutions, Behavior, and Public Policy) (1915-present)

    A. Prosperity Years

    B. The Modern Era

    C. Roaring Twenties

    D. Gilded Age

    E. Counter Culture

The answer is C.
The roaring twenties was the period of sustained economic prosperity with a distinctive cultural edge in many other major cities during the 1920s in the United States. E is incorrect because it represents a group that stood for the opposite of social norms. D and B both had times of economic growth but jazz and outlandish styles were not necessarily qualities of the era. A is non-factual

HISTORY OF THE UNITED STATES II

18. **What hate organization reached up to four million members in the 1920s, claiming membership of President Harding, and sympathies of President Wilson?**
    (Political Institutions, Behavior, and Public Policy) (1915-present)

    A. Aryan Nation

    B. The KKK

    C. American Nazi Party

    D. Communist Party

    E. Extreme Democrats

The answer is B.
The Ku Klux Klan is the largest hate group in American history. It consists of three waves. The KKK of the 1920s saw its most popularity with some estimating up to 12 million members. They emphasized in white separation. Many times Klan leaders down played violence in order to normalize the organization. A and C were hate groups but not nearly as popular as well as they have not had sympathies from any American president. D and E are not hate groups.

19. **What event officially ended the Great Depression?**
    (Political Institutions, Behavior, and Public Policy) (1915-present)

    A. The New Deal

    B. Keynesian Theory

    C. The election of Franklin Roosevelt

    D. Social Security

    E. The admission into War World II

The answer is E.
Despite the efforts of the New Deal America was still in a depression. When the war came so did jobs and resources boosting the economy. A through D are all played parts in helping the U.S get out of the Great Depression, but it was not fully out until the was started. After the war many of these programs were able to evolve.

HISTORY OF THE UNITED STATES II

20. **What is the New Deal?**
    (Political Institutions, Behavior, and Public Policy) (1915-present)

    A. President Franklin D. Roosevelt and Democrats different efforts to end the Great Depression and reform the American economy, principally by enlarging the United States government and its spending.

    B. A time period when President Harry S. Truman enlarged local governments and minimalized the federal government in order to bring more power back to the states.

    C. A series of events which eventually caused the Great Depression.

    D. President Harry S.Truman and Republican different efforts to end the Great Depression and reform the American economy, principally by enlarging the United States government and its spending.

    E. A time period when President Franklin D. Roosevelt enlarged local governments and minimalized the federal government in order to bring more power back to the states.

The answer is A.
The New Deal was a plan brought to America by Franklin D. Roosevelt. Its original plan was to get the United States out of the Great Depression by creating jobs, a larger government with larger social programs, and to increase spending. Thus B, C, D, and E are all incorrect.

21. **What event caused the United States of America to enter World War II?**
    (Political Institutions, Behavior, and Public Policy) (1915-present)

    A. Zimmerman Note

    B. The bombing of Pearl Harbor

    C. The invasion of France

    D. The invasion of Poland

    E. The Holocaust

The answer is B.
As in World War One, The U.S took a neutral stance and possibly would have stayed neutral had not the Japanese bomb the U.S Navy base in Pearl Harbor.

HISTORY OF THE UNITED STATES II

22. **What is the line called that separated the US, Britain, and France from the Soviet Union?**
    (Political Institutions, Behavior, and Public Policy) (1915-present)

    A. The Berlin Wall

    B. Soviet Union Border

    C. Satellite Border

    D. The Iron Curtain

    E. The Bronze Wall

The answer is D.
Although many of the answer represented parts of the real borders of the Soviet Union, answer D, the Iron curtain, was the term used to describe the entirety of the Soviet Union's borders.

23. **What was the fundamental theoretical problem that divided the US and the Soviet Union that caused the Cold War?**
    (Political Institutions, Behavior, and Public Policy) (1915-present)

    A. capitalism with liberal democracy vs totalitarian communism

    B. capitalism with conservative democracy vs totalitarian communism

    C. liberal democracy vs communism

    D. capitalism with liberal democracy vs mass communism

    E. capitalism with liberal democracy vs Trotskyite communism

The answer is A.
The United States and The Soviet Union main difference was an ideological one. The U.S believed in free trade and natural rights whereas the U.S.S.R believed in a strict form of communism, thus making everyone the same social class. B, C, and D all have non-factual terms. E is incorrect because the totalitarianism that was practiced by the U.S.S.R. Trotsky was exiled and assonated by the Soviet Union.

24. What general successfully won at the Battle of Inchon, turning the Korean War around; eventually leading to an invasion of North Korea?
    (Political Institutions, Behavior, and Public Policy) (1915-present)

    A. Robert A. Parson

    B. Dwight D. Eisenhower

    C. Douglas MacArthur

    D. Colin Powell

    E. Daniel McDaniel

The answer is C.
Douglas MacArthur was an American five-star general and Field Marshal of the Philippine Army. He was Chief of Staff of the United States Army during the 1930s and played a prominent role in the Pacific theater during World War II. Before MacArthur entered the Korean War, South Korea had almost been entirely taken over. General MacArthur forced the North Koreans all the way into China. However, China soon got involved and North Korea made its way back to its original border at the commencement of the war. MacArthur was then relieved as many politian, including President Truman, put the blame on him.

25. What was the policy in which Americans fought communist expansion where ever it occurred?
    (Political Institutions, Behavior, and Public Policy) (1915-present)

    A. Control Policy

    B. Anti-Communist Strategy

    C. Increase Liberty

    D. Containment Policy

    E. Pro- Capitalism Strategy

The answer is D.
Containment Policy was the idea that the United States would fight communism in-directly in a large number of small economical, diplomatic, and militaristic battles. Thus A, B, C, and D are non-factual.

HISTORY OF THE UNITED STATES II

26. **What did the outcome of the court case Roe v. Wade legalize in 1973?**
    (Political Institutions, Behavior, and Public Policy) (1915-present)

    A. Abortion

    B. Communism

    C. Alcohol consumption

    D. Women's right to vote

    E. Integrated school systems

The answer is A.
Roe v. Wade is a landmark decision by the United States Supreme Court on the issue of abortion. Decided simultaneously with a companion case, Doe v. Bolton, the Court ruled 7–2 that a right to privacy under the Due Process Clause of the 14th Amendment extended to a woman's decision to have an abortion, but that this right must be balanced against the state's two legitimate interests in regulating abortions: protecting women's health and protecting the potentiality of human life.

27. **What was the Civil Rights Act of 1964?**
    (Political Institutions, Behavior, and Public Policy) (1915-present)

    A. Prohibited individual citizens from carrying firearms

    B. A civil rights act that provided private solutions.

    C. Prohibited individuals to purchase or loiter in private sectors (super markets, bars, etc.) if unwanted.

    D. Outlawed discrimination based on race, color, religion, and national origin, but not sex.

    E. Outlawed discrimination based on race, color, religion, sex, or national origin.

The answer is E.
The Civil Rights Act was enacted in July 2, 1964. It outlawed discrimination based on race, color, religion, sex, or national origin.

HISTORY OF THE UNITED STATES II

28. Which three were famous African American Civil Rights activists that were assonated in the 1960s?
    (Political Institutions, Behavior, and Public Policy) (1915-present)

    A. Bull Connor, Nathan B. Forest, and Medgar Evans

    B. Bull Connor, Martin Luther King, and Medgar Evers

    C. Rev. George Lee, Martin Luther King, and Medgar Evers

    D. William Lewis Moore, Martin Luther King, and Medgar Evers

    E. Nathan B. Forest, Martin Luther King, and Medgar Evers

The answer is C.
Medger Evans was an American civil rights activist from Mississippi involved in efforts to overturn segregation at the University of Mississippi. After returning from overseas military service in World War II and completing his college education, he became active in the Civil Rights Movement. He became a field secretary for the NAACP. He was shot through the heart hours after John F. Kennedy's Civil Rights Address. George W. Lee was an African American civil rights leader, minister, and entrepreneur. He was a vice president of the Regional Council of Negro Leadership and head of the Belzoni, Mississippi branch of the National Association for the Advancement of Colored People. He was assassinated in 1955 for organizing African Americans to try to register to vote. Martin Luther King Jr. was an American Baptist minister, activist, humanitarian, and leader in the African-American Civil Rights Movement. He is best known for his role in the advancement of civil rights using nonviolent civil disobedience based on his Christian beliefs. He was assassinated on April 4, 1968.

HISTORY OF THE UNITED STATES II

29. **What program was a result of Lyndon B Johnson's "Great Societies" War on Poverty"?**
    (Political Institutions, Behavior, and Public Policy) (1915-present)

    A. Medicare

    B. Obama Care

    C. Johnson care

    D. Social Security

    E. Department of Education

The answer is A.
Medicare was just one of the social programs that came out of Lyndon B Johnsons "Great Society". The War on Poverty is the unofficial name for legislation first introduced by United States President Johnson during his State of the Union address on January 8, 1964. This legislation was proposed by Johnson in response to a national poverty rate of around nineteen percent.

30. **What was the multi-billion dollar research project for a missile defense system that could shoot down incoming Soviet missiles and eliminate the need for mutually assured destruction?**
    (Political Institutions, Behavior, and Public Policy) (1915-present)

    A. Missile Defense Program

    B. Star Wars (Strategic Defense Initiative)

    C. US Nuclear Program

    D. US Missile Security

    E. None of the above

The answer is B.
Star Wars (SDI) began in 1983. It was a proposed missile defense system intended to protect the United States from attack by ballistic strategic nuclear weapons.

HISTORY OF THE UNITED STATES II

31. **What Landmark Supreme Court decision declared that racial segregation in schools is unconstitutional?**
    (Political Institutions, Behavior, and Public Policy) (1915-present)

    A. Black v. Department of Education

    B. Rice v. Board of Education

    C. Sweatt v. Painter

    D. Brown v. Board of Education

    E. Roe v. Wade

The answer is D.
Brown v. Board of Education was a landmark United States Supreme Court case in which the Court declared state laws establishing separate public schools for black and white students to be unconstitutional. The decision overturned the Plessy v. Ferguson decision of 1896, which allowed state-sponsored segregation. Answer A is not factual. B, C, and E are not relevant.

32. **The Twenty-Sixth Amendment lowered the voting age from ___ to ___ in 1971?**
    (Political Institutions, Behavior, and Public Policy) (1915-present)

    A. 21 to 18

    B. 24 to 21

    C. 20 to 18

    D. 30 to 18

    E. The Twenty-Sixth Amendment had nothing to do with the voting age.

The answer is A.
Section 1 reads, "The right of citizens of the United States, who are eighteen years of age or older, to vote shall not be denied or abridged by the United States or by any State on account of age."

33. **McCarthyism in the 1950's was similar to the Palmer Raids (Red Scare) in the 1920s in what way?**
    (Political Institutions, Behavior, and Public Policy) (1915-present)

    A. American citizen's liberties were breached

    B. Immigrants were suspicious of white communists

    C. Anarchists were the biggest conspirators

    D. The Ku Klux Klan led the assault against "Anti-Americans"

    E. No immigrants entered the country during these time periods.

The answer is A.
During the 1950 to 1956 period in the United States, a period known as the Second Red Scare, characterized by heightened political repression against communists, as well as a campaign spreading fear of their influence on American institutions and of espionage by Soviet agents. Originally coined to criticize the anti-communist pursuits of Republican U.S. Senator Joseph McCarthy of Wisconsin.

34. **How did president Nixon Presidency end?**
    (Political Institutions, Behavior, and Public Policy) (1915-present)

    A. Impeachment

    B. Resignation

    C. Death

    D. Illness

    E. Like every other president, he was president for four years. However, he was not voted in again because of the Watergate scandal.

The answer is B.
After the Watergate scandal former President Nixon resigned because he was on the verge of federal charges that were going to be brought against him. After his resignation President Gerald Ford equated him of all federal charges.

35. **What hurt economic growth the most during the 1970s through the 1980s?**
    (Political Institutions, Behavior, and Public Policy) (1915-present)

    A. Decrease in manual labor

    B. Inflation on unique metals

    C. Increase in oil prices

    D. Lack of technology innovation

    E. Increase in water prices

The answer is C.
Many Middle Eastern nations came together a created the OPEC and drafted and put into place the Oil Embargo act which raised the price of oil to four times the normal cost.

36. **What island(s) in the Caribbean did the US invade in 1983 in order to stop a small Marxist faction with holding power?**
    (Political Institutions, Behavior, and Public Policy) (1915-present)

    A. Cuba

    B. Grenada

    C. Portugal

    D. Bermuda

    E. Virgin Islands

The answer is B.
The leftist New Jewel Movement, which was seen favorably by much of the Grenadian population, seized power in a coup in 1979, suspending the constitution. After a 1983 internal power struggle ended with the deposition and murder of revolutionary Prime Minister Maurice Bishop, the U.S. invaded the tiny island in the Caribbean. The war only lasted a few weeks and the island government was quickly replaced with a democratic system.

HISTORY OF THE UNITED STATES II

37. **Who was sworn in as the first woman Supreme court Justice?**
    (Political Institutions, Behavior, and Public Policy) (1915-present)

    A. Sandra Day O'Connor

    B. Ruth Bader Ginsberg

    C. Sonia Sotomayor

    D. Elena Kagan

    E. Condoleezza Rice

The answer is A.
In 1981 Ronald Reagan appointed Sandra Day O'Connor to be the first woman to serve as a Supreme Court justice. All the other answer except for E were Supreme Court justices afterwards.

38. **What were the economic policies of the former US president Ronald Reagan called that associated especially with the reduction of taxes and the promotion of unrestricted free-market activity?**
    (Political Institutions, Behavior, and Public Policy) (1915-present)

    A. Reaganomics

    B. Keynesian Economics

    C. Command Economics

    D. Traditional Economics

    E. Conservative Economics

The answer is A.
Reaganomics refers to the economic policies promoted by U.S. President Ronald Reagan during the 1980s. These policies are commonly associated with supply-side economics or trickle-down economics. Reaganomics consists of a policy that reduces the growth of government spending, reduces the federal income tax and capital gains tax, reduces government regulation, and tightens the money supply in order to reduce inflation. B is a progressive theory of economics, C and D are non-factual, and E is too vague, thus all incorrect.

HISTORY OF THE UNITED STATES II

39. Under what era did the United States have its longest time frame of economic prosperity?
(Political Institutions, Behavior, and Public Policy) (1915-present)

   A. Roaring Twenties

   B. Progressive Years

   C. Antebellum

   D. Reconstruction

   E. 1990s (Information Age)

The answer is E.
Because of the invention of the World Wide Web, it created revenue in a number of different markets across the world, including the U.S.

40. What was Truman Doctrine?
(Political Institutions, Behavior, and Public Policy) (1915-present)

   A. It was an American foreign policy during President Harry S. Truman's term to stop Soviet imperialism during the Cold War.

   B. President Harry S. Truman plan to give American citizens universal healthcare.

   C. President Franklin D. Roosevelts great depression bailout plan, though up by vice president Harry S. Truman.

   D. A set of rules brought to the U.N. by President Harry S. Truman to hinder fascist leaders from gaining power in former axis powers lands.

   E. A set of pro-Soviet laws enforced during President Harry S. Truman's candidacy.

The answer is A.
The Truman Doctrine was an American foreign policy to stop Soviet imperialism during the Cold War. It was announced to Congress by President Harry S. Truman on March 12, 1947 when he pledged to contain Soviet threats to Greece and Turkey.

HISTORY OF THE UNITED STATES II

41. What landmark piece of federal legislation was in 1964 in the United States lead by Lyndon B. Johnson prohibits racial discrimination in voting such as requiring some states (mostly in the south) that want to change its districts have to go through the department of justice?
    (Political Institutions, Behavior, and Public Policy) (1915-present)

    A. Public Law

    B. Help America Vote Act

    C. Voting Rights Act

    D. Patriot Act

    E. 15th Amendment

The answer is C.
The Voting Rights Act prohibits racial discrimination in voting. Examples range from the law prohibiting states that would manipulate votes by rearranging districts in order to get more votes to outlawing literacy test.

42. What was the initial reason of the First Persian Gulf War?
    (Political Institutions, Behavior, and Public Policy) (1915-present)

    A. U.N. need for oil

    B. American need for oil

    C. Saddam Hussein's genocide of northern Iraqis

    D. Iran's invasion of Iran

    E. Iraq's invasion of Kuwait

The answer is E.
Iraq accused Kuwait of stealing its oil through slant drilling. Iraq invaded Kuwait and set fire to over 600 oil fields. The US with the UN lead an invasion on the Iraqi forces.

HISTORY OF THE UNITED STATES II

43. **Which administration used the term "War on Terrorism" first when referring to terrorist?**
(Political Institutions, Behavior, and Public Policy) (1915-present)

   A. George H. W. Bush

   B. George W. Bush

   C. Ronald Reagan

   D. Bill Clinton

   E. Lyndon B. Johnson

The answer is C.
In 1984, the Reagan Administration used the term "war against terrorism" as part of an effort to pass legislation that was designed to freeze assets of terrorist groups and marshal the forces of government against them. Author Shane Harris asserts this was a reaction to the 1983 Beirut barracks bombing, which killed 241 U.S. and 58 French peacekeepers.

44. **What agreement in 1994 tried to eliminate barriers to trade and investment between the U.S., Canada and Mexico?**
(Political Institutions, Behavior, and Public Policy) (1915-present)

   A. North American Nationality Organization (NANO)

   B. Western Alliance, Sect II

   C. The North American Triple Alliance (NTATA)

   D. North American Free Trade Agreement (NAFTA)

   E. Canada–United States Free Trade Agreement

The answer is D.
North American Free Trade Agreement goal was to eliminate barriers to trade and investment between the U.S., Canada and Mexico. All other names labeled are nonfactual, except for E, which was the former trade agreement.

HISTORY OF THE UNITED STATES II

45. **What is the traditional view of why the United States "won" the Cold War?**
    (Political Institutions, Behavior, and Public Policy) (1915-present)

    A. During the Carter and Reagan Administrations the United States upped military spending. The USSR tried to keep up, however, could not afford it and eventually collapsed.

    B. During the Bush and Clinton Administrations the United States upped military spending. The USSR tried to keep up, however, could not afford it and eventually collapsed.

    C. The Soviet Union eastern satellite nations won independence, severing the USSR economy.

    D. The USSR could not evoke desire in its citizens to work, therefore the economy eventually collapsed.

    E. Covert successful CIA mission missions in Afghanistan against Soviets led to a total breakdown of Soviet military and then later economy.

The answer is A.
After the Korean and the controversial Vietnam War politicians were not eager into getting into a full throttle war with communists. The United States figured if they remain the containment policy then the larger communists states would break, During the Carter and Reagan Administrations the United States upped military spending. The USSR tried to keep up, however, could not afford it and eventually collapsed.

HISTORY OF THE UNITED STATES II

46. **What was the label President John F Kennedy's give the 1960s with its unknown opportunities and perils such as uncharted areas of science and space, unsolved problems of peace and war, unconquered problems of ignorance and prejudice, unanswered questions of poverty and surplus?**
    (Political Institutions, Behavior, and Public Policy) (1915-present)

    A. The Beat Generation

    B. The Lost Generation

    C. The New Age

    D. The Peace Age

    E. The New Frontier

The answer is E.
President Kennedy coined the 1960s with its unknown opportunities and perils such as uncharted areas of science and space, unsolved problems of peace and war, unconquered problems of ignorance and prejudice, unanswered questions of poverty and surplus the New Frontier because the old American frontier of the west was gone. A was a segment within this time period President Kennedy was talking about however, it is not a full answer. B is the wrong time. C and D are not factual.

47. **The New Left in the 1960s and 70s sympathized with what school of thought?**
    (Political Institutions, Behavior, and Public Policy) (1915-present)

    A. Frankfurt School of Critical Theory

    B. Taoism

    C. Functionalism

    D. Classic Liberalism

    E. Republicanism

The answer is A.
The New Left was a political movement in the 1960s and 1970s consisting of educators, agitators and others who sought to implement a broad range of reforms on issues such as gay rights, abortion, gender roles, and drugs, in contrast to earlier leftist or Marxist movements. The New Left supported the Frankfurt School of thought which was critical of both capitalism and Soviet socialism, their writings pointed to the possibility of an alternative path to social development.

HISTORY OF THE UNITED STATES II

48. **What was the plans that was enacted in 1947 that goals were to rebuild war-devastated regions, remove trade barriers, modernize industry, make Europe prosperous again, and prevent the spread of communism called?**
    (Political Institutions, Behavior, and Public Policy) (1915-present)

    A. Dawes Plan

    B. Marshall Plan

    C. Truman Plan

    D. Morganthau Plan

    E. Versailles Compromise

The answer is B.
The Marshall plan was an effort by the United States to help European nations build themselves up after the ending of World War Two.

49. *What was the difference between First New Deal and Second New Deal?*
    (Political Institutions, Behavior, and Public Policy) (1915-present)

    A. The First New Deal regulated the private sector of society, however, the Second New Deal focused on regulating the corporate sector.

    B. The First New Deal focused more or the war effort, whereas the Second New Deal was more about poverty.

    C. The First New Deal was an effort to reshape the American electoral. landscape whereas the Second New Deal focused on ending poverty.

    D. At first it was just trying to find an immediate stop the depression. Relief, Recovery and Reform. The second was to have government regulate labor, housing, and farms.

    E. There really was no difference except Franklin D. Roosevelt changed the name in order to invoke more votes because of the popularity of the first deal.

The answer is D.
The difference between the first New Deal and the second New Deal lies in ideology. The first was more economical while the Second Deal dealt with political issues.

HISTORY OF THE UNITED STATES II

50. Before ratification of the 22nd amendment in 1951, most presidents served no more than two terms because of
(Political Institutions, Behavior, and Public Policy) (1915-present)

A. Tradition

B. Federal law

C. Supreme Court Decision

D. The Eight Year Clause

E. Anti-tyranny laws

The answer is A.
After George Washington turned down the third election every president after him followed suit until Franklin D. Roosevelt. Broke that tradition in 1940. There were many factors at play, particularly the fact that the United States was in World War II.

51. The 15th Amendment allowed former African American slaves to _____.
(Social developments) (1865-1914)

A. buy land

B. vote

C. acquire ownership of a public facility

D. return back to Africa for free

E. be compensated for free labor

The answer is B.
The Fifteenth Amendment prohibits the federal and state government from preventing American citizens to vote based on race, color, or previous condition of servitude. All other answers are nonfactual.

HISTORY OF THE UNITED STATES II

52. **What were Jim Crow Laws?**
    (Social developments)(1865-1914)

    A. State and local laws enforcing racial segregation predominantly in the South. Enacted after the Reconstruction period, these laws continued in force until 1965.

    B. Racist laws enforced by Alabama Governor Jim Crow. Northerner politicians coined the universal racist laws in the South after him.

    C. Laws that supported black rights during the Reconstruction period.

    D. Laws enforced by the national government to restrict African. Americans directly after the Civil War.

    E. Racist laws enforced by South Carolina Governor Jim Crow. Northerner politicians coined the universal racist laws in the South after him.

The answer is A.
Jim Crow laws were state and local laws enforcing racial segregation in the Southern United States.

53. **What was a key device for the removal of ex-Confederates from the political arena during the Reconstruction of the United States in the 1860s, requiring every white male to swear they had never borne arms against the Union or supported the Confederacy (in the Wade–Davis Bill)?**
    (Social developments)(1865-1914)

    A. Reconstruction Plan

    B. Fourteenth Amendment

    C. Ten-Percent Plan

    D. Ironclad Oath

    E. Republican Circle

The answer is D.
The Ironclad Oath was a devise by radical republicans in order to take away ex-confederates the right to vote.

HISTORY OF THE UNITED STATES II

54. What was the series of acts of Congress that promoted the construction of a "transcontinental railroad" through authorizing the issuance of government bonds and granting Native American, private, and government lands to railroad companies?
(Social developments) (1865-1914)

   A. Pacific Railroad Acts

   B. Transcendental Acts

   C. Johnson Acts

   D. West Acts

   E. The Gilead Acts

The answer is A.
The Pacific Railroad Acts were enforced in order to create the transcontinental railroad. B through E are all nonfactual.

55. Congress passed ten-year restrictions on _____ immigration in 1882 and 1892 and a permanent exclusion act in 1902.
(Social developments) (1865-1914)

   A. German

   B. Irish

   C. Japanese

   D. Italian

   E. Chinese

The answer is E.
The Chinese Exclusions Act was the first law implemented to prevent a specific ethnic group from immigrating to the United States.

HISTORY OF THE UNITED STATES II

56. What was the idea called, led by William Graham Sumner, that argued the best equipped to win the struggle for survival was the American businessman, and concluded that taxes and regulations serve as dangers to his survival?
(Social developments) (1865-1914)

   A. Marxism

   B. Social Darwinism

   C. Capitalism

   D. Laissez Faire

   E. Imperialism

The answer is B.
Social Darwinism American Social Darwinism held that the social classes had no obligation towards those unequipped or under-equipped to compete for survival. C and D are incorrect because they represent capitalist ideas and A and E Marxist ideas.

57. What was the name given to the cultural, social, and artistic explosion that took place in Harlem between the end of World War I and the middle of the 1930s?
(Social developments)   (1865-1914)

   A. Civil Rights Movement

   B. Black Lives Matter

   C. Reconstruction Era

   D. African American Rights

   E. Harlem Renaissance

The answer is E.
The Harlem Renaissance was from 1919 to 1929 where African Americans from all over the United States came together and produced new forms of literature, fashion, and, lifestyles.

HISTORY OF THE UNITED STATES II

58. **What genre of dancing was famous from 1900 to 1918, beginning in African American communities?**
    (Social developments)   (1865-1914)

    A. The Waltz

    B. Swing Dance

    C. Ragtime

    D. Modern Dance

    E. Balboa

The answer is C.
The Ragtime was a dance that was very popular in the late 19thcenury and early twentieth century. It originated from African Americans and made its way across America.

59. **What was the process in which people moved (or migrated) toward the city in the early twentieth century in order to work in the booming industrial era?**
    (Social developments)   (1865-1914)

    A. Urbanization

    B. Modernization

    C. Counterurbanization

    D. Reconstruction

    E. City Overhaul

The answer is A.
American citizens began to grow contempt for major cities. With rise in economic gains Urbanization of outside city limits began to proceed.

HISTORY OF THE UNITED STATES II

60. **During the Progressive era what was supported in order to bring about a more "purer" vote to the American elections?**
    (Social developments)   (1865-1914)

    A. Prohibition laws

    B. African American rights

    C. Woman Suffrage

    D. Anti-Immigration laws

    E. Immigration laws

The answer is C.
Progressives thought women as more virtuous being, as did most of the United States, therefore, they believed women should vote to bring about more virtuous results. Thus Progressives supported the Women's Suffrage movement.

61. **What did President Wilson's "New Freedom" campaign seek to reform?**
    (Social developments) (1915-present)

    A. Tariff, Business, and Banking

    B. Tariff, Race, and State Rights

    C. Business, Race, and Banking

    D. Race, Tariff, and Banking

    E. Federal Rights, State Rights, and Tariff

The answer is A.
New Freedom is a series of the Progressive programs enacted by Wilson as president during his first term. There were three different phases, each one dealing with a different issue: Banking, Business, and Tariff reforms.

HISTORY OF THE UNITED STATES II

62. **Before World War I, what was the general reaction towards external conflicts by American citizens?**
    (Social developments) (1915-present)

    A. Interventionism

    B. Indirect Interference

    C. Interference

    D. Isolationism

    E. Reactionary

The answer is D.
Many Americans held and Isolationist attitude when referring to World War I. It was not until the Zimmerman note was found and the sinking of the Lusitania, killing 1198 citizens, that the US actually truly considered going to war.

63. **What was one reason the US entered World War I?**
    (Social developments) (1915-present)

    A. Invasion of Poland

    B. The sinking of the Lusitania

    C. Pearl Harbor

    D. Invasion of Austria

    E. Attacks on Britain

The answer is B.
1198 passengers were killed when the Lusitania was struck down by a German U boat torpedo. The US believed this was an infringement upon their isolationism, thus they declared war on Germany, entering into World War One.

HISTORY OF THE UNITED STATES II

64. Two Senators and fifty Representatives voted against the war resolution, including the first female ever to sit in Congress, _____ of Montana.
(Social developments) (1915-present)

    A. Joni Ernst

    B. Hattie Caraway

    C. Rebecca Felton

    D. Jeannette Rankin

    E. Ruth Elandor

The answer is D.
Jeanne Rankin was elected by the state of Montana in 1916 to sit in on Congress, making her the first women to do so.

65. What authorized the federal government to raise a national army for the American entry into World War I through the compulsory enlistment of people?
(Social developments) (1915-present)

    A. Draft

    B. Selective Service Act

    C. Draft Lottery

    D. Conscription Act

    E. There was no draft during WWI

The answer is B.
The Selective Service Act authorized the federal government to raise a national army for the American entry into World War I through the compulsory enlistment of people.

HISTORY OF THE UNITED STATES II

66. **The widespread use of what technological advancement in the 1920s revolutionized dating, education, change in work patters as well as an increase in recreational time?** *(Social developments) (1915-present)*

    A. Radio

    B. Train

    C. Automobile

    D. Airplane

    E. Bicycle

The answer is C.
Wide scale of the Automobile changed life dramatically. Things that took much longer, such as shopping, took less time, giving Americans ore time for reacreation.

67. **The American Mafia, an Italian-American organized-crime network with operations in cities across the United States, particularly New York and Chicago, rose to power through its success in the illicit _____ during the 1920s Prohibition era.** *(Social developments) (1915-present)*

    A. Illicit narcotic drug trade

    B. Alcohol trade

    C. Firearms trade

    D. Assignations of corporate leaders

    E. Burglary

The answer is B.
The American Mafia participated in all of the answers, however, alcohol trade initiated as well as gave these crime organizations its largest revenues.

HISTORY OF THE UNITED STATES II

68. What was the series of raids in 1919- 1920 called that focused on eastern Europeans and sympathizers of communist and anarchist ideology?
(Social developments) (1915-present)

    A. Second Red Scare

    B. McCarthyism

    C. Anti-Communism

    D. Swift Raids

    E. Palmer Raids

The answer is E.
The Palmer Raids were a series of raids by the United States Department of Justice intended to capture, arrest and deport radical leftists, especially anarchists, from the United States.

69. What was one result of the Great depression?
(Social developments) (1915-present)

    A. Increase in divorce rates

    B. Crime rates dropped

    C. Recreations activities dropped such as watching movies in a cinema.

    D. Migration from rural areas to urban

    E. Individuals in rural areas stayed stationary (cities were expensive and the transportation procedure was too expensive)

The answer is D.
Many families could not find work in rural areas, therefore, they were forced to live in larger cities to work in factories.

70. **Prodded by Eleanor Roosevelt, FDR created women's auxiliary forces for?**
    (Social developments) (1915-present)

    A. Transportation system

    B. Conservation

    C. Agriculture

    D. Universities

    E. Military

The answer is E.
World War Two needed every hand it could get. First lady Elinor Roosevelt saw the opportunity and supplanted women into jobs that were usually taken for men.

71. **What attributed to the rise in suburbia in the 1950s?**
    (Social developments) (1915-present)

    A. Increase in revenue

    B. Outburst of population from rural areas

    C. Overpopulation

    D. Racial fears, affordable living, avoidance of the "dirtiness" of the city

    E. Growth of conservative citizens that could not stand the normally progressive stance held by cities

The answer is D.
After the Great Depression and World War Two, the economy was town beginning to turn around. Many whites did not like the dirtiness and racial tension of the city. Suburbs began to be created on the outskirts of the city to fill this void.

HISTORY OF THE UNITED STATES II

72. What groups of individuals, led by writers such as Jack Kerouac and Alan Ginsberg, were specifically known for their refusal to conform to social norms?
    (Social developments) (1915-present)

    A. Renaissance Era

    B. Post-Moderns

    C. Baby Boomers

    D. Beat Generation

    E. Lost Generation

The answer is D.
The Beat Generation was known for their counter cultural style, literature, and wild lifestyles.

73. What Supreme Court decision overruled the Plessy v. Ferguson case and declared that in the field of public education the doctrine of separate but equal' has no place. *Separate educational facilities are inherently unequal.*
    (Social developments) (1915-present)

    A. Plessy v. Ferguson II

    B. Brown v. Board of Education

    C. Shelley v. Kraemer

    D. Powell v. Anderson

    E. Powell v. Alabama

The answer is B.
Brown v. Board of Education declared that schools that enforced segregation was unconstitutional. A and D is nonfactual. B and C all are race case, however, they enforce segregation.

74. **The Maoist tenet "Political power comes through the barrel of a gun" was adopted by which group?**
    (Social developments) (1915-present)

    A. Nation of Yahweh

    B. Black Back To Africa

    C. Black Panther

    D. NAACP

    E. United Nuwaubian Nation of Moors

The answer is C.
The black Panthers were a far extreme black power group in the Civil Rights Movement. They were known for their military like actions.

75. **What war started because France was determined to reclaim all its territories after World War II? This war was unique because American tradition dictated sympathy for the revolutionaries over any colonial power. However, supporting the Marxist in this given circumstance was unthinkable, given the new strategy of containing communism.**
    (Social developments) (1915-present)

    A. Korean War

    B. Afghanistan

    C. Vietnam War

    D. Geneva Island

    E. Chile Civil War

The answer is C.
France tried to keep its colonies abroad by trying to still a communist rebellion in Vietnam. It ended up being a very costly war in Vietnam.

HISTORY OF THE UNITED STATES II

76. Who was the first US President to visit China after the communist takeover?
(Social developments) (1915-present)

    A. Franklin D. Roosevelt

    B. Dwight D. Eisenhower

    C. Harry Truman

    D. Lyndon B. Johnson

    E. Richard Nixon

The answer is E.
President Nixon visit to China in 1972 ended 25 years of silence between the two nations. Prior to his visit no President had stepped foot on the People Republic of China since the takeover of the communist party.

77. What was one aspect that feminists such as Margret Sanger fought for in the early 1960s?
(Social developments) (1915-present)

    A. The use of contraceptives

    B. The right to vote

    C. The enforcement of prohibition laws

    D. Improved childcare laws

    E. Free Trade

The answer is A.
Feminist fought for a number of different things during the Civil Rights movement such as contraceptives. They believed their body belongs to them, therefore, they can say what will happen to it.

HISTORY OF THE UNITED STATES II

78. **What did the New Right consist of?**
    (Social developments) (1915-present)

    A. Extremist immigrants groups

    B. Extremist political groups, conservative Christians, and CEO's of corporations

    C. Fringe political groups, Christian evangelicals, and higher ups of corporations

    D. Extreme Libertarians

    E. Followers of Reagan

The answer is C.
As President Reagan was coming into power, a new sect of Republicans arrised. This group was filled with conservative Christian, fringe political groups, and CEOs.

79. **With the growing economy, many middle-class Americans rushed to invest in the stock market and to flaunt their newly acquired wealth. What group of people supplanted the hippies of the former generation?**
    (Social developments) (1915-present)

    A. Young Urban Professionals

    B. Rockers

    C. Punk rockers

    D. Society of X's

    E. Baby Boomers

The answer is A.
Young Urban Professionals were a group of young financially well off Americans.

HISTORY OF THE UNITED STATES II

80. What was the historic time called throughout 1997–2000 during which stock markets in industrialized nations saw their equity value rise rapidly from growth in the Internet sector and related fields (especially with the invention of the World Wide Web)?
    (Social developments) (1915-present)

    A. The Information Age

    B. Dot-Com Bubble

    C. Great Moderation

    D. Golden Age of Capitalism

    E. World Wide Consumerism

The answer is B.
The Dot Com Bubble was a period in the 1990s that saw a great increase in revenue due to the expansion of the World Wide Web. A and E are small parts of what caused the Dot Com Bubble, but they are incomplete.

81. The rapid expansion of _____ led to real wage growth of 60% between 1860 and 1890.
    (Economic Developments) (1865-1914)

    A. Agriculture

    B. Racial equality

    C. Industrialization

    D. Emigration

    E. Progressive ideals

The answer is C.
With the addition of factories, trains, and other forms of electricity, the standard of living sky rocketed.

HISTORY OF THE UNITED STATES II

82. In 1869, the First Transcontinental Railroad opened new areas of opportunity in _____.
(Economic Developments) (1865-1914)

   A. Far-west mining and ranching regions

   B. South American mining

   C. African American mobility

   D. Oil Revenue

   E. Exotic fur trade

The answer is A.
Before the transcontinental railroad it was extremely dangerous and long to move out west. The railroad system brought the East to the West within one to two days.

83. The Reconstruction era brought many changes to the very poor and broken South such as _____.
(Economic Developments) (1865-1914)

   A. Higher Education

   B. Equality

   C. Republicanism

   D. Mercantilism

   E. Sharecropping

The answer is E.
After slavery was banished Jim Crow laws were established. Blacks worked for very low wages and sometimes for free.

HISTORY OF THE UNITED STATES II

84. **What was the US financial crisis called that took place over a three-week period starting in mid-October, when the New York Stock Exchange fell almost 50% from its peak the previous year? Panic occurred, and eventually spread throughout the nation when many state and local banks and businesses entered bankruptcy.**
    (Economic Developments) (1865-1914)

    A. Depression of 1910

    B. Great Depression

    C. Panic of 1907

    D. The End of the Industrial Age

    E. The Second Great Depression

The answer is C.
The Panic of 1907 was a time when the stock market fell by 50 percent in the midst of a recession. The Great Depression happened a few years later. All other question are made up.

85. **The Federal road building program ended in 1818, 98 year gap, leaving states to build roads until the _____.**
    (Economic Developments) (1865-1914)

    A. Car and Road Act 1916

    B. Autobahn

    C. Dwight D. Eisenhower National System of Interstate and Defense Highways

    D. Federal Road Act of 1916

    E. Highway act of 1916

The answer is D.
With the creation of automobile roads became a necessity. D is correct. President Eisenhower did try to enhance the highway, however, much later. All other answers are nonfactual.

86. **In order to deal with the crisis in banking at the time of his inauguration, President Franklin D Roosevelt.**
    (Economic Developments) (1915-present)

    A. Closed the banking system for four days giving them a "banking holiday."

    B. Enlarged the Federal Bank.

    C. Prohibited for more than 1000 USD to be taking from any accounts that were to be used for recreational purposes.

    D. Fired all the Federal Bank board members and replaced them with Keynesian theorists

    E. President Roosevelt did nothing, he thought the bank would come out of its cycle if left alone.

The answer is A.
Banks feared that their customers were going take out all of their money because of the Great Depression. President Franklin Roosevelt gave them a four day "holiday" so that the banks had a chance to catch up.

87. **What was the policy adopted by the United States in 1939 to preserve neutrality while aiding the Allies? Britain and France could buy goods from the United States if they paid in full and transported them.**
    (Economic Developments) (1915-present)

    A. Isolation act

    B. Cash and Carry

    C. Prohibition Act

    D. Debt Default Act

    E. New Deal

The answer is B.
Cash and Carry was an act that took place of the Neutrality Act. It allowed The United states to trade with Great Britain and France as long as they used their own ships in picking up the goods.

HISTORY OF THE UNITED STATES II

88. What is one reason the US has had a dramatic increase in economic since the 1950s? *(Economic Developments) (1915-present)*

    A. The end of the Korean War

    B. The end of the Vietnam War

    C. Oil prices have decreased

    D. More of a focus is agriculture

    E. Baby Boomers

The answer is E.
After World War Two there was increase in pregnancies so much so that it was the most child births recorded in the United States history.

89. What policy did the Office of Economic Opportunity originate from? *(Economic Developments) (1915-present)*

    A. Personal Responsibility and Work Opportunity Act

    B. War on Poverty

    C. VISTA

    D. New Deal

    E. None of the Above

The answer is B.
President Lyndon B Johnson started the war on poverty in 1964. The office of Economic Opportunity becomes the administration program for this policy.

90. **The 1973 Oil Crisis began when**
    (Economic Developments) (1915-present)

    A. OAPEC proclaimed an oil embargo- raising the price of oil to four times as much.

    B. OPEC proclaimed and oil embargo- raising the price of oil to four times as much.

    C. large Oil fields caught on fire in Saudi Arabia, causing global oil prices to rise.

    D. the United States congress voted against drilling in Alaska and Texas, raising oil prices to three times as much.

    E. There was no Oil crisis in 1973.

The answer is A.
OAPEC proclaimed an oil embargo- raising the price of oil to four times as much. B is partially correct, however, it does not include Egypt and Syria, therefore, incorrect. All other answers are non-factual, thus, incorrect.

91. **What was one term used to define President Reagan's economic policy to cut both federal spending and taxes to release private revenue for future investments?**
    (Economic Developments) (1915-present)

    A. Supply-side

    B. Reagan Conservatism

    C. Laissez-faire

    D. New Conservative Economics

    E. Capitalism

The answer is A.
Supply side economics stems from Reaganomics. Policies consist of lowering barriers of productions of goods and services as well as investing capital. Supply-side economics usually is synonymous with tax cuts.

HISTORY OF THE UNITED STATES II

92. **What was reason for the longest and largest economic boom in the 1990s?**
    (Economic Developments) (1915-present)

    A. Cost of living decreased

    B. Lower taxes

    C. The ending of the food tax

    D. The creation of the World Wide Web

    E. Invasion of Iraq

The answer is D.
The creation of the World Wide Web allowed individuals to buy and sell without restraints. It also allowed information to travel fast. Thus revenue was created. E is incorrect because it did the opposite. A, B, and C are all incorrect because they are all nonfactual.

93. **What organization formed after the ending of the Civil War in 1865, later became known as the largest hate organization known in the United States?**
    (Cultural and intellectual developments 1865-1914)

    A. White Aryan Resistance

    B. Southern Democrats

    C. Ku Klux Klan

    D. Anti-Defense League

    E. White Supremists

The answer is C.
The Ku Klux Klan had three waves. The first wave (directly after the civil War) was mainly ex-confederate soldiers that would terrorize blacks. The Second Wave KKK turned its attention to whites as a whole and watered down their message. This was its most popular phase. The third way, is much smaller and nt as politically dangerous than its predecessor, however, more they are if not the same as the first, more physically dangerous.

94. **The idea (that originated in the 1880s by farmers and their associates) that the government was being made up of industrialists and bankers was called?**
   (Cultural and intellectual developments 1865-1914)

   A. Progressivism

   B. Populism

   C. Conservatism

   D. True Liberalism

   E. Free Republicanism

The answer is B.
Populism was founded during the gilded Age. Farmers and associates thought that corporations had corrupted politics. Populist sought to transform the government by ridding it of elites.

95. **Many of the middle class in the beginning of the 20th century believed that unfair election systems, exploitation of workers, women and children, corruption in the business class and the legal system all meant that there was an unfair political system. These people were called?**
   (Cultural and intellectual developments 1865-1914)

   A. Progressivism

   B. Populism

   C. Conservatism

   D. True Liberalism

   E. Free Republicanism

The answer is A.
Progressives main objectives were to eliminate corruption in government and bring about reforms within the society (conservation, technological change, etc.). B is incorrect because it focuses more on economic corruption. And A, B, and C might have focused on these attributes but it would have been a minor theme to their overarching beliefs in either natural rights (Liberalism) or state rights (conservatism and republicanism).

HISTORY OF THE UNITED STATES II

96. What was the genre of writing called that appeared after the Civil War and had great effect on the American populist all the wat into the Twentieth Century? The style of writing derived from the presentation of the features and peculiarities of a particular locality and its inhabitants.
    (Cultural and intellectual developments 1865-1914)

    A. Beat Generation

    B. Transcendentalism

    C. Realism

    D. Local Colour

    E. Expressionism

The answer is D.
Local Colour emphasized regional practicalities, as seen with Mark Twain in Huck Finn and the use of illicit language towards African Americans.

97. What did Jeffries V. Johnson boxing fright prove to the United States populace?
    (Cultural and intellectual developments 1865-1914)

    A. The United States was the strongest nation

    B. Anyone can fulfil the American dream

    C. Whites were more intelligent

    D. Blacks were equals

    E. That blacks were not meant to live in cities

The answer is D.
Social Darwinism was on the rise and many whites believed in the supremacy of their own race. Jack Johnson win over James Jeffries shocked the U.S. as they saw it as the best of the African Americans beat the best of the Caucasian Americans.

HISTORY OF THE UNITED STATES II

98. The NAACP was developed in order to?
(Cultural and intellectual developments) (1915-present)

    A. Fight radical black activism.

    B. Defend Jim Crow laws.

    C. To fight for equality on a national front.

    D. Support Ku Klux Klan

    E. Support Progressive politicians

The answer is C.
Founders of the NAACP: Moorfield Storey, Mary White Ovington and W.E.B. Du Bois. The Race Riot of 1908 in Abraham Lincoln's hometown of Springfield, Illinois, had highlighted the urgent need for an effective civil rights organization in the U.S. This event is often cited as the catalyst for the formation of the NAACP.

99. Conscription policies in the First and Second World Wars differed significantly in that in the First World War
(Cultural and intellectual developments) (1915-present)

    A. The draft began before the US entered

    B. Blacks were enlisted

    C. German skepticism

    D. Airplanes were not used

    E. Automatic weapons were not used

The answer is A.
The United States was surprise attacked by the Japanese at Pearl Harbor. They immediately declared war. This gave them not enough time to draft before the war had actually started.

HISTORY OF THE UNITED STATES II

100. What were the northern, urban, single, young, middle-class women from the 1920s called who enjoyed dancing to jazz music, wearing dresses at their knees, wearing short hair, and participating in night life?
(Cultural and intellectual developments) (1915-present)

- A. Revolutionists
- B. Hippies
- C. Valley girls
- D. Flappers
- E. Victorians

The answer is D.
Flappers were mostly middle class women that defied the gender roles and sexuality. They are known for their excessive style, interest in Jazz music, dancing, drinking, and smoking in the 1920s America.

101. What was the third largest political party in 1920?
(Cultural and intellectual developments) (1915-present)

- A. Republicans
- B. Democrats
- C. Socialist
- D. Communists
- E. Whig

The answer is C.
Led by Presidential candidate Eugene V. Debs, the Socialist party gained more votes than any third place party had in the history of the United States. Many during this time sympathized with healthcare and labor laws giving the socialist party more favor then usual

102. **In 1925 Tennessee passed what law that prohibited the teaching of Darwin's theory of evolution in schools?**
    (Cultural and intellectual developments) (1915-present)

    A. Bryan Laws

    B. Religious Freedom Law

    C. Creationism act

    D. Separate but Equal act

    E. Butler Law

The answer is E.
The rise of Social Darwinism scared many conservative Protestants. Tennessee led the way by outlawing the theory in all public schools by passing Butler law. Many states followed suit, largely in the South.

103. **What is the term for the practice of making accusations of subversion or treason without proper regard for evidence originating from the Second Red Scare, characterized by heightened political repression against communists?**
    (Cultural and intellectual developments) (1915-present)

    A. Anti-Soviet

    B. McCarthyism

    C. Palmerizing

    D. False allegations

    E. Anti-American

The answer is B.
McCarthyism is the practice of making accusations of subversion or treason without proper regard for evidence. The name stems back to the Second Red Scare in which Senator Joseph McCarthy led a campaign in depleting the United State of any communists, anarchists, or affiliates.

HISTORY OF THE UNITED STATES II

104. What was the Indian Termination Policy?
(Cultural and intellectual developments) (1915-present)

    A. President Franklin Roosevelts plan to destroy all Native American ancestry in the US

    B. President Dwight Eisenhower's policy to shape a series of laws and policies with the intent of assimilating Native Americans into mainstream American society fairly quickly (ending reservations and Native American sovereignty)

    C. President Franklin Roosevelts policy to shape a series of laws and policies with the intent of assimilating Native Americans into mainstream American society fairly quickly (ending reservations and Native American sovereignty)

    D. President Franklin Roosevelts plant to end Americans plans to destroy Native American plans by creating suburbs on Native American reservations.

    E. President Harry Truman's plan to end Native American ancestry in the US

The answer is B.
Dwight D. Eisenhower's Indian termination policy was nothing new to America except for its focus on quickness. Within one term period Eisenhower had managed to close a majority of Native American reservations as well as end Native Americans claims to sovereignty.

105. What was the anti-establishment cultural phenomenon in the 1950s and 1960s called?
(Cultural and intellectual developments) (1915-present)

    A. The Counter-Culture

    B. Brights Movement

    C. Ecofeminism

    D. Cultural Movement

    E. Human Rights Movement

The answer is A.
The Counter Culture of the 50 and 60s beliefs differed drastically from mainstream culture norms. The use of drugs, explicit writing, and outlandish (bum like) styles, created and absolutely diverse subculture in America.

HISTORY OF THE UNITED STATES II

106. What is one difference in first and second wave feminism?
(Cultural and intellectual developments) (1915-present)

   A. First wave feminism pursued the right to vote while second wave feminism sought equality in the workforce

   B. First wave feminism was much more radical than its counterparts

   C. Second wave feminism was more focused on woman outside the United States

   D. First wave feminism pursued the equality in the work place, second wave feminism focused on solely education

   E. Second wave feminism was more ideological

The answer is A.
First Wave feminist focused on rights to vote and the ability to seek education. Second wave feminism focused on equal opportunity/pay, reproductive rights, ending blatant sexism in the media.

107. Why did (/do) the majority of African American women not participate in all three feminist movements?
(Cultural and intellectual developments) (1915-present)

   A. They did not like white people

   B. The majority of the movement was made up of middle class white women. Blacks felt they could not relate with the white experience.

   C. All three movements did not admit African Americans.

   D. Black women were not educated enough.

   E. Question is incorrect, the majority of the feminist movement was black.

The answer is B.
Most of the feminist organizations were and are majority white women from middle class backgrounds. African American women felt and feel that their experiences are different from these women thus their issues are different.

HISTORY OF THE UNITED STATES II

108. What started the Montgomery Bus Boycott and was one reason that sparked the Civil Rights movement?
(Cultural and intellectual developments) (1915-present)

   A. Rosa Parks refusal to move on a Montgomery bus.

   B. Martin Luther King's organization of the Montgomery Bus riots.

   C. The assignation of Rosa Parks.

   D. Ralph Abernathy, King formed the Southern Christian Leadership Conference (SCLC), which invoked African Americans to riot, including bus riots.

   E. Malcom X refusal to get off a Montgomery all white bus

The answer is A.
After coming home from a long day of work Rosa Park was sitting on the bus when a Caucasian man told her she had to move for him and two of his friends. She told him she was not going to move. Other African American activists heard about this and followed suit setting off what is now called the Montgomery bus riots.

109. From the beginning of the decade until the end of the 90s, new forms of entertainment, commerce, research, work, and communication became commonplace in the United States. The driving force behind much of this change was an innovation popularly known as the Internet. This age is known as the _____?
(Cultural and intellectual developments) (1915-present)

   A. Information age

   B. Modernity

   C. Education age

   D. Consumer age

   E. Baby Boomers

The answer is A.
The Information Age is a period in human history characterized by the shift from traditional industry that the Industrial Revolution brought through industrialization, to an economy based on information computerization.

HISTORY OF THE UNITED STATES II

110. **What was the term for the 1970s decade when many young people were focused on themselves, rather than the world at large?**
    (Cultural and intellectual developments) (1915-present)

    A. Me Decade

    B. The Counter Culture

    C. Hippies

    D. Civil Rights

    E. Rockers

The answer is A.
The Me Decade was a time period when the majority of young Americans were focused more on themselves than international problems or even national problems. The sixties were filled with people trying to fix society, where the 70s seemed as if they wanted to return to the 1920s political atmosphere, where people distanced themselves for politics. The word was termed after Tom Wolfe's book *The Me generation and the Third Great Awakening*.

111. **_____ was one of the most significant restrictions on free immigration in US history, prohibiting all immigration of Chinese laborers.**
    (Diplomacy and international relations) (1865-1914)

    A. Anti-Chinese Act

    B. Chinese Exclusion Act

    C. Civil Rights Act

    D. Magnuson Act

    E. Immigration and Nationality Act

The answer is B.
The Chinese Exclusion Act was one of the most significant restrictions on free immigration in US history, prohibiting all immigration of Chinese laborers. The act was initially intended to last for 10 years, but was renewed in 1892 and made permanent in 1902. The Chinese Exclusion Act was the first law implemented to prevent a specific ethnic group from immigrating to the United States. It was finally repealed by the Magnuson Act on December 17, 1943.

HISTORY OF THE UNITED STATES II

112. **What was the policy proposed in 1899 to keep China open to trade with all countries on an equal basis?**
     (Diplomacy and international relations) (1865-1914)

     A. Immigration Act

     B. Mutual Security Act

     C. Foreign Assistance Act

     D. Open Door Policy

     E. Act for International Development

The answer is D.
The policy proposed to keep China open to trade with all countries on an equal basis. This kept one country form monopolizing the area. The U.S. announced its Open Door Policy with the dual intentions of avoiding the actual political division of China and taking financial advantage.

113. **What did the Roosevelt Corollary mean for the US international position?**
     (Diplomacy and international relations) (1865-1914)

     A. It allowed the United States to intervene in Russian affairs.

     B. It allowed the United States to intervene in the Middle East.

     C. Being an addition to the Monroe doctrine, it allowed the United States to interfere in Europe and South American countries.

     D. It ended a hundred year suppression on Native American lands.

     E. It allowed the ending of colonization in South America.

The answer is C.
The Monroe Doctrine stated the America could get involved with any war that had to with European colonizing. President Teddy Roosevelt used this to interfere with South American and Caribbean countries, particularly with Venezuela, whom President Roosevelt feared could not pay its debt to European powers.

HISTORY OF THE UNITED STATES II

114. Why is the Alaska Purchase sometimes called "Seward folly"?
(Diplomacy and international relations) (1865-1914)

   A. Because he had to pay Russia and then he had to pay Siberia for it.

   B. Secretary of State William Seward bought Alaska on behalf of the US and died in Alaska when trying to relocate the territories capital.

   C. The purchase threatened British colonies in the Pacific west, causing Britain to put tariffs on Western United States goods.

   D. People were critical of the deal and thought Secretary State William Seward payed too much for a piece of land that was mostly unexplored.

   E. Secretary of State William Seward killed thousands of local tribes trying to inhabit the newly purchased land.

The answer is D.
Many criticized Senator William Seward for heading up the deal between Russia and the United States of America. They said that the land was largely unexplored and had no known resources. The U.S. paid seven million dollars for the entirety of the land, outraging the critics.

115. What did the United States Congress in the 1930s, do in response to the growing turmoil in Europe and Asia that eventually led to World War II?
(Diplomacy and international relations) (1915-present)

   A. Ludlow Amendments

   B. McGovern–Hatfield Amendment

   C. World War II Acts

   D. Spot Resolutions

   E. Neutrality Acts of the 1930s

The answer is E.
The Neutrality Acts of the 1930s were and effort by politicians to keep the United States out of the affairs of Europe, particularly World War One. Many believed that it was inevitable for the U.S. to get in the Great War if they traded with Allie nations, thus the Neutrality Acts were in place to keep the U.S. from trading and participating in giving resources to nations that were in the midst of the Great War.

HISTORY OF THE UNITED STATES II

116. What was the first international difficulty the U.S. had with the U.S.S.R.?
(Diplomacy and international relations) (1915-present)

    A. Yugoslavia revolt

    B. Cuban Missile Crisis

    C. Bay of Pigs

    D. Berlin Blockade

    E. War in Vietnam

The answer is D.
On April 1, 1948 to 12 May 1949, the Soviet Union blocked all roads, canals, and railways around the Soviet sided Berlin, encircling the west Allies Berlin. In response Western countries dropped off supplies via Airplanes almost not stop for one year until the Soviets gave in.

117. How did the U.S. help stop communism in Afghanistan form 1979-1989?
(Diplomacy and international relations) (1915-present)

    A. Created sanctions against the Soviet Union.

    B. Fought Soviet Union directly in Afghanistan.

    C. Assonated rebel leader Zulfikar Ali Bhutto

    D. Practiced the doctrine of containment by giving military aid to Afghanistan rebels.

    E. All are incorrect. The U.S. stayed neutral in this particular situation.

The answer is D.
The Afghanistan government was taken over by a communist coup. However, soon after the Soviet Union got involved and murdered the communist leaders and began to put in to place Soviet communism. The U.S. backed rebel groups such as the Mujahedeen and the Afghanistan rebels eventually won their freedom.

HISTORY OF THE UNITED STATES II

118. What example would best describe Reagan doctrine?
(Diplomacy and international relations) (1915-present)

    A. Giving covert aid to anti-communist militia

    B. Creating an isolationist society

    C. Creating open trade diplomacy with the USSR

    D. Creating open trade with every country except the USSR

    E. Fight the Soviet Union with a direct military offensive.

The answer is A.
Reagan held a hard stance against communism. Seeing the past failures in total war in Vietnam and Korea, Reagan decided to keep the containment policy but added to it by trying to outspend the U.S.S.R. until they went bankrupt.

119. What was the largest military operation after Vietnam War in the United States?
(Diplomacy and international relations) (1915-present)

    A. Persian Gulf war

    B. Somalia

    C. Yugoslavia

    D. Grenada

    E. India-Pakistan War

The answer is A.
The U.S. sent the largest amount of troops to liberate Kuwait from Iraq, because Iraq at the time had the world's fourth largest standing army.

120. Journalist organization, WikiLeaks, released a United States cable leak describing *(Diplomacy and international relations) (1915-present)*

A. classified receipts of illegal transactions of military weapons sent from the U.S. government.

B. classified information about the Iraq War

C. classified cables that had been sent to the U.S. State Department by 274 of its consulates, embassies, and diplomatic missions around the world.

D. classified information about the U.S military presence in eastern European countries.

E. falsified information that supposedly exposed U.S. senate members of embezzling money.

The answer is C.
Cablegate began on November 28, 2010. A nonprofit journalist organization called WikiLeaks released 274 cables from diplomats from around the world addressing things from analyses on world leaders to assessments of diplomat's house country.

WESTERN CIVILIZATION I

Description of the Examination

The Western Civilization I: Ancient Near East to 1648 examination covers material that is usually taught in the first semester of a two-semester course in Western Civilization. Questions deal with the civilizations of Ancient Greece, Rome, and the Near East; the Middle Ages; the Renaissance and Reformation; and early modern Europe. Candidates may be asked to choose the correct definition of a historical term, select the historical figure whose political viewpoint is described, identify the correct relationship between two historical factors, or detect the inaccurate pairing of an individual with a historical event. Groups of questions may require candidates to interpret, evaluate, or relate the contents of a passage, a map, or a picture to other information, or to analyze and utilize the data contained in a graph or table.

The examination contains approximately 120 questions to be answered in 90 minutes. Some of these are pretest questions that will not be scored. Any time candidates spend on tutorials and providing personal information is in addition to the actual testing time. This examination uses the chronological designations b.c.e. (before the common era) and c.e. (common era). The labels correspond to b.c. (before Christ) and a.d. (anno Domini), which are used in some textbooks.

Knowledge and Skills Required

Questions on the Western Civilization I examination require candidates to demonstrate one or more of the following abilities.

- Ability to understand important factual knowledge of developments in Western Civilization
- Ability to identify the causes and effects of major historical events
- Ability to analyze, interpret, and evaluate textual and graphic historical materials
- Ability to distinguish the relevant from the irrelevant
- Ability to reach conclusions on the basis of facts

The subject matter of the Western Civilization I examination is drawn from the following topics. The percentages next to the main topics indicate the approximate percentage of exam questions on that topic.

8%–10% **Ancient Near East**
- Political evolution
- Religion, culture, and technical developments in and near the Fertile Crescent

15%–17% **Ancient Greece and Hellenistic Civilization**
- Political evolution to Periclean Athens
- Periclean Athens through the Peloponnesian Wars
- Culture, religion, and thought of Ancient Greece
- The Hellenistic political structure
- The culture, religion, and thought of Hellenistic Greece

15%–17% **Ancient Rome**
- Political evolution of the Republic and of the Empire (economic and geographical context)
- Roman thought and culture
- Early Christianity
- The Germanic invasions
- The late empire

WESTERN CIVILIZATION I

23%–27% **Medieval History**
- Byzantium and Islam
- Early medieval politics and culture through Charlemagne
- Feudal and manorial institutions
- The medieval Church
- Medieval thought and culture
- Rise of the towns and changing economic forms
- Feudal monarchies
- The late medieval church

13%–17% **Renaissance and Reformation**
- The Renaissance in Italy
- The Renaissance outside Italy
- The New Monarchies
- Protestantism and Catholicism reformed and reorganized

10%–15% **Early Modern Europe, 1560-1648**
- The opening of the Atlantic
- The Commercial Revolution
- Dynastic and religious conflicts
- Thought and culture

WESTERN CIVILIZATION I

SAMPLE TEST

DIRECTIONS: Read each item and select the best response.

1. **The Ganges River empties into the:**
   (Ancient near East)

   A. Bay of Bengal

   B. Arabian Sea

   C. Red Sea

   D. Arafura Sea

   E. Indian Ocean

2. **The circumference of the earth, which greatly contributed to geographic knowledge, was calculated by:**
   (Ancient Greece and Hellenistic Civ)

   A. Ptolemy

   B. Eratosthenes

   C. Galileo

   D. Strabo

   E. Pythagoras

3. **Which nation colonized most of South America in the 1600s?**
   (Early Modern Europe, 1560 -1648)

   A. England

   B. France

   C. Spain

   D. The Dutch Republic

   E. Belgium

4. **Which ancient civilization is credited with being the first to develop irrigation techniques through the use of canals, dikes, and devices for raising water?**
   (Ancient near East)

   A. The Sumerians

   B. The Egyptians

   C. The Babylonians

   D. The Akkadians

   E. The Hittites

5. **What people group are thought to create some of the world's first cities?**
   (Ancient near East)

   A. Egyptians

   B. Semites

   C. Sumerians

   D. Babylonians

   E. Greeks

6. One of the first ancient civilization to introduce and practice monotheism was the:
   (Ancient near East)

   A. Sumerians

   B. Minoans

   C. Phoenicians

   D. Christians

   E. Hebrews

7. The "father of political science" is considered to be:
   (Ancient Greece and Hellenistic Civ)

   A. Aristotle

   B. John Locke

   C. Plato

   D. Thomas Hobbes

   E. Marcus Aurelius

8. Which early cultural group from 1500 B.C.E. - 300 B.C.E. were known as the greatest sailors?
   (Ancient Greece and Hellenistic Civ)

   A. Greeks

   B. Persians

   C. Minoans

   D. Phoenicians

   E. Egyptians

9. Bathtubs, hot and cold running water, and sewage systems with flush toilets were developed by the _____.
   (Ancient Greece and Hellenistic Civ)

   A. Minoans

   B. Mycenaeans

   C. Phoenicians

   D. Greeks

   E. Sumerians

10. Geography was first systematically studied by _____.
    (Ancient near East)

    A. the Egyptians

    B. the Greeks

    C. the Romans

    D. the Arabs

    E. the French

11. Development of a solar calendar, invention of the decimal system, and contributions to the development of geometry and astronomy are all the legacy of:
    (Ancient near East)

    A. The Babylonians

    B. The Persians

    C. The Sumerians

    D. The Egyptians

    E. The Greeks

WESTERN CIVILIZATION I

12. **Which of the following is an example of a direct democracy?**
    (Ancient Greece and Hellenistic Civ)

    A. Elected representatives

    B. Greek city-states

    C. The United States Senate

    D. The United States House of Representatives

    E. The Egyptian priesthood

13. **What term is used to describe a complex human society, that began between 8000 B.C.E to 5500 B.C.E, with a high level of cultural and technological development**
    (Ancient near East)

    A. Lifestyle

    B. Modernism

    C. Civilization

    D. Agricultural Revolution

    E. Barbarianism

14. **Which one of the following is not an important legacy of the Byzantine Empire?**
    (Medieval History)

    A. It protected Western Europe from various attacks from the East by such groups as the Persians, Ottoman Turks, and Barbarians

    B. It played a part in preserving the literature, philosophy, and language of ancient Greece

    C. It created the Orthodox Church

    D. It kept the legal traditions of Roman government, collecting and organizing many ancient Roman laws

    E. Its military organization was the foundation for modern armies

15. **Charlemagne's most important influence on Western civilization is seen today in:**
    (Medieval History)

    A. Relationship of church and state

    B. Strong military for defense

    C. The criminal justice system

    D. Education of women

    E. Strong sense of nationalism

16. The "divine right" of kings was the key political characteristic of:
    (Renaissance and Reformation)

    A. The Age of Absolutism

    B. The Age of Reason

    C. The Age of Feudalism

    D. The Age of Despotism

    E. The Age of Empire

17. Which one of the following is not a reason why Europeans came to the New World?
    (Early Modern Europe, 1560-1648)

    A. To find resources in order to increase wealth

    B. To empower Native Americans

    C. To increase a ruler's power and importance

    D. To spread Christianity

    E. To look for alternative shipping routes

18. In Western Europe, the achievements of the Renaissance were unsurpassed and made these countries outstanding cultural centers on the continent. All of the following were accomplishments except:
    (Renaissance and Reformation)

    A. Invention of the printing press

    B. A rekindling of interest in the learning of classical Greece and Rome

    C. Growth in literature and philosophy

    D. Better military tactics

    E. New techniques applied in art

19. What idea during the Renaissance changed artists and scholars focus from religion to human beings and their interaction with the world?
    (Renaissance and Reformation)

    A. Realism

    B. Humanism

    C. Individualism

    D. Intellectualism

    E. Surrealism

20. The "father of anatomy" is considered to be:
    (Renaissance and Reformation)

    A. Vesalius

    B. Servetus

    C. Galen

    D. Harvey

    E. Scipio

21. Which one of the following did not contribute to the early medieval European civilization?
    (Medieval History)

    A. The heritage from the classical cultures

    B. The Christian religion

    C. The influence of the German Barbarians

    D. The spread of ideas through trade and commerce

    E. Feudalism

22. Who is considered to be the most important figure in the spread of Protestantism across Switzerland?
    (Renaissance and Reformation)

    A. More

    B. Zwingli

    C. Munzer

    D. Leyden

    E. Calvin

23. The Age of Exploration begun in the 1400s was led by:
    (Early Modern Europe, 1560-1648)

    A. The Portuguese

    B. The Spanish

    C. The English

    D. The Dutch

    E. The French

24. The Italian born explorer who gave England its claim to North America was:
    (Early Modern Europe, 1560-1648)

    A. Raleigh

    B. Hawkins

    C. Drake

    D. Cabot

    E. Columbus

25. The societies from _____ suffered from the outcomes of the Renaissance, Enlightenment, Commercial and Industrial Revolutions.
    (Early Modern Europe, 1560-1648)

    A. Asia

    B. Latin America

    C. Africa

    D. Middle East

    E. Europe

WESTERN CIVILIZATION I

26. The end to hunting, gathering, and fishing of prehistoric people was due to: *(Ancient near East History)*

    A. Domestication of animals

    B. Building crude huts and houses

    C. Development of agriculture

    D. Organized government in villages

    E. Scarcity of resources

27. The ideas and innovations during the Renaissance were spread throughout Europe mainly because of: *(Renaissance and Reformation)*

    A. Extensive exploration

    B. Craft workers and their guilds

    C. The invention of the printing press

    D. Increased travel and trade

    E. Warfare

28. The Roman Empire gave so much to the world, especially the Western world. Of the legacies below which was the most influential, effective, and lasting? *(Ancient Rome)*

    A. The language of Latin

    B. Roman law, justice, and political system

    C. Engineering methods

    D. The writings of its poets and historians

    E. Buildings

29. Which city-states fought in the Peloponnesian Wars? *(Ancient Greece and Hellenistic Civilization)*

    A. Alexandria and Athens

    B. Sparta and Rome

    C. Alexandria and Rome

    D. Sparta and Athens

    E. Athens and Rome

30. Which of the following was characteristic of Athenian democracy? *(Ancient Greece and Hellenistic Civilization)*

    A. A bicameral legislature

    B. All males could vote in the assembly

    C. Three voting assemblies

    D. Classification of citizens by economic status

    E. Both men and women could vote

31. **The significance of the Norman conquest was that it:**
    (Medieval History)

    A. Was an invasion of Normandy

    B. Was a victory for the British

    C. Kept the French from the British throne

    D. Infused French concepts into English culture

    E. Marked the start of the British Empire

32. **The Byzantine Empire was taken over by the:**
    (Medieval History)

    A. Turks

    B. Mongols

    C. Mughals

    D. Muslims

    E. Latins

33. **The vast majority of people living in Europe during the Middle Ages were:**
    (Medieval History)

    A. Aristocrats

    B. Warriors

    C. Peasants

    D. Noblemen

    E. Knights

34. **What element, more than any, helped the church to dominate in Europe between the ninth and thirteenth centuries?**
    (Medieval History)

    A. The caste system

    B. The class system

    C. Monarchy

    D. Renaissance

    E. Feudalism

35. **Sultan Mehmed II led which group in its capture of Constantinople?**
    (Medieval History)

    A. Byzantines

    B. Ottoman Turks

    C. Suleiman the Magnificent

    D. Visigoths

    E. The Latins

36. **The trade routes in the sub-Sahara connected all of the following areas except:**
    (Medieval History)

    A. India

    B. China

    C. Northern Africa

    D. Western Europe

    E. Eastern Europe

WESTERN CIVILIZATION I

37. **The Catholic Reformation was undertaken to:**
    (Renaissance and Reformation)

    A. Gain religious tolerance

    B. More opportunities for education

    C. Respond to the Protestant Reformation

    D. Respond to growing criticism

    E. All of the above

38. **Cortés conquered the Aztecs in Mexico with the help of:**
    (Early Modern Europe, 1560-1648)

    A. Pizarro

    B. Native American tribes

    C. Montezuma

    D. The Incas

    E. The British

39. **Human settlements began in areas that:**
    (Ancient near East)

    A. Had good soil

    B. Offered natural resources

    C. Permitted division of labor

    D. Offered opportunities for animal husbandry

    E. Were already unoccupied

40. **Why was the Fertile Crescent called the "Cradle of Civilization"?**
    (Ancient near East)

    A. Agriculture allowed people to remain in one place throughout the year

    B. It had rich agricultural lands

    C. The area developed complex societies

    D. The area hosted the earliest civilizations

    E. It was shaped exactly like a crescent

41. **Which document provides the basis of English constitutional liberties?**
(Medieval History)

   A. Magna Carta

   B. Hammurabi's Code of Laws

   C. Declaration of Independence

   D. Code of Justinian

   E. The Twelve Tables

42. **How did the Minoans and Mycenaeans differ?**
(Ancient Greece and Hellenistic Civilization)

   A. The Minoans lived in the Peloponnese

   B. The Mycenaeans lived on Crete

   C. The Minoans were traders until about 2700 BCE

   D. The Mycenaeans were warriors and conquerors

   E. They didn't; they were the same group

43. **What revolutionized the trans-Sahara trade in West Africa?**
(Medieval History)

   A. Silk

   B. Gold

   C. Camels

   D. Slaves

   E. Water bladders

44. **Which of the following is not true about Egypt during ancient times?**
(Ancient near East)

   A. It was occupied by Alexander the Great

   B. It became a Roman province

   C. Its cultural center was Cairo

   D. It became an important center for Christianity

   E. It spawned many architectural marvels

45. **How did politics contribute to the collapse of the Roman Empire?**
(Ancient Rome)

   A. Diocletian's reforms encouraged revolution

   B. The "divine-right" monarchy lessened the burden of ruling

   C. Constantine's efforts demoralized the city-states

   D. Landlords controlled more of the large villas and commerce

   E. There were too many treaties with the different Barbarian tribes

WESTERN CIVILIZATION I

46. **Which of the following was not an effect of the Crusades?**
    (Medieval History)

    A. Increased military authority of the Roman Catholic Church

    B. Establishment of political authority of the Pope

    C. The Spanish Inquisition

    D. Migration of Scandinavian tribes into modern day Germany

    E. The establishment of Latin kingdoms in the Holy Land

47. **Which statement is true about colonization in what became Canada in the 1600s?**
    (Early European History)

    A. The Dutch built a plantation society in South America

    B. The British controlled much of Central America

    C. The British controlled the Mississippi

    D. The French controlled most of northern North America, including much of the Great Lake area.

    E. Only large military groups colonized North America

48. **Which of the following was not a painter during the Renaissance?**
    (Renaissance and Reformation)

    A. da Vinci

    B. Donatello

    C. el Greco

    D. Montaigne

    E. Botticelli

49. **Which ancient king created and distributed one of the oldest set of laws that were cataloged in great detail that include laws on established minimum wage and establishes one of the earliest examples of the presumption of innocence?**
    (Near Ancient East)

    A. Montezuma

    B. Hammurabi

    C. Caesar

    D. Xerxes

    E. Alexander

50. **Homer's epic poem, "The Iliad," covered the war between the Trojans and which other group of people?**
(Ancient Greece and Hellenistic Civilization)

   A. The Spartans

   B. The Egyptians

   C. The Babylonians

   D. The Greeks

   E. The Amazons

51. **The _____ modeled their society and government on Greek ideals.**
(Ancient Greece and Hellenistic Civilization)

   A. Corinthians

   B. Romans

   C. Byzantines

   D. Egyptians

   E. Hittites

52. **The war between Hannibal of Carthage and the Romans, led by Scipio Amelianus, was known as:**
(Ancient Rome)

   A. The First Punic War

   B. The Second Punic War

   C. The Peloponnesian War

   D. The War of the Alps

   E. The Third Punic War

53. **One lasting effect of the Second Crusade was:**
(Medieval History)

   A. An increase in power in the Latin Kingdoms

   B. A steady alliance between the Islamic powers and the Crusaders

   C. A decline in Byzantine prestige

   D. An increase in Islamic prestige and power

   E. The establishment of a new Latin kingdom

54. The First Crusade was called by Pope Urban II as an attempt to free the city of _____ from Muslim control.
(Medieval History)

   A. Jerusalem

   B. Bethlehem

   C. Constantinople

   D. Mecca

   E. Antioch

55. Which of the following statements about the medieval social structure of feudalism is false?
(Medieval History)

   A. Peasants were tied to land owned by their liege lords.

   B. The lands held by the nobility were heredity and could not be taken by the Crown.

   C. Vassals were obliged to provide military service when called upon.

   D. There was a distinct lack of social mobility.

   E. Feudalism declined after the 1500s because of a combination of factors such as warfare, the plague and social unrest.

56. Which of the following religious orders was established to care for pilgrims traveling to the Holy Land?
(Medieval History)

   A. The Knights Templar

   B. The Franciscans

   C. The Knights Hospitaller

   D. The Red Cross

   E. The Cistercian Monks

57. This queen accompanied her husband, King Louis VII, on the Second Crusade.
(Medieval History)

   A. Eleanor of Aquitaine

   B. Blanche of Castile

   C. Boudicca

   D. Isabella of France

   E. Isabella of Spain

58. Which crusade temporarily ended the Byzantine Empire and created a Latin Kingdom?
(Medieval History)

   A. The First Crusade

   B. The Second Crusade

   C. The Third Crusade

   D. The Fourth Crusade

   E. The Fifth Crusade

59. **Flying buttresses, large stained glass windows and vaulted ceilings are characteristic of which architectural style?**
    (Medieval History)

    A. Neo-classical

    B. Pre-modern

    C. Renaissance

    D. Baroque

    E. Gothic

60. **The Bubonic Plague killed what percentage of Europe's population at its peak in 1347?**
    (Medieval History)

    A. 13 percent

    B. 25 percent

    C. 33 percent

    D. 49 percent

    E. 65 percent

61. **Dante Alighieri's Divine Comedy was written in what language?**
    (Medieval History)

    A. Greek

    B. French

    C. Latin

    D. Italian

    E. English

62. **The Bayeux Tapestry describes and represents the military victories of _____?**
    (Medieval History)

    A. Julius Caesar

    B. William the Conqueror

    C. Edward II of England

    D. Henry I of France

    E. Richard the Lionheart

63. **Which of the following was NOT an effect of the Crusades?**
    (Medieval History)

    A. Several Latin kingdoms were established

    B. Trade between the Holy Land and Western Europe began to flourish

    C. An exchange of thoughts and ideas began between the European kingdoms and the Islamic territories

    D. Feudalism was strengthened as the number of Crusades rose

    E. Pilgrims and travelers began to move between the Europe and the Middle East

64. The Hundred Years' War was characterized by England's desire to conquer which country:
    (Medieval History)

    A. Spain

    B. France

    C. Portugal

    D. Italy

    E. Byzantium

65. Which English king completed the conquest and incorporation of Wales?
    (Medieval History)

    A. Henry III

    B. Edward I

    C. John

    D. Henry VII

    E. William the Conqueror

66. The Lombards were a Germanic-speaking people who conquered a large portion of Italy in the 700s, ousting which major power from the area?
    (Medieval History)

    A. The Byzantines

    B. The Romans

    C. The Papal States

    D. The French

    E. The Franks

67. The first Holy Roman Emperor was:
    (Medieval History)

    A. Constantine the Great

    B. Charlemagne

    C. Lothair I

    D. Louis the German

    E. Drogo of Champagne

68. The War of the Roses was primarily a fight for:
    (Medieval History)

    A. Trade rights in Italy

    B. An end of feudalism in England

    C. Succession of the crown of England

    D. English control of the French crown

    E. English control over Scotland

69. During the Renaissance what is the term for the art form that focused on authentic emotions and life-like proportions?
    (Renaissance and Reformation)

    A. Baroque

    B. Realism

    C. Neo-classicism

    D. Surrealism

    E. Impressionism

WESTERN CIVILIZATION I

70. **A popular type of song in the Middle Ages involved multiple people singing the melody one after the other. What was this called?**
    (Medieval History)

    A. Pavan

    B. Carol

    C. Solo

    D. Round

    E. Chant

71. **Which of these emperors was NOT a aspirant contender during the Year of the Four Emperors in 69 CE?**
    (Ancient Rome)

    A. Galba

    B. Otho

    C. Vitellius

    D. Vespasian

    E. Nero

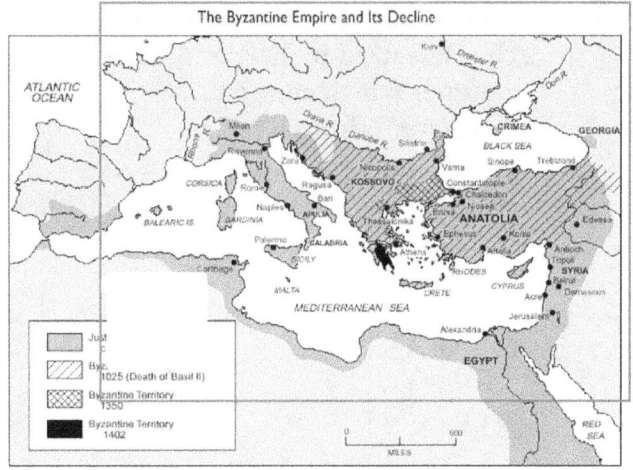

"The Byzantine Empire and its Decline." *All Empires.* 2015. http://www.allempires.com/empires/byzantine1/map09_01.gif.

72. **The dark gray shaded region shows the extent of the Byzantine Empire under which emperor?**
    (Medieval History)

    A. Justinian

    B. Constantine

    C. Manuel I

    D. Zeno

    E. Basil I

73. **The Roman Empire was divided into four sections under which emperor?**
    (Ancient Rome)

    A. Constantine

    B. Domitian

    C. Diocletian

    D. Tiberius

    E. Augustus

74. **Which of the following is a false statement about women's lives in Rome?**
    (Ancient Rome)

    A. Women were able to consistently wield large amounts of political power

    B. The role of matriarch was glorified in Roman society

    C. A woman could rule as regent if her son was underage or her husband was absent

    D. Women enjoyed a great deal of social mobility and freedom

    E. There were religious roles that only women could perform

75. **One version of Rome's early history indicates the belief that its earliest founder was a fugitive from what war?**
    (Ancient Rome)

    A. The Trojan War

    B. The Punic War

    C. The Peloponnesian War

    D. The Greco-Persian Wars

    E. The Corinthian War

76. **This philosopher-emperor was a successful general and author of Stoic Philosophy.**
    (Ancient Rome)

    A. Nero

    B. Titus

    C. Marcus Aurelius

    D. Augustus

    E. Justinian

77. **Which emperor was not among those classically referred to as the "Five Good Emperors"?**
    (Ancient Rome)

    A. Nerva

    B. Trajan

    C. Hadrian

    D. Augustus

    E. Antoninus Pius

78. **What was Rome's typical reaction when encountering unknown or opposing religious values in regions it conquered?**
    (Ancient Rome)

    A. Rome would stamp out any of the native religion and install priests to instruct the new province about Roman ways.

    B. Rome would adopt the religion and gods of the province as its own.

    C. The citizens were offered the option of following Roman religions and gods.

    D. Romans only spread the cult of emperor worship.

    E. Rome would find parallels between the provinces' gods and its own and assume the provinces' gods were incarnations of Roman deities.

79. **The name of the ineffectual and largely ceremonial last emperor of Rome was what?**
    (Ancient Rome)

    A. Amelianus

    B. Honorius

    C. Theodosius I

    D. Romulus

    E. Valentinian III

80. **Rome's early military history involved attacking neighboring cities in Italy to expand its territory. Which war marked the start of expansion outside the borders of Italy?**
    (Ancient Rome)

    A. The Samnite Wars

    B. The First Punic War

    C. The Latin Wars

    D. The Pyrrhic War

    E. The Second Punic War

81. **Which of the following was a fact about Roman citizenship?**
    (Ancient Rome)

    A. Both men and women enjoyed the rights of full Roman citizenship.

    B. Slaves could eventually become full citizens after their manumissions.

    C. Residents in Roman territories were automatically granted citizenship.

    D. Roman citizenship was used as a method of influencing nearby territories.

    E. Roman citizenship was not seen as a desirable state.

82. **In what year did the western half of the Roman Empire fall?**
(Ancient Rome)

   A. 284 CE

   B. 312 CE

   C. 372 CE

   D. 454 CE

   E. 476 CE

83. **The Crisis of the Third Century was marked by all but what?**
(Ancient Rome)

   A. Multiple claimants to the throne over a short period of time

   B. Population growth in the Roman Empire

   C. A loss of Roman territory and prestige

   D. Hyperinflation and a weak economy

   E. Breakdown of trade relations across the Roman Empire

84. **Which of the following was NOT a social rank in the Roman Empire?**
(Ancient Rome)

   A. Patrician

   B. Plebian

   C. Equestrian

   D. Slave

   E. Serf

"Arch-of-Titus."*Britannica*.Undefined. 2015.http://www.britannica.com/place/Arch-of-Titus.

85. **The Arch of Titus, seen above, displayed what historical event?**
(Ancient Rome)

   A. Julius Caesar's conquest of Gaul

   B. The destruction of the Temple in Jerusalem

   C. The defeat of Hannibal

   D. The conquest of Britannia

   E. The establishment of Roman law

WESTERN CIVILIZATION I

86. **The Greek philosophy of Stoicism was characterized by all but what?**
(Ancient Greece and Hellenistic Civ)

   A. Focusing on what is said rather than what is done

   B. Focusing on what is done rather than what is said

   C. The application of logic to daily life

   D. The pursuit of a virtuous existence

   E. The belief in self-control and self-determination

87. **The Islamic Golden Age refers to a time of social, military and scientific expansion and cultivation. What marked the end of this period?**
(Medieval History)

   A. Increasing Christian pressure from Europe and the Mongols from the east

   B. Muslim focus on military matters

   C. Internal revolt and uprisings

   D. A "brain drain" to Europe

   E. An increased focus on religious life

88. **The ancient ruler Sargon the Great conquered Sumerian city-states to form what empire?**
(Ancient near East)

   A. Babylonian

   B. Neo-Assyrian

   C. Akkadian

   D. Hittite

   E. Assyrian

89. **Achievements of the so-called "New Monarchies" included all but what?**
(Renaissance and Reformation)

   A. Internal stability

   B. Efficient taxation

   C. A strong focus on nationalism

   D. Increased trade and interaction

   E. Maintaining a standing army

90. **The Commercial Revolution was a period of economic expansion and diversification during the Middle Ages. Which statement can be concluded to be FALSE regarding the Commercial Revolution's effect on society?**
(Medieval History)

   A. Increased interaction between different kingdoms allowed for more trade

   B. Increased production of goods allowed for the merchant class to grow

   C. Increased competition between the European powers rapidly advanced maritime science

   D. Advances in trade and science did not encourage exploration

   E. Modern banking developed to handle the increased demand for loans and money storage

91. **Who were the Huguenots?**
(Renaissance and Reformation)

   A. English Protestants

   B. English Catholics

   C. French Protestants

   D. French Catholics

   E. Dutch Protestants

92. **Which of the following was not a complaint made by Protestants against the Catholic Church?**
(Renaissance and Reformation)

   A. The improper selling of indulgences

   B. Churches held too much land

   C. Too much money remaining in the hands of Church officials

   D. The influence of the Church needed to be increased

   E. The Church had become hopelessly corrupt and indulgent

93. **The Reformation in England resulted in which of the following?**
(Renaissance and Reformation)

   A. A clear and uncompromising break with the Roman Church

   B. The destruction and dissolution of monasteries

   C. The monarchy immediately adopted Protestantism as the religion of England

   D. All citizens were forced to convert to Protestantism

   E. All Catholic churches in England were eventually dissolved

94. **The man bellow opposed King Henry VIII and the Protestant Reformation in England. What is his name?**
    (Renaissance and Reformation)

    Birzer, Bradley. "Sir Thomas More, Humanist." *College of Arts and Science, University of Colorado Boulder.*n.d.http://artsandsciences.colorado.edu/ctp/2014/08/the-utopia-of-thomas-more/.

    A. Martin Luther

    B. Thomas Cranmer

    C. Thomas More

    D. Cardinal Wolsey

    E. George Boleyn

95. **Which of the following monarchs was not Protestant?**
    (Renaissance and Reformation)

    A. Elizabeth I

    B. Mary Tudor

    C. Edward VI

    D. William and Mary

    E. James VI

96. **Early modern Europe was noted for all but which of the following:**
    (Early Modern Europe, 1560-1648)

    A. Religious reformation

    B. Religious persecution

    C. A decline in scientific advancement

    D. An increase of exploration and trade

    E. New advancements in philosophy

97. **The Thirty Years' War began as a struggle between which two powers?**
    (Early Modern Europe, 1560-1648)

    A. Protestants and Catholics

    B. England and France

    C. England and Germany

    D. Protestants and Huguenots

    E. Spain and France

WESTERN CIVILIZATION I

98. **Which of the following was a result of the Peloponnesian War?**
    (Ancient Greece and Hellenistic Civilization)

    A. Sparta lost influence in the Adriatic

    B. Athens gained territory and influence

    C. Sparta gained influence and prestige over Athens

    D. The Peloponnesian League was dissolved

    E. Democracy continued without interruption in Athens

99. **The Persian Wars were a series of engagements between the Greek states and the Persian Empire over fifty years. Who is the primary contemporary source of information during this time?**
    (Ancient Greece and Hellenistic Civilization)

    A. Plato

    B. Livy

    C. Herodotus

    D. Plutarch

    E. Aristotle

100. **Which king led the Second Crusade?**
     (Medieval History)

     A. Louis VII of France

     B. Conrad III of Germany

     C. John of England

     D. Richard the Lionheart

     E. Both A and B

101. **Sea power was crucial for most of the European powers. In 1588, the English navy defeated the navy of which country, an action that established England as the major rising power in Europe?**
     (Early Modern Europe, 1560-1648)

     A. France

     B. The Netherlands

     C. Germany

     D. Spain

     E. The Portuguese

102. **The English Civil War resulted from complaints about all of the following except:**
(Early Modern Europe, 1560-1648)

   A. Parliament would not grant Charles I funds

   B. Parliament and the people of England did not support Charles' Catholic bride

   C. Constitutional guarantees were not being made by the king

   D. Parliament did not feel it was being consulted enough by the king

   E. The king's lack of enforcement of Divine Right

103. **Nation-states comprised groups of people united by:**
(Early Modern Europe, 1560-1648)

   A. Common language

   B. Geography

   C. Traditions

   D. History

   E. All of the above

104. **The Roman Cult of Mithras was made up primarily of whom?**
(Ancient Rome)

   A. Women

   B. Slaves

   C. Soldiers

   D. Freemen

   E. Senators

Feitscherg. "Map Gallia Tribes Towns."*wikimedia*.2015.https://commons.wikimedia.org/wiki/File:Map_Gallia_Tribes_Towns.png.

105. **This above Roman province is known as what?**
(Ancient Rome)

   A. Britannia

   B. Gaul

   C. Hispania

   D. Londinium

   E. Dacia

106. **In 1492, an edict was issued that expelled Jews from which country?**
(Medieval History)

   A. England

   B. France

   C. Portugal

   D. Spain

   E. The Netherlands

107. **Baroque art, which gained popularity in the 1600s, can be distinguished by:**
(Renaissance and Reformation)

   A. Its return to Greek and Roman styles

   B. Clean, uncomplicated aesthetic

   C. Heavily ornate architecture and paintings

   D. Unemotional figures in paintings

   E. Experimentations with the representation of human form

108. **The Renaissance was a great leap ahead in terms of science, architecture and art. What was another effect of the Renaissance on political culture outside of Italy?**
(Renaissance and Reformation)

   A. Independent city-states were established across Europe

   B. Religious thought stagnated

   C. Trade decreased as cities and kingdoms sought to protect their advancements

   D. Monarchies declined in power compared to the Church

   E. Nation-states were created

109. **The Age of Enlightenment emphasized what schools of thought?**
(Renaissance and Reformation)

   A. Reason and logic

   B. Emotion

   C. Absolute monarchy

   D. Religion was supreme above science

   E. Isolationism

110. **What is the truest statement about the First and Second Crusades?**
(Medieval History)

   A. The First Crusade had trouble gathering enough soldiers and pilgrims while the Second Crusade had enough men

   B. The First Crusade increased Muslim power while the Second Crusade decreased it

   C. The First Crusade decreased Muslim power while the Second Crusade increased it

   D. Both crusades were ultimately unsuccessful

   E. Both crusades achieved their objectives

111. **What type of government did Sparta have?**
(Ancient Greece and Hellenistic Civilization)

   A. Oligarchy

   B. Representative democracy

   C. Theocracy

   D. Democracy

   E. Anarchy

112. **Which of the following was NOT a member of the Delian League?**
(Ancient Greece and Hellenistic Civilization)

   A. Neopolis

   B. Athens

   C. Sparta

   D. Byzantium

   E. Chalcedon

113. **New Monarchs achieved all of the following except:**
(Renaissance and Reformation)

   A. Increase in power of nobility

   B. The unification of their kingdoms

   C. Creation of national identity

   D. Increase in trade

   E. Creation of a standing army

114. **The type of writing first used in early civilizations was called what?**
(Ancient near East)

   A. Hieroglyphics

   B. Cuneiform

   C. Alphabet

   D. Pictograms

   E. Demotic

WESTERN CIVILIZATION I

115. **Greek political independence ended after the conquest by:**
(Ancient Greece and Hellenistic Civilization)

   A. Alexander the Great

   B. The Romans

   C. The Persians

   D. The Spartans

   E. The Trojans

116. **The body of water surrounding most of the Grecian Islands is called what?**
(Ancient Greece and Hellenistic Civilization)

   A. Black Sea

   B. Indian Ocean

   C. Libyan Sea

   D. Aegean Sea

   E. Mediterranean

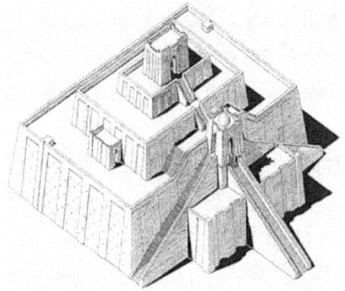

"Ziggurat." *Many Prophets One Message*. undefined. 2014. http://www.manyprophetsonemessage.com/2014/10/14/quran-reveals-lost-knowledge-about-prophet-abraham/.

117. **The above image is called a what?**
(Ancient near East)

   A. Pyramid

   B. Ziggurat

   C. Temple

   D. Burial mound

   E. Obelisk

118. **Which country was least effected by Protestant Reformation?**
(Renaissance and Reformation)

   A. France

   B. England

   C. Germany

   D. Spain

   E. Italy

119. **The Anglican Church was considered to be only a partial concession to Protestant pressure because it:**
(Renaissance and Reformation)

   A. Reverted back to Catholicism

   B. Maintained Popish ceremonies and décor

   C. Stayed in communication with the Pope

   D. Supported Catholic claims to the throne

   E. Suppressed Protestant supporters

120. **The Roman Inquisition, which was charged with stamping out heresy that resulted from the Protestant Reformation, famously brought which Italian to trial?**
(Ancient Rome)

   A. Dante Alighieri

   B. Lucrezia Borgia

   C. Leonardo da Vinci

   D. Michelangelo

   E. Galileo Galilei

WESTERN CIVILIZATION I

ANSWER KEY

Question Number	Correct Answer	Your Answer	Question Number	Correct Answer	Your Answer	Question Number	Correct Answer	Your Answer
1	A		41	A		81	D	
2	B		42	D		82	E	
3	C		43	C		83	B	
4	A		44	C		84	E	
5	C		45	C		85	B	
6	E		46	D		86	A	
7	A		47	D		87	A	
8	D		48	D		88	C	
9	A		49	E		89	C	
10	B		50	D		90	D	
11	D		51	B		91	C	
12	B		52	B		92	D	
13	C		53	D		93	B	
14	E		54	A		94	C	
15	A		55	B		95	B	
16	A		56	C		96	C	
17	B		57	A		97	A	
18	D		58	D		98	C	
19	B		59	E		99	C	
20	A		60	C		100	E	
21	D		61	D		101	D	
22	E		62	B		102	E	
23	A		63	D		103	E	
24	D		64	B		104	C	
25	C		65	B		105	B	
26	C		66	A		106	D	
27	C		67	B		107	C	
28	B		68	C		108	E	
29	D		69	B		109	A	
30	B		70	D		110	C	
31	D		71	E		111	A	
32	A		72	A		112	C	
33	C		73	C		113	A	
34	E		74	A		114	B	
35	B		75	A		115	B	
36	D		76	C		116	D	
37	E		77	D		117	B	
38	B		78	E		118	D	
39	B		79	D		119	B	
40	D		80	B		120	E	

WESTERN CIVILIZATION I

RATIONALES

1. **The Ganges River empties into the:**
   (Ancient near East)

   A. Bay of Bengal

   B. Arabian Sea

   C. Red Sea

   D. Arafura Sea

   E. Indian Ocean

The answer is A.
The Ganges River runs 1,560 miles, northeast through India across the plains to the Bay of Bengal in Bangladesh. The Ganges is considered to be the most sacred river in India according to the Hindus.

2. **The circumference of the earth, which greatly contributed to geographic knowledge, was calculated by:**
   (Ancient Greece and Hellenistic Civ)

   A. Ptolemy

   B. Eratosthenes

   C. Galileo

   D. Strabo

   E. Pythagoras

The answer is B.
There is no doubt of Ptolemy and Galileo's influence as astronomers. (A) Ptolemy as an earlier theorist and (C) Galileo as a founder of modern scientific knowledge of astronomy and our place in the galaxy. However, it was (B) Eratosthenes (275 B.C. – 195 B.C.), the Greek writer, philosopher, and astronomer, who is credited with measuring the earth's circumference as well as the distances between Earth, sun, and moon. (D) Strabo was more concerned with geography and history than astronomy.

WESTERN CIVILIZATION I

3. **Which nation colonized most of South America in the 1600s?**
   (Early Modern Europe, 1560 -1648)

   A. England

   B. France

   C. Spain

   D. The Dutch Republic

   E. Belgium

The answer is C.
Spain and Portugal were the only two nations to have dominated the South American region during this time. Britain, the Dutch, and France at this time were more focused on North America.

4. **Which ancient civilization is credited with being the first to develop irrigation techniques through the use of canals, dikes, and devices for raising water?**
   (Ancient near East)

   A. The Sumerians

   B. The Egyptians

   C. The Babylonians

   D. The Akkadians

   E. The Hittites

The answer is A.
The ancient (A) Sumerians of the Fertile Crescent of Mesopotamia are credited with being the first to develop irrigation techniques through the use of canals, dikes, and devices for raising water. The (B) Egyptians also practiced controlled irrigation but that was primarily through the use of the Nile's predictable flooding schedule. The (C) Babylonians were more noted for their revolutionary systems of law than their irrigation systems.

WESTERN CIVILIZATION I

5. **What people group are thought to create some of the world's first cities?**
   (Ancient near East)

   A. Egyptians

   B. Semites

   C. Sumerians

   D. Babylonians

   E. Greeks

The answer is C.
Along with developing irrigation techniques the Sumer was one of the first nations to create cities. The abundance of food grown in the rich mud in the Fertile Crescent made it possible for large numbers of people to live together in cities. Population growth and a surplus of food led to specialization of labor and the leisure time necessary for civilization. Egyptians, Babylonians, and Greeks were not yet in the same time period. Semites were in the same time period, however, they were largely disorganized. There were a number of different East Semitic Akkadians within the Sumer kingdom. However, they are not accredited to creating the first cities.

6. **One of the first ancient civilization to introduce and practice monotheism was the:**
   (Ancient near East)

   A. Sumerians

   B. Minoans

   C. Phoenicians

   D. Christians

   E. Hebrews

The answer is E.
The (A) Sumerians and (C) Phoenicians both practiced religions in which many gods and goddesses were worshipped. Often these gods/goddesses were based on a feature of nature such as a sun, moon, weather, rocks, water, etc. The (B) Minoan culture shared many religious practices with the Ancient Egyptians. It seems that the king was somewhat of a god figure and the queen, a goddess. Much of Minoan art points to worship of multiple gods. The (D) Christians are monotheistic, but are from a later time than the Hebrews. Therefore, only the (E) Hebrews introduced and fully practiced monotheism, or the belief in one God.

7. **The "father of political science" is considered to be:**
   (Ancient Greece and Hellenistic Civ)

   A. Aristotle

   B. John Locke

   C. Plato

   D. Thomas Hobbes

   E. Marcus Aurelius

The answer is A.
(D) Thomas Hobbes (1588-1679) wrote the important work *Leviathan* in which he pointed out that people are by all means selfish, individualistic animals that will always look out for themselves and, therefore the state must combat this natural desire. (B) John Locke (1632-1704) whose book *Two Treatises of Government* has long been considered a founding document on the rights of people to rebel against an unjust government was an important figure in the founding of the US Constitution and on general politics of the American Colonies. (C) Plato (427-347 B.C.) and Aristotle (384-322 B.C.) both contributed to the field of political science.

Both believed that political order would result in the greatest stability. In fact, Aristotle studied under Plato. Both Plato and Aristotle studied the ideas of causality and the Prime Mover, but their conclusions were different. Aristotle, however, is considered to be "the father of political science" because of his development of systems of political order the true development, a scientific system to study justice and political order.

8. **Which early cultural group from 1500 B.C.E. - 300 B.C.E. were known as the greatest sailors?**
   (Ancient Greece and Hellenistic Civ)

   A. Greeks

   B. Persians

   C. Minoans

   D. Phoenicians

   E. Egyptians

The answer is D.
Although the Greeks were quite able sailors and developed a strong navy in their defeat of the Persians at sea in the Battle of Marathon, it was the Eastern Mediterranean culture of the Phoenicians dominated the high seas. The Phoenicians were fantastic shipbuilders who could create very tough fast ships to reach long distance in order to trade. They are credited in being able to use the North Star at night while navigating. Many believe that they sailed as far as North Africa and Britain (And some saying even as far as North America). The Minoans were an advanced early civilization off the Greek coast on Crete more noted for their innovations in terms of sewage systems, toilets, and running water.

WESTERN CIVILIZATION I

9. **Bathtubs, hot and cold running water, and sewage systems with flush toilets were developed by the _____.**
   (Ancient Greece and Hellenistic Civ)

   A. Minoans

   B. Mycenaeans

   C. Phoenicians

   D. Greeks

   E. Sumerians

The answer is A.
The (A) Minoans were one of the earliest Greek cultures and existed on the island of Crete and flourished from about 1600 B.C. to about 1400 B.C. During this time, the (B) Mycenaean were flourishing on the mainland of what is now Greece. However, it was the Minoans on Crete that are best known for their advanced ancient civilization in which such advances as bathtubs, hot and cold running water, sewage systems and flush toilets were developed. The (C) Phoenicians also flourished around 1250 B.C.; however, their primary development was in language and arts. The Phoenicians created an alphabet that influenced alphabets still in use today. The great developments of the (D) Greeks were primarily in the fields of philosophy, political science, and early ideas of democracy. The (E) Sumerians created laws and an early model of government.

10. **Geography was first systematically studied by _____.**
    (Ancient near East)

    A. the Egyptians

    B. the Greeks

    C. the Romans

    D. the Arabs

    E. the French

The answer is B.
The Greeks were the first to study geography, possibly because of the difficulties they faced as a result of geographic conditions. Greece had difficulty uniting early on as their steep, treacherous, mountainous terrain made it difficult for the city-states to be united. As the Greeks studied their geography, it became possible to defeat more powerful armies on their home turf, such as the great victory over the Persians at Marathon.

WESTERN CIVILIZATION I

11. **Development of a solar calendar, invention of the decimal system, and contributions to the development of geometry and astronomy are all the legacy of:**
    (Ancient near East)

    A. The Babylonians

    B. The Persians

    C. The Sumerians

    D. The Egyptians

    E. The Greeks

The answer is D

The (A) Babylonians of ancient Mesopotamia flourished for a time under their great contribution of organized law and code, called Hammurabi's Code (1750 B.C.), named after the ruler Hammurabi. The fall of the Babylonians to the Persians in 539 B.C. made way for the warrior-driver Persian Empire that expanded from Pakistan to the Mediterranean Sea until the conquest of Alexander the Great in 331 B.C. The (C) Sumerians of ancient Mesopotamia were most noted for their early advancements as one of the first civilizations and their contributions toward written language known as cuneiform. It was the (D) Egyptians who were the first true developers of a solar calendar, the decimal system, and made significant contributions to the development of geometry and astronomy.

WESTERN CIVILIZATION I

12. Which of the following is an example of a direct democracy?
    (Ancient Greece and Hellenistic Civ)

    A. Elected representatives

    B. Greek city-states

    C. The United States Senate

    D. The United States House of Representatives

    E. The Egyptian priesthood

The answer is B
The Greek city-states are an example of a direct democracy as their leaders were elected directly by the citizens and the citizens themselves were given voice in government. (A) Elected representatives in the United States as in the case of the presidential elections are actually elected by an electoral college that is supposed to be representative of the citizens. As we have learned from the elections of 2000, this is a flawed system. The United States Congress, the Senate, and the House of Representatives are also examples of indirect democracy as they represent the citizens in the legislature as opposed to having citizens represent themselves. The (E) Egyptian priesthood was a hierarchy and very carefully controlled.

13. What term is used to describe a complex human society, that began between 8000 B.C.E to 5500 B.C. E, with a high level of cultural and technological development
    (Ancient near East)

    A. Lifestyle

    B. Modernism

    C. Civilization

    D. Agricultural Revolution

    E. Barbarianism

The answer is C.
After the and during the Agricultural Revolution (starting in 8000 B.C.E.) groups of people began to conjugate for defense, trade regulation, maintenance of boundaries in their fields, and regulating and directing the economic activities of the people as they worked in groups. In other words civilizations or human societies with a high level of cultural and technological development were created. E is incorrect because it is the opposite. B is a advanced form of society. D is something that occurred to produce civilization. And A is someone's everyday life choices, therefore, it is not relevant.

14. **Which one of the following is not an important legacy of the Byzantine Empire?**
    (Medieval History)

    A. It protected Western Europe from various attacks from the East by such groups as the Persians, Ottoman Turks, and Barbarians

    B. It played a part in preserving the literature, philosophy, and language of ancient Greece

    C. It created the Orthodox Church

    D. It kept the legal traditions of Roman government, collecting and organizing many ancient Roman laws

    E. Its military organization was the foundation for modern armies

The answer is E.
The Byzantine Empire (330-1453) was the successor to the Roman Empire in the East and protected Western Europe from invaders such as the Persians and Ottomans. The Byzantine Empire was a Christian incorporation of Greek philosophy, language, and literature along with Roman government and law. The creation of the Orthodox Church is a legacy that remains today. Therefore, although regarded as having a strong infantry, cavalry, and engineering corps along with excellent morale amongst its soldiers, the Byzantine Empire is not particularly considered a foundation for modern armies.

15. **Charlemagne's most important influence on Western civilization is seen today in:**
    (Medieval History)

    A. Relationship of church and state

    B. Strong military for defense

    C. The criminal justice system

    D. Education of women

    E. Strong sense of nationalism

The answer is A.
Charlemagne was the leader of the Germanic Franks responsible for the promotion of the Holy Roman Empire across Europe. Although he unified governments and aided the Pope, he re-crowned himself in 802 A.D. to demonstrate that his power and right to rule was not a grant from the Pope, but rather a secular achievement. Therefore, although he used much of the Church's power in his rise to power, the Pope in turn used Charlemagne to ascend the Church to new heights. Thus, Charlemagne had an influence on the issues between Church and state.

16. **The "divine right" of kings was the key political characteristic of:**
    (Renaissance and Reformation)

    A. The Age of Absolutism

    B. The Age of Reason

    C. The Age of Feudalism

    D. The Age of Despotism

    E. The Age of Empire

The answer is A.
The "divine right" of kings was the key political characteristic of The Age of Absolutism and was most visible in the reign of King Louis XIV of France, as well as during the times of King James I and his son, Charles I. The divine right doctrine claims that kings and absolute leaders derive their right to rule by virtue of their birth alone. They see this both as a law of God and of nature.

17. **Which one of the following is not a reason why Europeans came to the New World?**
    (Early Modern Europe, 1560-1648)

    A. To find resources in order to increase wealth

    B. To empower Native Americans

    C. To increase a ruler's power and importance

    D. To spread Christianity

    E. To look for alternative shipping routes

The answer is B.
The Europeans came to the New World for a number of reasons; often they came to find new natural resources to extract for manufacturing. The Portuguese, Spanish and English were sent over to increase the monarch's power and spread influences such as religion (Christianity) and culture. Therefore, the only reason given that Europeans did not come to the New World was to establish the Native Americans. In fact they did the opposite- seizing their land, massacring many people groups, and enslaving many Native Americans.

18. **In Western Europe, the achievements of the Renaissance were unsurpassed and made these countries outstanding cultural centers on the continent. All of the following were accomplishments except:**
    (Renaissance and Reformation)

    A. Invention of the printing press

    B. A rekindling of interest in the learning of classical Greece and Rome

    C. Growth in literature and philosophy

    D. Better military tactics

    E. New techniques applied in art

The answer is D.
The Renaissance in Western Europe produced many important achievements that helped push immense progress among European civilization. Some of the most important developments during the Renaissance were Gutenberg's invention of the printing press in Germany and a reexamination of the ideas and philosophies of classical Greece and Rome that eventually helped Renaissance thinkers to approach more modern ideas. Also important during the Renaissance was the growth in literature (Petrarch, Boccaccio, Erasmus), philosophy (Machiavelli, More, Bacon) and art (Van Eyck, Giotto, da Vinci). Therefore, improved military tactics is the only possible answer as it was clearly not a characteristic of the Renaissance in Western Europe.

WESTERN CIVILIZATION I

19. **What idea during the Renaissance changed artists and scholars focus from religion to human beings and their interaction with the world?**
    (Renaissance and Reformation)

    A. Realism

    B. Humanism

    C. Individualism

    D. Intellectualism

    E. Surrealism

The answer is B.
Realism is a medieval philosophy that contemplated independence of existence of the body, the mind, and God. The idea of individualism is usually either a reference to an economic or political theory. Intellectualism is the placing of great importance and devotion to the exploring of the intellect. Surrealism is an art form that became popularized during the early 1900s. Therefore, the changing focus during the Renaissance when artists and scholars were less concerned with religion but centered their efforts on a better understanding of people and the world was called humanism.

20. **The "father of anatomy" is considered to be:**
    (Renaissance and Reformation)

    A. Vesalius

    B. Servetus

    C. Galen

    D. Harvey

    E. Scipio

The answer is A.
Andreas Vesalius (1514-1564) is considered to be the "father of anatomy" as a result of his revolutionary work on the human anatomy based on dissections of human cadavers. Prior to Vesalius, men such as Galen, (130-200) had done work in the field of anatomy, but they had based the majority of their work on animal studies.

WESTERN CIVILIZATION I

21. **Which one of the following did not contribute to the early medieval European civilization?**
    (Medieval History)

    A. The heritage from the classical cultures

    B. The Christian religion

    C. The influence of the German Barbarians

    D. The spread of ideas through trade and commerce

    E. Feudalism

The answer is D.
The heritage of the classical cultures such as Greece, the Christian religion which became dominant, and the influence of the Germanic Barbarians (Visigoths, Saxons, Ostrogoths, Vandals, and Franks) were all contributions to early medieval Europe and its plunge into feudalism. During this period, lives were often difficult and lived out on one single manor, with very little travel or spread of ideas through trade or commerce. Civilization seems to have halted progress during these years.

WESTERN CIVILIZATION I

22. **Who is considered to be the most important figure in the spread of Protestantism across Switzerland?**
    (Renaissance and Reformation)

    A. More

    B. Zwingli

    C. Munzer

    D. Leyden

    E. Calvin

The answer is E.
While Huldreich Zwingli (1484-1531) was the first to spread the Protestant Reformation in Switzerland around 1519, it was John Calvin (1509-1564), whose less radical approach to Protestantism who really made the most impact in Switzerland. Calvin's ideas separated from the Lutherans over the "Lord's Supper" debate over the sacrament, and his branch of Protestants became known as Calvinism. Calvin certainly built on Zwingli's early influence but really made the religion widespread throughout Switzerland. Thomas Munzer (1489-1525) was a German Protestant reformer whose radical and revolutionary ideas about God's will to overthrow the ruling classes and his siding with the peasantry got him beheaded. Munzer has since been studied and admired by Marxists for his views on class. Leyden (or Leiden) was a founder of the University of Leyden, a Protestant place for study in the Netherlands.

23. **The Age of Exploration begun in the 1400s was led by:**
    (Early Modern Europe, 1560-1648)

    A. The Portuguese

    B. The Spanish

    C. The English

    D. The Dutch

    E. The French

The answer is A.
Although the Age of Exploration had many important players among them, the Dutch, Spanish and English, it was the Portuguese who sent the first explorers to the New World.

WESTERN CIVILIZATION I

24. The Italian born explorer who gave England its claim to North America was:
(Early Modern Europe, 1560-1648)

    A. Raleigh

    B. Hawkins

    C. Drake

    D. Cabot

    E. Columbus

The answer is D.
Sir Walter Raleigh (1554-1618) was an English explorer and navigator, sent to the New World in search of riches. He founded the lost colony at Roanoke, Virginia, and was later imprisoned for a supposed plot to kill the King for which he was later released. Sir John Hawkins (1532-1595) and Sir Francis Drake (1540-1596) were both navigators who worked in the slave trade, made some voyages to the New World, and commanded ships against and defeated the Spanish Armada in 1588. John Cabot (1450-1498) was the Italian explorer who gave England claim to North America. Christopher Columbus, of course, was not English.

25. The societies from _____ suffered from the outcomes of the Renaissance, Enlightenment, Commercial and Industrial Revolutions.
(Early Modern Europe, 1560-1648)

    A. Asia

    B. Latin America

    C. Africa

    D. Middle East

    E. Europe

The answer is C.
The results of the Renaissance, Enlightenment, Commercial and Industrial Revolutions were quite beneficial for many people in much of the world. New ideas of humanism, religious tolerance, and secularism were spreading. Increased trade and manufacturing were surging economies in much of the world. The people of Africa, however, suffered during these times as they became largely left out of the developments. Also, the people of Africa were stolen, traded, and sold into slavery to provide a cheap labor force for the growing industries of Europe and the New World.

WESTERN CIVILIZATION I

26. **The end to hunting, gathering, and fishing of prehistoric people was due to:**
(Ancient near East History)

   A. Domestication of animals

   B. Building crude huts and houses

   C. Development of agriculture

   D. Organized government in villages

   E. Scarcity of resources

The answer is C.
Although the domestication of animals, the building of huts and houses and the first organized governments were all very important steps made by early civilizations, it was the development of agriculture that ended the once dominant practices of hunting, gathering, and fishing among prehistoric people. The development of agriculture provided a more efficient use of time and for the first time a surplus of food. This greatly improved the quality of life and contributed to early population growth.

27. **The ideas and innovations during the Renaissance were spread throughout Europe mainly because of:**
(Renaissance and Reformation)

   A. Extensive exploration

   B. Craft workers and their guilds

   C. The invention of the printing press

   D. Increased travel and trade

   E. Warfare

The answer is C.
The ideas and innovations of the Renaissance were spread throughout Europe for a number of reasons. While exploration, increased travel, and spread of craft may have aided the spread of the Renaissance to small degrees, nothing was as important to the spread of ideas as Gutenberg's invention of the printing press in Germany.

WESTERN CIVILIZATION I

28. The Roman Empire gave so much to the world, especially the Western world. Of the legacies below which was the most influential, effective, and lasting?
    (Ancient Rome)

    A. The language of Latin

    B. Roman law, justice, and political system

    C. Engineering methods

    D. The writings of its poets and historians

    E. Buildings

The answer is B.
Of the lasting legacies of the Roman Empire, it is their law, justice, and political system that has been the most effective and influential on our Western world today. The idea of a Senate and different houses is still maintained by our United States government and their legal justice system is also the foundation of our own. We still use many Latin words in our justice system, terms such as habeas corpus. English, Spanish, Italian, French, and others are all based on Latin. The Roman language, Latin itself has died out. Roman engineering and building and their writings and poetry have also been influential but not nearly to the degree that their government and justice systems have been.

29. Which city-states fought in the Peloponnesian Wars?
    (Ancient Greece and Hellenistic Civilization)

    A. Alexandria and Athens

    B. Sparta and Rome

    C. Alexandria and Rome

    D. Sparta and Athens

    E. Athens and Rome

The answer is D.
Sparta and Athens were city-states that fought in the Peloponnesian Wars. Rome did not fight in the Peloponnesian Wars, and Alexandria is a city in Egypt.

WESTERN CIVILIZATION I

30. **Which of the following was characteristic of Athenian democracy?**
(Ancient Greece and Hellenistic Civilization)

    A. A bicameral legislature

    B. All males could vote in the assembly

    C. Three voting assemblies

    D. Classification of citizens by economic status

    E. Both men and women could vote

The answer is B.
Option B is correct as an example of direct democracy in ancient Greece. Option A is an example of indirect democracy in the United States. Options C and D are examples of Roman democracy. Option E was not a characteristic of either Roman or Greek democracy.

31. **The significance of the Norman conquest was that it:**
(Medieval History)

    A. Was an invasion of Normandy

    B. Was a victory for the British

    C. Kept the French from the British throne

    D. Infused French concepts into English culture

    E. Marked the start of the British Empire

The answer is D.
The French-Norman victory over the British put a French-speaking monarch on the English throne and infused French concepts into English language and culture. Option A is incorrect because the Normans invaded England. Option B is incorrect because the Normans defeated the British. Option C is incorrect because William became king of England. Option E is incorrect because the concept of a British empire did not start for many more years.

WESTERN CIVILIZATION I

32. The Byzantine Empire was taken over by the:
(Medieval History)

    A. Turks

    B. Mongols

    C. Mughals

    D. Muslims

    E. Latins

The answer is A.
The Seljuk Turks took over most of the Asian territory of the Byzantines in the eleventh century. Constantinople fell to the Ottomans in 1453. Option B is incorrect because the Mongols captured territories from Southeast Asia to central Europe. Option C is incorrect because the Mughals ruled in India. Option D is incorrect because Muslims are followers of Islam. The (E) Latins briefly conquered the Byzantine Empire during the Fourth Crusade, but the Empire was restored after a short rule of Latin kings.

33. The vast majority of people living in Europe during the Middle Ages were:
(Medieval History)

    A. Aristocrats

    B. Warriors

    C. Peasants

    D. Noblemen

    E. Knights

The answer is C.
Noblemen and aristocrats accounted for a small minority of the population, and people in various walks of life served the armies of noblemen. Knights were also noblemen who had pledged service to a liege lord. Ninety percent of the population were peasants.

WESTERN CIVILIZATION I

34. **What element, more than any, helped the church to dominate in Europe between the ninth and thirteenth centuries?**
    (Medieval History)

    A. The caste system

    B. The class system

    C. Monarchy

    D. Renaissance

    E. Feudalism

The answer is E.
Option A is incorrect because the caste system was part of India's society. Option B is incorrect because it was ownership of land, not a class system, that helped the church dominate in Europe. Option D is incorrect because the Renaissance was a rebirth and reawakening of culture after the Middle Ages.

35. **Sultan Mehmed II led which group in its capture of Constantinople?**
    (Medieval History)

    A. Byzantines

    B. Ottoman Turks

    C. Suleiman the Magnificent

    D. Visigoths

    E. The Latins

The answer is B.
The siege of Constantinople took place in 1453. Option A is incorrect because the Byzantines were captured. Suleiman the Magnificent ruled the Ottoman Empire in the 1500s. The Visigoths did not attack Constantinople because they were diverted to cities in Greece. The Latins were led by Christian leaders, not Muslim.

WESTERN CIVILIZATION I

36. **The trade routes in the sub-Sahara connected all of the following areas except:**
    (Medieval History)

    A. India

    B. China

    C. Northern Africa

    D. Western Europe

    E. Eastern Europe

The answer is D.
Options A, B, and C are areas the African sub-Saharan trade routes connected.

37. **The Catholic Reformation was undertaken to:**
    (Renaissance and Reformation)

    A. Gain religious tolerance

    B. More opportunities for education

    C. Respond to the Protestant Reformation

    D. Respond to growing criticism

    E. All of the above

The answer is E.
The intent of the Catholic Reformation was to slow to stop the Protestant Revolution. Options A, B, C and D were results of the Catholic Reformation. The Counter Reformation (or Catholic Reformation) had its roots before the Reformation, however, the Reformation was definitely a catalyst. The Catholic Reformation (beginning in 1545 CE) came after the Reformation (beginning in 1517 CE). Therefore, E is correct.

38. **Cortés conquered the Aztecs in Mexico with the help of:**
    (Early Modern Europe, 1560-1648)

    A. Pizarro

    B. Native American tribes

    C. Montezuma

    D. The Incas

    E. The British

The answer is B.
When rumors were spread that the Aztecs were plotting against the Spanish, Cortés convinced some Native American tribes to help the Spanish attack the Aztecs. Option A is incorrect because Pizarro was the Spanish conqueror of the Incas. Option C is incorrect because Montezuma was the Aztec leader. Option D is incorrect because the Incas lived in South America. The British were also not allies of the Spanish.

39. **Human settlements began in areas that:**
    (Ancient near East)

    A. Had good soil

    B. Offered natural resources

    C. Permitted division of labor

    D. Offered opportunities for animal husbandry

    E. Were already unoccupied

The answer is B.
Option B is the best answer because natural resources support life. Option A is incorrect because good soil is just one type of resource. Options C and D are incorrect because division of labor can occur in any settlement and opportunities for animal husbandry are dependent upon natural resources. Option E is also not required for settlement.

WESTERN CIVILIZATION I

40. Why was the Fertile Crescent called the "Cradle of Civilization"?
(Ancient near East)

    A. Agriculture allowed people to remain in one place throughout the year

    B. It had rich agricultural lands

    C. The area developed complex societies

    D. The area hosted the earliest civilizations

    E. It was shaped exactly like a crescent

The answer is D.
The area in the present-day Middle East was home to the earliest civilizations. Options A, B, and C are true statements because the area was located around three rivers and the soil was good, causing people to develop settlements. However, the options do not explain why it was called the "Cradle of Civilization."

41. Which document provides the basis of English constitutional liberties?
(Medieval History)

    A. Magna Carta

    B. Hammurabi's Code of Laws

    C. Declaration of Independence

    D. Code of Justinian

    E. The Twelve Tables

The answer is A.
The Magna Carta was granted to English barons and nobles in 1215 by King John. It is considered to be the first modern document that sought to try to limit the powers of the state. The Code of Justinian was a reference work of laws, Hammurabi's Code was used in Mesopotamia, and the Declaration of Independence was written in 1776. The Twelve Tables were a set of Roman laws.

WESTERN CIVILIZATION I

42. **How did the Minoans and Mycenaeans differ?**
    (Ancient Greece and Hellenistic Civilization)

    A. The Minoans lived in the Peloponnese

    B. The Mycenaeans lived on Crete

    C. The Minoans were traders until about 2700 BCE

    D. The Mycenaeans were warriors and conquerors

    E. They didn't; they were the same group

The answer is D.
The Mycenaeans conquered the Minoans in the 1400s BCE. Options A, B, and C are incorrect because the Minoans lived on Crete, the Mycenaeans lived in the Peloponnese, and the Mycenaeans were traders until they developed a high level of agriculture in 2700 BCE. They were two distinctly different groups of people, so Option E is wrong.

43. **What revolutionized the trans-Sahara trade in West Africa?**
    (Medieval History)

    A. Silk

    B. Gold

    C. Camels

    D. Slaves

    E. Water bladders

The answer is C.
Camels could travel long distances in heat and dry conditions and needed little water. Option A is incorrect because silk was a product that was traded in Asia. Option B is incorrect because gold was a produce that was carried on the caravan routes but did not revolutionize the trade. Option D is incorrect because slaves were treated as commodities but did not revolutionize the trans-Sahara trade. Water bladders were a necessity, but did not revolutionize trans-Sahara trade.

WESTERN CIVILIZATION I

44. Which of the following is not true about Egypt during ancient times?
(Ancient near East)

    A. It was occupied by Alexander the Great

    B. It became a Roman province

    C. Its cultural center was Cairo

    D. It became an important center for Christianity

    E. It spawned many architectural marvels

The answer is C.
Alexandria, not Cairo, was the cultural center of Egypt. Alexandria was located at the mouth of the Nile and was a Mediterranean port. The Romans and Greeks conquered Egypt and Alexandria became an important business and cultural center.

45. How did politics contribute to the collapse of the Roman Empire?
(Ancient Rome)

    A. Diocletian's reforms encouraged revolution

    B. The "divine-right" monarchy lessened the burden of ruling

    C. Constantine's efforts demoralized the city-states

    D. Landlords controlled more of the large villas and commerce

    E. There were too many treaties with the different Barbarian tribes

The answer is C.
Constantine reunited the empire, but Diocletian had made many changes, including an oppressive taxation system and reconstruction of the empire. These efforts demoralized the people. Option A is incorrect because Diocletian's reforms demoralized the people. Option B is incorrect because the "divine right" of absolute monarchy also had a negative effect on the people. Option D is incorrect because the landlords' control of commerce was an economic, not political, reason for the collapse.

WESTERN CIVILIZATION I

46. Which of the following was not an effect of the Crusades?
(Medieval History)

A. Increased military authority of the Roman Catholic Church

B. Establishment of political authority of the Pope

C. The Spanish Inquisition

D. Migration of Scandinavian tribes into modern day Germany

E. The establishment of Latin kingdoms in the Holy Land

The answer is D.
Scandinavians tribes moved southwards around 1000 B.C.E, therefore incorrect because that is over 1500 years before the crusades. The other options are correct effects of the Crusades.

47. Which statement is true about colonization in what became Canada in the 1600s?
(Early European History)

A. The Dutch built a plantation society in South America

B. The British controlled much of Central America

C. The British controlled the Mississippi

D. The French controlled most of northern North America, including much of the Great Lake area.

E. Only large military groups colonized North America

The answer is D.
Option D is correct because the French laid claim to most of the land as well as dominated the fur trade industry until it lost its claim to the Mississippi after the French and Indian war. The other options are incorrect answers because they are false statements.

WESTERN CIVILIZATION I

48. Which of the following was not a painter during the Renaissance?
    (Renaissance and Reformation)

    A. da Vinci

    B. Donatello

    C. el Greco

    D. Montaigne

    E. Botticelli

The answer is D.
Option D is the correct answer because Montaigne was a French writer and philosopher. The other choices are correct because the men were artists. Donatello and da Vinci were Italian, and el Greco was Spanish.

49. Which ancient king created and distributed one of the oldest set of laws that were cataloged in great detail that include laws on established minimum wage and establishes one of the earliest examples of the presumption of innocence?
    (Near Ancient East)

    A. Montezuma

    B. Hammurabi

    C. Caesar

    D. Xerxes

    E. Alexander

The answer is E.
Option B is correct. Hammurabi's code of laws, created in the 18 century B.C.E, laid out in minute detail and covered questions over punishment, trade and harvest.

50. Homer's epic poem, "The Iliad," covered the war between the Trojans and which other group of people?
    (Ancient Greece and Hellenistic Civilization)

    A. The Spartans

    B. The Egyptians

    C. The Babylonians

    D. The Greeks

    E. The Amazons

The answer is D.
"The Iliad" covered the war between the Greeks and the Trojans.

51. The _____ modeled their society and government on Greek ideals.
    (Ancient Greece and Hellenistic Civilization)

    A. Corinthians

    B. Romans

    C. Byzantines

    D. Egyptians

    E. Hittites

The answer is B.
The Romans modeled their society after Greek law and ideals, though their religion was tempered by the addition of gods and practices from the neighboring Etruscans.

WESTERN CIVILIZATION I

52. **The war between Hannibal of Carthage and the Romans, led by Scipio Amelianus, was known as:**
    (Ancient Rome)

    A. The First Punic War

    B. The Second Punic War

    C. The Peloponnesian War

    D. The War of the Alps

    E. The Third Punic War

The answer is B.
The Second Punic War famously brought Hannibal over the Alps, where despite nearly annihilate the Roman legions, he failed to take Rome. The First and Third Punic Wars also involved Carthage, but were not led by Hannibal. The Peloponnesian War was between the Athenians and their allies and Sparta, while the War of the Alps did not happen.

53. **One lasting effect of the Second Crusade was:**
    (Medieval History)

    A. An increase in power in the Latin Kingdoms

    B. A steady alliance between the Islamic powers and the Crusaders

    C. A decline in Byzantine prestige

    D. An increase in Islamic prestige and power

    E. The establishment of a new Latin kingdom

The answer is D.
During the Second Crusade, most of the Latin gains made during the First Crusade were lost thanks to poor military decisions and lack of troops and supplies. The Byzantines actually benefited from these losses because they regained control of several territories the Latins had taken and formed an alliance with the Caliph. Therefore D is correct.

54. **The First Crusade was called by Pope Urban II as an attempt to free the city of _____ from Muslim control.**
    (Medieval History)

    A. Jerusalem

    B. Bethlehem

    C. Constantinople

    D. Mecca

    E. Antioch

    The answer is A.
    The capture of Jerusalem by the Muslims was what sparked the call for the First Crusade.

55. **Which of the following statements about the medieval social structure of feudalism is false?**
    (Medieval History)

    A. Peasants were tied to land owned by their liege lords.

    B. The lands held by the nobility were heredity and could not be taken by the Crown.

    C. Vassals were obliged to provide military service when called upon.

    D. There was a distinct lack of social mobility.

    E. Feudalism declined after the 1500s because of a combination of factors such as warfare, the plague and social unrest.

    The answer is B.
    All of the answers but B are true statements about feudalism. Lands were primarily hereditary, but could be claimed by the crown either as punishment or if there was no male heir.

WESTERN CIVILIZATION I

56. **Which of the following religious orders was established to care for pilgrims traveling to the Holy Land?**
    (Medieval History)

    A. The Knights Templar

    B. The Franciscans

    C. The Knights Hospitaller

    D. The Red Cross

    E. The Cistercian Monks

The answer is C.
The Knights Hospitaller set up waystations along the route to the Holy Land to assist pilgrims. The Franciscans and Cistercians were monks and did not travel unless required. The Knights Templar played a large role in the Crusades, but they were primarily warriors. The Red Cross is a service organization, but was not founded until the late 1800s.

57. **This queen accompanied her husband, King Louis VII, on the Second Crusade.**
    (Medieval History)

    A. Eleanor of Aquitaine

    B. Blanche of Castile

    C. Boudicca

    D. Isabella of France

    E. Isabella of Spain

The answer is A.
Eleanor of Aquitaine's thirst for adventure drove her to accompany her husband, Louis VII of France, on crusade. Blanche of Castile and both Isabellas did not go on crusade, and Boudicca was a British queen who famously led a revolt against the Romans.

58. **Which crusade temporarily ended the Byzantine Empire and created a Latin Kingdom?**
    (Medieval History)

    A. The First Crusade

    B. The Second Crusade

    C. The Third Crusade

    D. The Fourth Crusade

    E. The Fifth Crusade

The answer is D.
While all crusades were required to interact with the Byzantine Empire during crusades for safe passage and supplies, members of the Fourth Crusade grew frustrated with the empire's reluctance to offer additional aid. So they attacked and successfully sacked the nearly impregnable city.

59. **Flying buttresses, large stained glass windows and vaulted ceilings are characteristic of which architectural style?**
    (Medieval History)

    A. Neo-classical

    B. Pre-modern

    C. Renaissance

    D. Baroque

    E. Gothic

The answer is E.
Gothic architecture is defined by these traits. Neo-classical focuses on Roman and Greek aesthetic, while Renaissance architecture focuses less on angles and sharp lines and more on rounded arches. Baroque architecture is highly ornate, and pre-modern is a term used generally to describe architecture over several centuries.

60. **The Bubonic Plague killed what percentage of Europe's population at its peak in 1347?**
    (Medieval History)

    A. 13 percent

    B. 25 percent

    C. 33 percent

    D. 49 percent

    E. 65 percent

The answer is C.
The Bubonic Plague killed off nearly one-third, or 33 percent, of Europe's population.

61. **Dante Alighieri's Divine Comedy was written in what language?**
    (Medieval History)

    A. Greek

    B. French

    C. Latin

    D. Italian

    E. English

The answer is D.
Dante's "Divine Comedy" was famously written in the more common language of Italian rather than Latin since it allowed nominally educated people to read it.

WESTERN CIVILIZATION I

62. The Bayeux Tapestry describes and represents the military victories of _____?
(Medieval History)

   A. Julius Caesar

   B. William the Conqueror

   C. Edward II of England

   D. Henry I of France

   E. Richard the Lionheart

The answer is B.
The Bayeux Tapestry, which is actually a very long work of embroidery, detailed the arrival and conquest of England by William the Conqueror.

63. Which of the following was NOT an effect of the Crusades?
(Medieval History)

   A. Several Latin kingdoms were established

   B. Trade between the Holy Land and Western Europe began to flourish

   C. An exchange of thoughts and ideas began between the European kingdoms and the Islamic territories

   D. Feudalism was strengthened as the number of Crusades rose

   E. Pilgrims and travelers began to move between the Europe and the Middle East

The answer is D.
All of these except for D are true statements about the Crusades. The large the number of men going on crusade were taught new skills and strengths, which made it difficult for them to want to return to serfdom once the crusade was over. As a result, a larger merchant class started to develop, which in many countries signaled the end of feudalism.

WESTERN CIVILIZATION I

64. The Hundred Years' War was characterized by England's desire to conquer which country:
(Medieval History)

- A. Spain
- B. France
- C. Portugal
- D. Italy
- E. Byzantium

The answer is B.
England was attempting to exert a hereditary claim to the throne of France through a common ancestor.

65. Which English king completed the conquest and incorporation of Wales?
(Medieval History)

- A. Henry III
- B. Edward I
- C. John
- D. Henry VII
- E. William the Conqueror

The answer is B.
Though John and Henry III made excursions into Wales, Edward I was the king who ended major Welsh rebellion and incorporated the country into England.

WESTERN CIVILIZATION I

66. **The Lombards were a Germanic-speaking people who conquered a large portion of Italy in the 700s, ousting which major power from the area?**
    (Medieval History)

    A. The Byzantines

    B. The Romans

    C. The Papal States

    D. The French

    E. The Franks

The answer is A.
The Byzantines had expanded back into Rome as part of Emperor Justinian's vision of a renewed Roman Empire. The invasion of the Lombards pushed the Byzantines out of Italy for the last time.

67. **The first Holy Roman Emperor was:**
    (Medieval History)

    A. Constantine the Great

    B. Charlemagne

    C. Lothair I

    D. Louis the German

    E. Drogo of Champagne

The answer is B.
Constantine was the first emperor of Rome who set his capital in Byzantium and renamed it Constantinople. However, he was not Holy Roman Emperor. That position sprung from the Germanic kingdoms, and it was Charlemagne who was crowned by the Pope as a defender of the faith and Holy Roman Emperor.

68. **The War of the Roses was primarily a fight for:**
(Medieval History)

    A. Trade rights in Italy

    B. An end of feudalism in England

    C. Succession of the crown of England

    D. English control of the French crown

    E. English control over Scotland

The answer is C.
The War of the Roses began when two competing branches of the English royal family, the House of York and the House of Lancaster, competed for control of the crown. The House of Lancaster was temporarily defeated by Edward of York, who ruled as Edward IV. He was succeeded by his brother, Richard III, who was overthrown by a nominal Lancaster noble called Henry Tudor, who later became Henry VII.

69. **During the Renaissance what is the term for the art form that focused on authentic emotions and life-like proportions?**
(Renaissance and Reformation)

    A. Baroque

    B. Realism

    C. Neo-classicism

    D. Surrealism

    E. Impressionism

The answer is B.
Neither of the other art forms focus on emotion or life-like proportions. In fact, realism in arm at this time was the first major form of art to show genuine emotion rather than an idealized human form.

WESTERN CIVILIZATION I

70. A popular type of song in the Middle Ages involved multiple people singing the melody one after the other. What was this called?
    (Medieval History)

    A. Pavan

    B. Carol

    C. Solo

    D. Round

    E. Chant

    The answer is D.
    A round begins with one person singing a line of music, and at a certain point in the score, other singers join in singing the same line. The effect is a tiered musical experience.

71. Which of these emperors was NOT a aspirant contender during the Year of the Four Emperors in 69 CE?
    (Ancient Rome)

    A. Galba

    B. Otho

    C. Vitellius

    D. Vespasian

    E. Nero

    The answer is E.
    Nero preceded the Year of the Four Emperors. It was his suicide and lack of an heir that sparked competing claims to the throne.

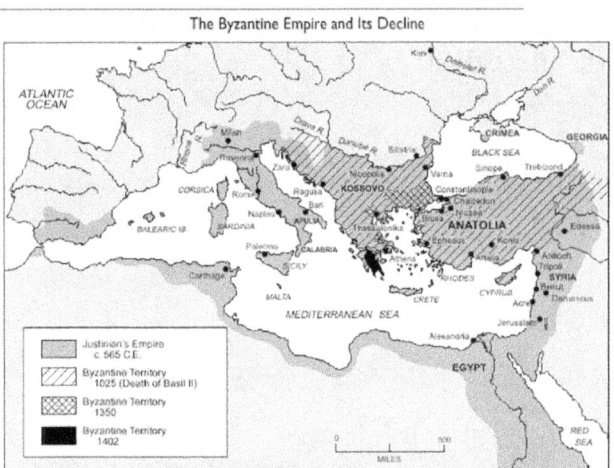

"The Byzantine Empire and its Decline." *All Empires.* 2015. http://www.allempires.com/empires/byzantine1/map09_01.gif.

72. **The dark gray shaded region shows the extent of the Byzantine Empire under which emperor?**
    (Medieval History)

    A. Justinian

    B. Constantine

    C. Manuel I

    D. Zeno

    E. Basil I

The answer is A.
The correct answer is Option A. Justinian's vision for the Eastern Roman Empire was for it to extend to its original borders. He mostly succeeded on this front and also contributed a large number of building projects and law recodification. However, his vision of a large Roman Empire died shortly after him, as such a large empire was doomed to attack on multiple fronts.

WESTERN CIVILIZATION I

73. **The Roman Empire was divided into four sections under which emperor?**
(Ancient Rome)

    A. Constantine

    B. Domitian

    C. Diocletian

    D. Tiberius

    E. Augustus

The answer is C.
Diocletian divided the overlarge empire into portions that would each be ruled by a Caesar in an attempt to manage the multiple borders and fronts of the extended empire. This tetrarchy lasted until the rise of Constantine, who slowly took power over the whole of the empire.

74. **Which of the following is a false statement about women's lives in Rome?**
(Ancient Rome)

    A. Women were able to consistently wield large amounts of political power

    B. The role of matriarch was glorified in Roman society

    C. A woman could rule as regent if her son was underage or her husband was absent

    D. Women enjoyed a great deal of social mobility and freedom

    E. There were religious roles that only women could perform

The answer is A.
All of these statements are true except A. While there were some notable women in Roman history, women were not allowed to wield too much power in daily life. Any woman who did was typically vilified in contemporary accounts.

WESTERN CIVILIZATION I

75. One version of Rome's early history indicates the belief that its earliest founder was a fugitive from what war?
(Ancient Rome)

    A. The Trojan War

    B. The Punic War

    C. The Peloponnesian War

    D. The Greco-Persian Wars

    E. The Corinthian War

The answer is A.
In an attempt to connect their fledgling city with a historical counterpart, one common early legend stated that Rome was founded by the soldier Aeneas, who was fleeing the Trojan War.

76. This philosopher-emperor was a successful general and author of Stoic Philosophy.
(Ancient Rome)

    A. Nero

    B. Titus

    C. Marcus Aurelius

    D. Augustus

    E. Justinian

The answer is C.
Though both Augustus and Justinian were noted scholars, it was Marcus Aurelius' contributions to the philosophy of Stoicism that made him both a power political and historical figure.

WESTERN CIVILIZATION I

77. **Which emperor was not among those classically referred to as the "Five Good Emperors"?**
    (Ancient Rome)

    A. Nerva

    B. Trajan

    C. Hadrian

    D. Augustus

    E. Antoninus Pius

The answer is D.
The Five Good Emperors were, with one exception, all adopted, which furthered the belief that merit by birth wasn't guaranteed, even if the child was the son of an emperor. All of these except Augustus were from the time period of the Five Good Emperors. Augustus was the nephew of Julius Caesar, who was later adopted by Caesar as his son and heir. His long rule allowed him to consolidate power and made him the first Emperor of Rome.

78. **What was Rome's typical reaction when encountering unknown or opposing religious values in regions it conquered?**
    (Ancient Rome)

    A. Rome would stamp out any of the native religion and install priests to instruct the new province about Roman ways.

    B. Rome would adopt the religion and gods of the province as its own.

    C. The citizens were offered the option of following Roman religions and gods.

    D. Romans only spread the cult of emperor worship.

    E. Rome would find parallels between the provinces' gods and its own and assume the provinces' gods were incarnations of Roman deities.

The answer is E.
Rome was remarkably tolerant of differing religious values as long as the deified emperors were worshipped and taxes were paid. Therefore E is correct, as Rome would often assume that gods and goddesses in other territories were simply manifestations of their own gods.

WESTERN CIVILIZATION I

79. **The name of the ineffectual and largely ceremonial last emperor of Rome was what?** *(Ancient Rome)*

    A. Amelianus

    B. Honorius

    C. Theodosius I

    D. Romulus

    E. Valentinian III

The answer is D.
Interestingly, the historical founder and last emperor of Rome was called Romulus, while the first and last emperor of the Byzantine Empire was called Constantine.

80. **Rome's early military history involved attacking neighboring cities in Italy to expand its territory. Which war marked the start of expansion outside the borders of Italy?** *(Ancient Rome)*

    A. The Samnite Wars

    B. The First Punic War

    C. The Latin Wars

    D. The Pyrrhic War

    E. The Second Punic War

The answer is B.
As Rome grew, it quickly fought and conquered the Latins and Samnites. The First Punic War, Option B, marked the first attempt by Rome to expand outside of the peninsula of Italy. The Pyrrhic War was a defense against a group of Greek allies who were attacking the Romans and Carthaginians.

WESTERN CIVILIZATION I

81. Which of the following was a fact about Roman citizenship?
(Ancient Rome)

    A. Both men and women enjoyed the rights of full Roman citizenship.

    B. Slaves could eventually become full citizens after their manumissions.

    C. Residents in Roman territories were automatically granted citizenship.

    D. Roman citizenship was used as a method of influencing nearby territories.

    E. Roman citizenship was not seen as a desirable state.

The answer is D.
Option A is incorrect because women were not allowed to vote. Option B is incorrect because slaves became freedmen, which were not considered to be full citizens under Roman law. While some citizens in new Roman provinces were granted citizenship as incentive to cooperate with Roman rulers, Option C is incorrect because that did not automatically happen after incorporation. Option E is incorrect because Roman citizenship was in fact highly desirable. Therefore, Option D is correct. The availability of Roman citizenship was a method used to incorporate new territories into Roman territory.

82. In what year did the western half of the Roman Empire fall?
(Ancient Rome)

    A. 284 CE

    B. 312 CE

    C. 372 CE

    D. 454 CE

    E. 476 CE

The answer is E.
The western half of the empire fell after the final sack of Rome by Odoacer and his Gothic tribes in 476 CE.

83. **The Crisis of the Third Century was marked by all but what?**
    (Ancient Rome)

    A. Multiple claimants to the throne over a short period of time

    B. Population growth in the Roman Empire

    C. A loss of Roman territory and prestige

    D. Hyperinflation and a weak economy

    E. Breakdown of trade relations across the Roman Empire

The answer is B.
The Crisis of the Third Century was a period of turmoil that began the decline of the Western Roman Empire. This period was defined by all of the answer choices except for B, population growth. With economic and political turmoil rising, residents of Rome fled the city for the Eastern Roman Empire.

84. **Which of the following was NOT a social rank in the Roman Empire?**
    (Ancient Rome)

    A. Patrician

    B. Plebian

    C. Equestrian

    D. Slave

    E. Serf

The answer is E.
All of these were ranks in Roman life except for serfs. The concept of feudalism, where serfs were tied to land owned by members of the nobility, did not arise until the early Middle Ages.

"Arch-of-Titus."*Britannica*.Undefined.
2015.http://www.britannica.com/place/Arch-of-Titus.

85. **The Arch of Titus, seen above, displayed what historical event?**
(Ancient Rome)

A. Julius Caesar's conquest of Gaul

B. The destruction of the Temple in Jerusalem

C. The defeat of Hannibal

D. The conquest of Britannia

E. The establishment of Roman law

The answer is B.
The Arch of Titus details the Emperor Titus' conquest and destruction of the great Temple in Jerusalem. The Arch also details the spoils that were claimed from the temple, including the large menorah.

86. **The Greek philosophy of Stoicism was characterized by all but what?**
    (Ancient Greece and Hellenistic Civ)

    A. Focusing on what is said rather than what is done

    B. Focusing on what is done rather than what is said

    C. The application of logic to daily life

    D. The pursuit of a virtuous existence

    E. The belief in self-control and self-determination

The answer is A.
Stoicism, which began in Greece and later found a following in famous Romans, such as Cato the Younger and Marcus Aurelius, focused on a sparse, logical and controlled existence with little dissembling. Therefore Option A is not characteristic of stoicism as it focuses on words rather than actions performed.

87. **The Islamic Golden Age refers to a time of social, military and scientific expansion and cultivation. What marked the end of this period?**
    (Medieval History)

    A. Increasing Christian pressure from Europe and the Mongols from the east

    B. Muslim focus on military matters

    C. Internal revolt and uprisings

    D. A "brain drain" to Europe

    E. An increased focus on religious life

The answer is A.
The Islamic Golden Age occurred while most of Europe was considered to be in the Dark Ages and was a time of mathematical, scientific and religious innovation. It was also the age of conquest and expansion for the Muslim armies of the Middle East, so Options B through D would be incorrect. Instead, it was the start of the First Crusade as well as the rise of Genghis Khan to the East that brought the Islamic Golden Age to an end.

WESTERN CIVILIZATION I

88. The ancient ruler Sargon the Great conquered Sumerian city-states to form what empire?
    (Ancient near East)

    A. Babylonian

    B. Neo-Assyrian

    C. Akkadian

    D. Hittite

    E. Assyrian

The answer is C.
Sargon the Great led a series of military campaigns that resulted in the creation of the Akkadian Empire.

89. Achievements of the so-called "New Monarchies" included all but what?
    (Renaissance and Reformation)

    A. Internal stability

    B. Efficient taxation

    C. A strong focus on nationalism

    D. Increased trade and interaction

    E. Maintaining a standing army

The answer is C.
The New Monarchs were characteristic Renaissance rulers focused on redefining the role of the monarchy in an enlightened society. During this time, focus on stability was primary. This meant that taxation, trade and a standing army all contributed to that sense of security. However the concept of nationalism as it is understood today did not exist at this time. Therefore, Option C is the correct answer.

90. **The Commercial Revolution was a period of economic expansion and diversification during the Middle Ages. Which statement can be concluded to be FALSE regarding the Commercial Revolution's effect on society?**
    (Medieval History)

    A. Increased interaction between different kingdoms allowed for more trade

    B. Increased production of goods allowed for the merchant class to grow

    C. Increased competition between the European powers rapidly advanced maritime science

    D. Advances in trade and science did not encourage exploration

    E. Modern banking developed to handle the increased demand for loans and money storage

The answer is D.
The Commercial Revolution was the direct result of technological advancements in production in agriculture, textiles and manufacturing that allowed for a growing merchant class, the modern banking system and a competitive atmosphere as kingdoms raced to be the first to complete new inventions. All of the answers are true except for D. These advances in science and manufacturing allowed the first explorers to set sail for the New World.

91. **Who were the Huguenots?**
    (Renaissance and Reformation)

    A. English Protestants

    B. English Catholics

    C. French Protestants

    D. French Catholics

    E. Dutch Protestants

The answer is C.
The Huguenots were French Protestants who called for an end to the extravagances of the French Catholic Church.

92. **Which of the following was not a complaint made by Protestants against the Catholic Church?**
    (Renaissance and Reformation)

    A. The improper selling of indulgences

    B. Churches held too much land

    C. Too much money remaining in the hands of Church officials

    D. The influence of the Church needed to be increased

    E. The Church had become hopelessly corrupt and indulgent

The answer is D.
Martin Luther famously had a long list of grievances against the Catholic Church, but the correct answer here is D. No Protestant believed the power of the church needed to be increased. Rather, the church needed to bend to the will of the people, cut excess and revise its policies on selling indulgences and lands.

93. **The Reformation in England resulted in which of the following?**
    (Renaissance and Reformation)

    A. A clear and uncompromising break with the Roman Church

    B. The destruction and dissolution of monasteries

    C. The monarchy immediately adopted Protestantism as the religion of England

    D. All citizens were forced to convert to Protestantism

    E. All Catholic churches in England were eventually dissolved

The answer is B.
England's step into Reformation was less extreme than many other countries. Though Henry VIII ordered the destruction and dissolution of all Catholic monasteries in England, this was done primarily for financial rather than religious reasons. The newly formed Anglican Church maintained ceremonies very similar to the Catholic Church, which caused some more extreme Protestants to complain that England's conversion wasn't forceful enough. Some of these people eventually left England as Puritans to settle in the New World.

94. The man below opposed King Henry VIII and the Protestant Reformation in England. What is his name?
(Renaissance and Reformation)

Birzer, Bradley. "Sir Thomas More, Humanist." *College of Arts and Science, University of Colorado Boulder.* n.d. http://artsandsciences.colorado.edu/ctp/2014/08/the-utopia-of-thomas-more/.

A. Martin Luther

B. Thomas Cranmer

C. Thomas More

D. Cardinal Wolsey

E. George Boleyn

The answer is C.
Option A, Martin Luther, famously began the Protestant Reformation, so he would not have opposed its spread in England. Thomas Cranmer was an archbishop who also supported the Reformation. Cardinal Wolsey died before the Reformation began in England, and George Boleyn was Anne Boleyn's brother. Both Boleyns were supporters of the Reformation. The painting depicts Thomas More, who denied both the Reformation and the role of Henry VIII as head of the Anglican Church. He was executed in 1535.

WESTERN CIVILIZATION I

95. **Which of the following monarchs was not Protestant?**
    (Renaissance and Reformation)

    A. Elizabeth I

    B. Mary Tudor

    C. Edward VI

    D. William and Mary

    E. James VI

The answer is B.
All of the monarchs were famous Protestants except for Option B, Mary Tudor. Queen Mary rose to the throne after the death of her 15-year-old brother Edward VI. She sought to undo England's shift to Protestantism by ruthlessly persecuting known Protestant leaders, leading her to be famously dubbed "Bloody Mary."

96. **Early modern Europe was noted for all but which of the following:**
    (Early Modern Europe, 1560-1648)

    A. Religious reformation

    B. Religious persecution

    C. A decline in scientific advancement

    D. An increase of exploration and trade

    E. New advancements in philosophy

The answer is C.
Early modern Europe saw religious reformation and persecution, increases in exploration and new advancements in philosophy, all characteristic of the beginning of the Age of Reason. This period is not noted for a decline in scientific advancement, therefore Option C is the correct answer.

WESTERN CIVILIZATION I

97. **The Thirty Years' War began as a struggle between which two powers?**
    (Early Modern Europe, 1560-1648)

    A. Protestants and Catholics

    B. England and France

    C. England and Germany

    D. Protestants and Huguenots

    E. Spain and France

The answer is A.
The Thirty Years' War was a violent clash between Protestants and Catholics that eventually drew in most of Europe's major powers, with each pursuing their goals. Initially it was a war between Protestant and Catholic states in the fragmenting Holy Roman Empire, it gradually developed into a more general conflict involving most of the great powers of Europe, becoming less about religion and more a continuation of the France–Habsburg rivalry for European political pre-eminence. The end result of the war was the protection of Protestantism, the decline of Hapsburg power in the German states, and the decline of feudalism.

98. **Which of the following was a result of the Peloponnesian War?**
    (Ancient Greece and Hellenistic Civilization)

    A. Sparta lost influence in the Adriatic

    B. Athens gained territory and influence

    C. Sparta gained influence and prestige over Athens

    D. The Peloponnesian League was dissolved

    E. Democracy continued without interruption in Athens

The answer is C.
The Peloponnesian War was a war between Athens and Sparta, with various allies on either side. The main cause of the war was an attempt to check Athens' power in the Greek islands. By the end of the war, Sparta and its allies had defeated Athens, so Option C is correct.

99. **The Persian Wars were a series of engagements between the Greek states and the Persian Empire over fifty years. Who is the primary contemporary source of information during this time?**
    (Ancient Greece and Hellenistic Civilization)

    A. Plato

    B. Livy

    C. Herodotus

    D. Plutarch

    E. Aristotle

The answer is C.
Herodotus' writings are the main source of information about the Persian wars. Plato and Aristotle were both philosophers, not historians, while Livy and Plutarch were Romans who wrote about Greek history from secondary sources.

100. **Which king led the Second Crusade?**
    (Medieval History)

    A. Louis VII of France

    B. Conrad III of Germany

    C. John of England

    D. Richard the Lionheart

    E. Both A and B

The answer is E.
Louis VII of France and Conrad III of Germany jointly led the Second Crusade back into the Holy Land to support the Latin Kingdoms that were created after the First Crusade.

WESTERN CIVILIZATION I

101. **Sea power was crucial for most of the European powers. In 1588, the English navy defeated the navy of which country, an action that established England as the major rising power in Europe?**
(Early Modern Europe, 1560-1648)

   A. France

   B. The Netherlands

   C. Germany

   D. Spain

   E. The Portuguese

The answer is D.
King Philip II of Spain sent an armada to defeat the British navy in hopes of ending privateering. Due to a combination of bad weather and skill on the part of the British navy captains, the armada was completely destroyed, which left England mostly unopposed at sea.

102. **The English Civil War resulted from complaints about all of the following except:**
(Early Modern Europe, 1560-1648)

   A. Parliament would not grant Charles I funds

   B. Parliament and the people of England did not support Charles' Catholic bride

   C. Constitutional guarantees were not being made by the king

   D. Parliament did not feel it was being consulted enough by the king

   E. The king's lack of enforcement of Divine Right

The answer is E.
Charles I believed very firmly in Divine Right, meaning that he believed he was appointed by and answerable only to God. This led to an uncompromising attitude that caused his Parliament to refuse him funds until he made constitutional guarantees to the people. His refusal to do so led to the Civil War that resulted in his execution and the brief suspension of the monarchy. Option E is correct.

WESTERN CIVILIZATION I

103. **Nation-states comprised groups of people united by:**
(Early Modern Europe, 1560-1648)

   A. Common language

   B. Geography

   C. Traditions

   D. History

   E. All of the above

The answer is E.
Option E is correct as all of the traits shown were characteristic of nation-states.

104. **The Roman Cult of Mithras was made up primarily of whom?**
(Ancient Rome)

   A. Women

   B. Slaves

   C. Soldiers

   D. Freemen

   E. Senators

The answer is C.
The Romans had many gods, and most Romans honored multiple gods. However it was not uncommon for a family to have a specific god it honored as a protector. The cult of Mithras, which became a sort of secret society in Roman times, comprised mostly soldiers who looked to the Persian warrior god as a protector.

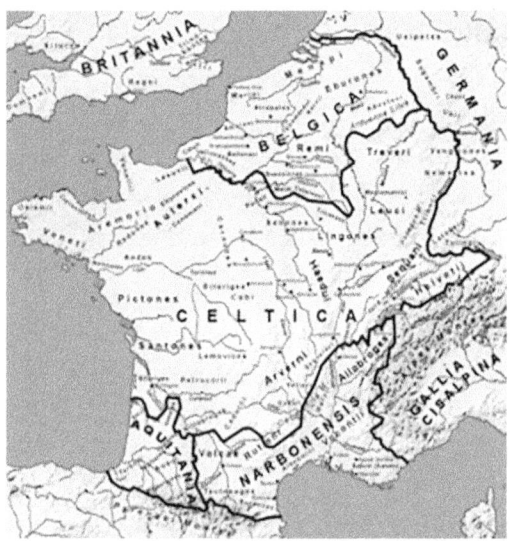

Feitscherg. "Map Gallia Tribes Towns." *wikimedia*.2015.https://commons.wikimedia.org/wiki/File:Map_Gallia_Tribes_Towns.png.

105. **This above Roman province is known as what?**
     (Ancient Rome)

     A. Britannia

     B. Gaul

     C. Hispania

     D. Londinium

     E. Dacia

The answer is B.
The map shows the province of Gaul, modern day France. It was famously conquered by Julius Caesar, who wrote about his experiences in the province. Caesar invaded Gaul in 58 B.C.E. killing as many as a million people (probably 1 in 5 of the Gauls) and enslaving another million.

WESTERN CIVILIZATION I

106. In 1492, an edict was issued that expelled Jews from which country?
(Medieval History)

    A. England

    B. France

    C. Portugal

    D. Spain

    E. The Netherlands

The answer is D.
In 1492, King Ferdinand and Queen Isabella issued a proclamation that expelled the Jews from Spain. This was done either by threat of death or forcible conversions.

107. Baroque art, which gained popularity in the 1600s, can be distinguished by:
(Renaissance and Reformation)

    A. Its return to Greek and Roman styles

    B. Clean, uncomplicated aesthetic

    C. Heavily ornate architecture and paintings

    D. Unemotional figures in paintings

    E. Experimentations with the representation of human form

The answer is C.
Greek and Roman artistic ideals are known as Neo-classicism, while an uncomplicated aesthetic is more typical of Renaissance art. Baroque art, however, is defined by ornate altarpieces, architecture and extremely detailed works of art. Option C is correct.

WESTERN CIVILIZATION I

108. **The Renaissance was a great leap ahead in terms of science, architecture and art. What was another effect of the Renaissance on political culture outside of Italy?** *(Renaissance and Reformation)*

    A. Independent city-states were established across Europe

    B. Religious thought stagnated

    C. Trade decreased as cities and kingdoms sought to protect their advancements

    D. Monarchies declined in power compared to the Church

    E. Nation-states were created

The answer is E.
The Renaissance in Italy famously brought about an artistic and military revolution. These progressive ideas were carried along trade routes. In much of the Rhine region, small kingdoms were constantly warring. Under Renaissance ideals, these smaller kingdoms began to combine, either through conquest or alliance, and form larger nation-states.

109. **The Age of Enlightenment emphasized what schools of thought?** *(Renaissance and Reformation)*

    A. Reason and logic

    B. Emotion

    C. Absolute monarchy

    D. Religion was supreme above science

    E. Isolationism

The answer is A.
The Age of Enlightenment sought to apply the Scientific Method to every aspect of life in a pursuit of reason and order.

WESTERN CIVILIZATION I

110. What is the truest statement about the First and Second Crusades?
(Medieval History)

    A. The First Crusade had trouble gathering enough soldiers and pilgrims while the Second Crusade had enough men

    B. The First Crusade increased Muslim power while the Second Crusade decreased it

    C. The First Crusade decreased Muslim power while the Second Crusade increased it

    D. Both crusades were ultimately unsuccessful

    E. Both crusades achieved their objectives

The answer is C.
The First Crusade was a great success for the Latin allies. Jerusalem was reconquered, and several Latin kingdoms were formed from cities taken from the Muslims. However the Second Crusade saw the loss of Latin territory and prestige. Option C is correct.

111. What type of government did Sparta have?
(Ancient Greece and Hellenistic Civilization)

    A. Oligarchy

    B. Representative democracy

    C. Theocracy

    D. Democracy

    E. Anarchy

The answer is A.
Sparta was ruled by an oligarchy. An oligarchy is a power structure were power rest with a small number of people.

112. **Which of the following was NOT a member of the Delian League?**
    (Ancient Greece and Hellenistic Civilization)

    A. Neopolis

    B. Athens

    C. Sparta

    D. Byzantium

    E. Chalcedon

The answer is C.
The Delian League was the collection of Athens and her allies who opposed Sparta during the Peloponnesian War. Option C is therefore correct as Sparta led the Peloponnesian League.

113. **New Monarchs achieved all of the following except:**
    (Renaissance and Reformation)

    A. Increase in power of nobility

    B. The unification of their kingdoms

    C. Creation of national identity

    D. Increase in trade

    E. Creation of a standing army

The answer is A.
New Monarchs were figureheads of Renaissance ideals. Much of their power came from the creation of a national identity, which was reinforced by a standing army and increases in trade and wealth. Most monarchs were able to accomplish this by reducing, not increasing, the powers of the nobility. Therefore Option A is correct.

WESTERN CIVILIZATION I

114. The type of writing first used in early civilizations was called what?
(Ancient near East)

    A. Hieroglyphics

    B. Cuneiform

    C. Alphabet

    D. Pictograms

    E. Demotic

The answer is B.
Both hieroglyphics and Demotic were Egyptian scripts. The Alphabet as it is used in modern English was a derivation of the Phoenician scripts. Pictograms are general terms for images that convey an idea. But the first type of writing was cuneiform, which was used by the Sumerians.

115. Greek political independence ended after the conquest by:
(Ancient Greece and Hellenistic Civilization)

    A. Alexander the Great

    B. The Romans

    C. The Persians

    D. The Spartans

    E. The Trojans

The answer is B.
While Alexander the Great consolidated power in the Greek cities his father, Phillip of Macedon, had conquered, the cities were allowed to run as they had for centuries. However, under Roman rule, Greek political independence ceased.

WESTERN CIVILIZATION I

116. **The body of water surrounding most of the Grecian Islands is called what?**
(Ancient Greece and Hellenistic Civilization)

   A. Black Sea

   B. Indian Ocean

   C. Libyan Sea

   D. Aegean Sea

   E. Mediterranean

The answer is D.
The Aegean Sea is the most correct answer since the majority of the Greek Islands are located in it.

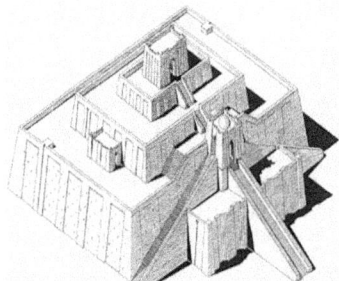

"Ziggurat." *Many Prophets One Message*. undefined. 2014. http://www.manyprophetsonemessage.com/2014/10/14/quran-reveals-lost-knowledge-about-prophet-abraham/.

117. **The above image is called a what?**
(Ancient near East)

   A. Pyramid

   B. Ziggurat

   C. Temple

   D. Burial mound

   E. Obelisk

The answer is B.
The image showed a ziggurat, which was a type of early pyramid used for religious rites and for storage. Several of these, including the famous Ziggurat of Ur, still stand today.

118. **Which country was least effected by Protestant Reformation?**
(Renaissance and Reformation)

   A. France

   B. England

   C. Germany

   D. Spain

   E. Italy

The answer is D.
The Protestant Reformation had great success in France, England and Germany. The Reformation even managed to gain a foothold in Italy, though the success there was limited after the start of Papal Inquisitions. Spain is the correct answer since the monarchy was very quick to execute any suspected Protestant sympathizers.

119. **The Anglican Church was considered to be only a partial concession to Protestant pressure because it:**
(Renaissance and Reformation)

   A. Reverted back to Catholicism

   B. Maintained Popish ceremonies and décor

   C. Stayed in communication with the Pope

   D. Supported Catholic claims to the throne

   E. Suppressed Protestant supporters

The answer is B.
The Anglican Church did separate from Rome, but received criticism from other Protestant countries because it did not completely strip out the pomp and ceremony of the Catholic mass.

WESTERN CIVILIZATION I

120. **The Roman Inquisition, which was charged with stamping out heresy that resulted from the Protestant Reformation, famously brought which Italian to trial?**
(Ancient Rome)

    A. Dante Alighieri

    B. Lucrezia Borgia

    C. Leonardo da Vinci

    D. Michelangelo

    E. Galileo Galilei

The answer is E.
The Papal or Roman Inquisitions originally began as an attempt to stamp out heresy and Protestant sympathizers. These trials famously included Galileo Galilei, who was persecuted and sentenced to house arrest for expanding on Copernicus' theory that the Earth in fact orbited the Sun.

WESTERN CIVILIZATION II

Description of the Examination

The Western Civilization II: 1648 to the Present examination covers material that is usually taught in the second semester of a two-semester course in Western Civilization. Questions cover European history from the mid-seventeenth century through the post-Second World War period including political, economic, and cultural developments such as Scientific Thought, the Enlightenment, the French and Industrial Revolutions, and the First and Second World Wars. Candidates may be asked to choose the correct definition of a historical term, select the historical figure whose political viewpoint is described, identify the correct relationship between two historical factors, or detect the inaccurate pairing of an individual with a historical event. Groups of questions may require candidates to interpret, evaluate, or relate the contents of a passage, a map, a picture, or a cartoon to the other information, or to analyze and use the data contained in a graph or table.

The examination contains 120 questions to be answered in 90 minutes. Some of these are pretest questions that will not be scored. Any time candidates spend on tutorials and providing personal information is in addition to the actual testing time.

Knowledge and Skills Required

Questions on the Western Civilization II examination require candidates to demonstrate one or more of the following abilities:

- Understanding important factual knowledge of developments in Western Civilization
- Ability to identify the causes and effects of major historical events
- Ability to analyze, interpret, and evaluate textual and graphic materials
- Ability to distinguish the relevant from the irrelevant
- Ability to reach conclusions on the basis of facts

The subject matter of the Western Civilization II examination is drawn from the following topics. The percentages next to the main topics indicate the approximate percentages of exam questions on those topics.

7%–9% **Absolutism and Constitutionalism, 1648–1715**
- The Dutch Republic
- The English Revolution
- France under Louis XIV
- Formation of Austria and Prussia
- The "westernization" of Russia

4%–6% **Competition for empire and economic expansion**
- Global economy of the eighteenth century
- Europe after Utrecht, 1713–1740
- Demographic change in the eighteenth century

5%–7% **The scientific view of the world**
- Major figures of the scientific revolution
- New knowledge of man and society
- Political theory

WESTERN CIVILIZATION II

7%–9% **Period of Enlightenment**
- Enlightenment thought
- Enlightened despotism
- Partition of Poland

10%–13% **Revolution and Napoleonic Europe**
- The Revolution in France
- The Revolution and Europe
- The French Empire
- Congress of Vienna

7%–9% **The Industrial Revolution**
- Agricultural and industrial revolution
- Causes of revolution
- Economic and social impact on working and middle class
- British reform movement

6%–8% **Political and cultural developments, 1815–1848**
- Conservatism
- Liberalism
- Nationalism
- Socialism
- The Revolutions of 1830 and 1848

8%–10% **Politics and diplomacy in the Age of Nationalism, 1850–1914**
- The unification of Italy and Germany
- Austria-Hungary
- Russia
- France
- Socialism and labor unions
- European diplomacy, 1871–1900

7%–9% **Economy, culture, and imperialism, 1850–1914**
- Demography
- World economy of the nineteenth century
- Technological developments
- Science, philosophy, and the arts
- Imperialism in Africa and Asia

10%–12% **The First World War and the Russian Revolution**
- The causes of the First World War
- The economic and social impact of the war
- The peace settlements
- The Revolution of 1917 and its effects

7%–9% **Europe between the wars**
- The Great Depression
- International politics, 1919–1939
- Stalin's five-year plans and purges
- Italy and Germany between the wars
- Interwar cultural developments

8%-10% **The Second World War and contemporary Europe**
- The causes and course of the Second World War
- Postwar Europe
- Science, philosophy, the arts, and religion
- Social and political developments

WESTERN CIVILIZATION II

SAMPLE TEST

DIRECTIONS: Read each item and select the best response.

1. **What was the initial reason the Thirty Year War began?**
   (Absolutism and Constitutionalism 1648-1715)

   A. Protestantism opposition to Roman Catholicism domination in the Netherlands and Germany

   B. French imperialism over Nordic European countries

   C. Roman Catholicism opposition to Protestantism domination in the Netherlands and Germany

   D. Spanish imperialism over France

   E. Spanish protestant churches revolted

2. **What principle was the result of the end of the Thirty Year War at the Treaty of Westphalia in 1648?**
   (Absolutism and Constitutionalism 1648-1715)

   A. That religion was more powerful than politics

   B. National dominion was clearly resilient and remained to serve as the basis for the system on imperialism and colonialism

   C. State sovereignty emerged and serves as the basis for the modern system of nation-states

   D. That state sovereignty could not work

   E. That politics were more powerful than religion

3. **What type monarchical government, such as Louis XIV of France government, has absolute power among his or her people, wielding unrestricted political power over the sovereign state and its people?**
   (Absolutism and Constitutionalism 1648-1715)

   A. Tyrannical Monarchism

   B. Constitutional Monarchism

   C. Monarchism

   D. Aristocracy Monarchism

   E. Absolute Monarchism

4. What is a document outlining the fundamental laws and principles that govern a nation.
   (Absolutism and Constitutionalism 1648-1715)

   A. Judicial Review

   B. Canon Law

   C. Treaty

   D. Parliament document

   E. Constitution

5. What is the Glorious Revolution?
   (Absolutism and Constitutionalism 1648-1715)

   A. Event against King James II (sometimes called the bloodless revolution) that consisted of Whig and Tories forcing him to leave

   B. Religious reformers from Calvinist and Luther sects fight a bloody reformation against Anglicans

   C. French imperialist come to England and displace King James II

   D. French revolutionist come to England and displace King James II

   E. Dutch Republic solidify Catholicism by force.

6. What was one outcome of the English Revolution?
   (Absolutism and Constitutionalism 1648-1715)

   A. Bill of Rights of 1689 created

   B. English sovereignty over the Dutch Republic

   C. English constitution of 1690 created

   D. Parliament created

   E. King James II remained in power

7. What was one outcome of the War of the Austrian Succession?
   (Absolutism and Constitutionalism 1648-1715)

   A. Prussia and France became allies

   B. France and Britain became allies

   C. Prussia became a prominent world leader

   D. Austria lost its sovereignty

   E. The war ended all wars

8. **Define Boyars:**
   (Absolutism and Constitutionalism 1648-1715)

   A. a member of the old aristocracy in Russia, next in rank to a prince

   B. a member of the Austrian aristocracy

   C. a reformer in the Russian Orthodox church

   D. a member belonging by rank, title, or birth to the aristocracy in the British parliament

   E. an agricultural laborer bound by the feudal system who was tied to working on his lord's estate

9. **Peter the Great revolutionized Russia by**
   (Absolutism and Constitutionalism 1648-1715)

   A. Introducing communism

   B. Introducing western ideas on education, economy, culture, politics, and military exploits

   C. Allying itself with Nordic countries such as Sweden

   D. Introducing eastern ideas on education, economy, culture, politics, and military exploits

   E. Establishing the Roman Catholic church

10. **What was one main difference between western European powers economies in the 18th century than in the 17th century?**
    (Competition for Empire and Economic Expansion)

    A. Wealth is gold and silver

    B. Free trade will create the best world

    C. There was finite amounts of wealth

    D. Mercantilism ideals

    E. Government should control economy

11. **What is the political ideologies, led by Adam Smith and John Locke, called that advocates civil liberties and political freedom with representative democracy under the rule of law and emphasizes economic freedom?**
    (Competition for Empire and Economic Expansion)

    A. Liberalism

    B. Classical Liberalism

    C. Modern Liberalism

    D. Democratic Liberalism

    E. Conservative Liberalism

12. **What was one main difference in France and Britain after the treaty of Utrecht in 1714?**
    (Competition for Empire and Economic Expansion)

    A. Monarchism spread in Britain and Conservatism in France

    B. French became rich while Britain became poor

    C. Britain stopped colonizing, while France increased in colonization

    D. Communism spread in France and socialism in Britain

    E. Absolutism spread in France and Constitutionalism in Britain.

13. **What did the Treaty of Utrecht mean for Europe?**
    (Competition for Empire and Economic Expansion)

    A. It kept the Dutch from taking over Europe

    B. It stopped the English from invading Spain

    C. It ended French hegemony and kept the balance of power

    D. It ended the subjugation of Russia and started the empire of Portugal

    E. The union of Versailles was created

14. **Why did populations in major western nations grow so rapidly in the 18th century?**
    (Competition for Empire and Economic Expansion)

    A. Society began to share wealth amongst poorer classes

    B. Humans had more children at earlier ages

    C. Humans became better at safeguarding food, creation of new advance medicines; ending of the bubonic plague

    D. The death of textile industries

    E. Populations did not grow, however, decreased

15. **Why did large European inhabits move towards bigger cities by the 1750s?**
    (Competition for Empire and Economic Expansion)

    A. Textile industry

    B. Open-field system

    C. Wartime atrocities does to farms scared the people

    D. mercantilism

    E. Increase in diseases from rural areas

16. Who was the inventor of deductive reasoning which in turn created the idea if Deism?
    (The Scientific View of the World)

    A. Leonard Fuchs

    B. Albert Einstein

    C. Galileo Galilie

    D. Samuel Hartlib

    E. Rene Descartes

17. What scientist created the laws of universal gravitation?
    (The Scientific View of the World)

    A. Rene Descartes

    B. Leonard Fuchs

    C. Isaac Newton

    D. Samuel Hartlib

    E. John Napier

18. What used observation and experimentation to explain theories on the workings of the universe such as government, environment, religion, society, and culture? This process removed blind adherence to tradition from science Scientific Revolution.
    (The Scientific View of the World)

    A. The Scientific Method

    B. Natural Rights

    C. Checks and Balances

    D. Religious Thought

    E. Enlightened Despots

19. John Locke's book, *Two Treatises of Government,* he explains that all men have Natural Rights, which are
    (The Scientific View of the World)

    A. Sleep, Eat, and Work

    B. Life, Liberty, and Property

    C. Speech, Writing, and Action

    D. Life, Liberty, and the Pursuit of Happiness

    E. Autonomy, Democracy, and Conventionality

20. Enlightenment thinker Thomas Hobbes created the idea of Social Contract, which stated that human beings were inherently
    (The Scientific View of the World)

    A. greedy, selfish, and cruel

    B. merciful, caring, and agreeable

    C. powerless

    D. religious, dutiful, and ardent

    E. collective

21. Which belief stated that man was inherently good but society and its unequal distribution of wealth was problematic?
    (Period of Enlightenment)

    A. Checks and Balances

    B. Absolute Monarch

    C. Individualism

    D. Classic Liberalism

    E. The General Will

22. This work by Montesquieu called for a separation of powers and heavily influenced the formation of American government
    (Period of Enlightenment)

    A. Democratic Ideals

    B. Republic

    C. The Spirit of Laws

    D. Liberty Bells

    E. Natural Rights

23. What is the philosophy stressing the recognition of every person as a valuable individual with inalienable, inborn rights.
    (Period of Enlightenment)

    A. Humanity

    B. Conformity

    C. Individualism

    D. Democracy

    E. Libertarian

24. **What is the separation of powers?**
    (Period of Enlightenment)

    A. The belief that on country should not have more/less power than another

    B. The concept that all governments should become one universal order

    C. The idea that monarchies have all the power and the people should have none, therefore, separating their powers

    D. The idea that power in government should be divided into separate branches in order to ensure that no one branch of a governing body can gain too much authority

    E. The ideas that no government is the best government

25. **What was the main difference between monarchies prior to the Enlightenment and those during who practiced Enlightened Absolutism**
    (Period of Enlightenment)

    A. Those during the Enlightenment tended to allow religious toleration, freedom of speech and the press, and the right to hold private property. Most fostered the arts, sciences, and education.

    B. Those prior to the Enlightenment tended to allow religious toleration, freedom of speech and the press, and the right to hold private property. Most fostered the arts, sciences, and education

    C. Leaders that practiced ideals of Enlightened Absolutism were extremely intolerable. Any new forms of religion, culture, freedom speech, press, and the ability to hold private property were all banned.

    D. Monarchies prior to the Enlightenment believed more so in rational thinking rather than belief in in an outside divinity.

    E. None of the above, they were absolutely the same. Only thinkers and philosophers ideals were changing during these periods.

26. **What is the idea of Devine Right?**
    (Period of Enlightenment)

    A. That lords were allowed to take the newly wife of any of its servants for the first night

    B. That the God had appointed the people to rule

    C. That no one held rights except for the monarch

    D. That monarchs were appointed and held their office by the grace of God

    E. That only leaders of parliament were appointed by God

27. **How was the Polish Enlightenment different than Western countries such as Prussia or France?**
    (Period of Enlightenment)

    A. Those in the west wrote about the need for more checks and balances on their kings, Polish Enlightenment was geared towards fighting the abuses stemming from too many checks and balances

    B. The Polish Enlightenment boasted no real political shifts

    C. Not one enlightened theory came from Poland

    D. There was no bloodshed over the governmental takeover of the libertarian parties. King Stanisław August Poniatowski voluntarily stepped own

    E. Western powers ideals on Enlightenment were based on reasoning while Polish scholars still based ideas on divinity.

28. **What proceeded to happen after the third Partition of Poland?**
    (Period of Enlightenment)

    A. Russia took over and became the most powerful portioning power in Poland. Enlightenment supporters were forced to flee the country

    B. France became the most powerful nation in Europe

    C. Poland was revolutionized by Enlightenment thinkers and a true democracy was short lived

    D. Prussia, France, and Russia split Poland

    E. Poland remained a monarchy

29. **What changed during the French Revolution in the political sphere?**
    (Revolution and Napoleonic Europe)

    A. King Louis XVI's monarchy was empowered

    B. All high ranking members of the French aristocracy became Lords of several pieces of lands

    C. Taxes were raised

    D. It abolished the feudal system and absolute monarchy

    E. Conservative republicanism was implanted

30. **What concepts influenced the French Revolution?**
    (Revolution and Napoleonic Europe)

    A. Totalitarianism

    B. Romanticism

    C. Socialistic and domesticate rights

    D. Popular sovereignty and inalienable rights.

    E. Classicism

31. **Why did the French Revolution begin?**
    (Revolution and Napoleonic Europe)

    A. Extravagant lifestyles of the monarchy brought France to the verge of bankruptcy

    B. Maria Antoinette statement, "let them eat cake," infused rage in Parisians

    C. King Louis XVI was assonated and had no known heir

    D. German insurgents invaded eastern France

    E. It was a phenomena. No one knows the cause.

32. What were the three main classes in 18th Century France?
(Revolution and Napoleonic Europe)

   A. Peasant, Serf, and Noble

   B. First Estate, Second Estate and the Third Estate

   C. Upper, Middle, Lower

   D. Lower, Bourgeoisie, and Aristocrat

   E. Lower, Middle, and Gentry

33. Over 50 countries were affected but the Revolution in Europe in the 19th century. However, they had no coordination or cooperation among the revolutionaries in different countries. What were some shared factors involved:
(Revolution and Napoleonic Europe)

   A. Demands for more participation in government and democracy; demands for freedom of press; the regrouping of the reactionary forces based on the royalty, the aristocracy, the army, the church and the peasants.

   B. Demands for less participation of peasants; demand for stable monarchy.

   C. Every monarch was destroyed and replaced by a democratic republic.

   D. The working (middle) class always led each revolution

   E. The poor (lower) class always led the revolution

34. In the 1840s what did the term "democracy" mean?
(Revolution and Napoleonic Europe)

   A. Freedom from government

   B. Consent of the governed and the restriction of church and state power, republican government, freedom of the press and the individual

   C. Universal male suffrage

   D. Uniting people bound by (some mix of) common languages, culture, religion, shared history, and of course immediate geography

   E. More power to workers

35. What did the Corn Laws of 1815 enact?
(Revolution and Napoleonic Europe)

   A. imposed restrictions and tariffs on imported grain in Great Britain

   B. restricted farmers from growing only a limited amount of grain products in Great Britain

   C. ratified taxes on grains in United States

   D. decreed every household was allotted one bushel of grain from the government yearly in Germany

   E. restricted grain trade in United States

36. What was the Frankfurt Parliament in 1848?
(Revolution and Napoleonic Europe)

   A. The Assembly of German Aristocrats

   B. The first freely elected parliament in Germany

   C. The Prussian monarchies assembly

   D. The first Belgian freely elected parliament

   E. It was a treaty that sectioned off the southern part of Germany (Bavaria and Saxon) to the Austrians

37. Which country did NOT experience a Revolution in 1848?
(Revolution and Napoleonic Europe)

   A. France

   B. Denmark

   C. Poland

   D. Russia

   E. Italy

38. How far east did Napoleon Empire reach in Europe?
(Revolution and Napoleonic Europe)

   A. Russia

   B. Germany

   C. Austria

   D. Denmark

   E. Poland

39. What was the French civil code established in 1804 that forbade privileges based on birth, allowed freedom of religion, and specified that government jobs should go to the most qualified?
(Revolution and Napoleonic Europe)

   A. Napoleonic Code

   B. Natural Rights

   C. French Code

   D. Bill of Rights

   E. Rights

40. What were the series of major conflicts (1803-1815) pitting the French Empire led by Emperor Napoleon I against an array of European powers formed into various coalitions?
    (Revolution and Napoleonic Europe)

    A. The Great War

    B. Napoleonic Wars

    C. The Rebellion

    D. The Napoleonic Struggle

    E. The French Wars

41. Which country was the reason why the first great French Empire collapsed?
    (Revolution and Napoleonic Europe)

    A. Great Britain

    B. Austria

    C. Russia

    D. Prussia

    E. Napoleon never lost

42. What was the congress of ambassadors of European States that in 1814 arose because of the French Revolution and the Napoleonic Wars?
    (Revolution and Napoleonic Europe)

    A. Europeans Allies

    B. NATO

    C. European Union

    D. Congress of Vienna

    E. Congress of Paris

43. What was the Congress of Vienna's main objective?
    (Revolution and Napoleonic Europe)

    A. Congress was to provide a long-term peace plan

    B. To convict Britain of all its atrocities

    C. To unify Europe and invade Asia provinces

    D. To stop revolutions and support monarchies

    E. To serve the peasants of every European country

WESTERN CIVILIZATION II

44. **What treaty ended the Napoleonic Wars between France and the Sixth Coalition in 1814?**
    (Revolution and Napoleonic Europe)

    A. Treaty of Vienna

    B. The Sixth Coalition Agreement

    C. Treaty of Paris

    D. Peace of Paris

    E. Second Treaty of Paris

45. **What treaty ended Napoleons rule as emperor in France?**
    (Revolution and Napoleonic Europe)

    A. Treaty of Fontainebleau

    B. Treaty of Paris

    C. Second Treaty of Paris

    D. Treaty of Vienna

    E. The Sixth Coalition Agreement

46. **What was the Enclosure Act?**
    (The Industrial Revolution)

    A. An act that pushed all British citizens north of England into bigger cities

    B. The creation of industrial zoning areas

    C. Stated that every citizen of Britain had land rights, regardless of gender or ethnicity

    D. It created legal property rights to land that was previously considered common without the request of parliament

    E. None of the above

47. **How did Britain's Agricultural Revolution influence the industrial Revolution?**
    (The Industrial Revolution)

    A. It did not influence the industrial Revolution

    B. It started strife between industrial merchants and agricultural suppliers; often leading to bloody conflicts.

    C. Increased levels of technology produced less jobs.

    D. Increased levels of food increased population. The rise in productivity accelerated the decline of the agricultural share of the labor force, adding to the urban workforce

    E. Decreased levels of technology and increased jobs

48. **A number of technological advances throughout the 18th century made possible the large-scale production of which of the following?**
(The Industrial Revolution)

   A. Weaponry

   B. Ships

   C. Money

   D. Textiles

   E. Furniture

49. **What was one cause of the Industrial Revolution?**
(The Industrial Revolution)

   A. Embargo Act of 1807

   B. Treaty of Tripoli

   C. The Stamp Act

   D. The Revolutionary War

   E. Agricultural decline

50. **What was one effect of the Industrial Revolution?**
(The Industrial Revolution)

   A. The emergence of the middle class

   B. Manufacturing decreased

   C. Trade decreased

   D. Longer transportation times

   E. Population of lower class increased

51. **What two new classes did the Industrial Revolution create?**

   A. Republicans and Liberals

   B. merchants, and slaves

   C. bourgeoisie and land owners

   D. capitalists and the workers

   E. lower and middle

52. **Industrialization led to the creation of**
(The Industrial Revolution)

   A. factories

   B. boats

   C. wooden houses

   D. leather

   E. paper

53. **What did the Reform Bill of 1832 do for Great Britain society?**
(Political and Cultural Developments, 1815-1848)

   A. It redistributed the districts to reflect population changes and changed voting qualifications

   B. It made women eligible to work and vote.

   C. Allowed workers to be compensated for work injuries

   D. Abolished child labor

   E. Allowed aristocrats more use of common lands

54. **Republicans in 1815-1840 sought**
    (Political and Cultural Developments, 1815-1848)

    A. economic equality for all

    B. support from monarchies

    C. land in the Middle East

    D. complete political equality in the form of universal suffrage

    E. government control

55. **Jeremy Bentham is said to be the founder of?**
    (Political and Cultural Developments, 1815-1848)

    A. conservatism

    B. socialism

    C. modern utilitarianism

    D. liberalism

    E. economics

56. **What two countries did classic liberalism begin in?**
    (Political and Cultural Developments, 1815-1848)

    A. Britain and France

    B. Germany and France

    C. Prussia and Belgium

    D. Spain and France

    E. Russia and Prussia

57. **Classic liberalism consisted of mostly:**
    (Political and Cultural Developments, 1815-1848)

    A. businessman and professionals

    B. the lower class

    C. aristocrats

    D. nobility

    E. slaves

58. **What is the definition of Nationalism?**
    (Political and Cultural Developments, 1815-1848)

    A. the idea that one's own nation-state is abysmal

    B. based on the premise that the individual's loyalty and devotion to the nation-state surpass other individual or group interests

    C. complete universal equality

    D. all states are equal

    E. the attitude or policy of placing the interests of the entire world above those of individual nations

59. **Conservatism argues**
    (Political and Cultural Developments, 1815-1848)

    A. for prudent and gradual change to be made as slowly as possible.

    B. for no change

    C. for quick social changes

    D. that society should promote distribution of wealth

    E. for the ending of government

60. **What is the definition of socialism?**
    (Political and Cultural Developments, 1815-1848)

    A. small government

    B. complete political equality in the form of universal suffrage

    C. that one person should rule over a large mass

    D. no government

    E. economic equality for all

61. **What best describes the idea of *Laissez Faire*?**
    (Political and Cultural Developments, 1815-1848)

    A. when all of society is controlled by the government

    B. is an economic system in which transactions between private parties are free from government interference

    C. when government is done away with

    D. the term the men were called when fighting in the French Revolution

    E. is an economic system in which transactions between private parties are dependent on government interference

62. **Charles Fourier created "phalansteries." What were they?**
(Political and Cultural Developments, 1815-1848)

   A. groups in which everyone would be able to do whatever work they wanted and all be paid the same wages

   B. areas were absolute anarchy was enforced

   C. houses where socialism could be practiced

   D. military forces that would usually invade small nation-sates and set up governments that revolved around socialism

   E. none of the above

63. **What happened on the "July Days" of 1830?**
(Political and Cultural Developments, 1815-1848)

   A. Queen Elizabeth I married into Charles X dynasty

   B. The Belgium rebellion broke out

   C. French stormed Bastille

   D. Napoleon became emperor

   E. the Bourbon King, Charles X, was overthrown and replaced by Louis-Philippe, Duke of Orléans

64. **What was so significant?**
(Political and Cultural Developments, 1815-1848)

   A. King Louis head was taken off

   B. A Belgium constitution was created that protected individual freedom

   C. the substitution of the principle of popular sovereignty for hereditary right

   D. the first English-French royal connection was created

   E. the beginning of the French empire had begun

65. **What 19th century ideology closely resembles "conservatism" in the United States today?**
(Political and Cultural Developments, 1815-1848)

   A. Conservatism

   B. Liberalism

   C. Socialism

   D. Anarchism

   E. Republicanism

66. **What was Karl Marx and Friedrich Engels most notable work in 1848?**
    (Political and Cultural Developments, 1815-1848)

    A. *The Communist Manifesto*

    B. *The Difference Between the Democritean and Epicurean Philosophy of Nature*

    C. *Atheistic Archives*

    D. "Introduction to a Contribution to the Critique of Hegel's Philosophy of Right"

    E. *Capital*

67. **What was the first country to implement a government social welfare system?**
    (Politics and Diplomacy in the Age of Nationalism, 1850—1914)

    A. Sweden

    B. England

    C. France

    D. Germany

    E. Russia

68. **What two European countries (one having over 310 nation-states) was unified in 1871?**
    (Politics and Diplomacy in the Age of Nationalism, 1850—1914)

    A. Italy and France

    B. Poland and Prussia

    C. Germany and Italy

    D. Serbia and Bosnia

    E. Austria and Ottoman Empire

69. **What type of government did Austria-Hungary have?**
    (Politics and Diplomacy in the Age of Nationalism, 1850—1914)

    A. Dictatorship

    B. Dual monarchy

    C. Republic

    D. Democracy

    E. Socialist

70. **What was the Compromise of 1867?**
(Politics and Diplomacy in the Age of Nationalism, 1850—1914)

   A. established Prussia as a nation east of Leipzig

   B. established the dual monarchy of Austria-Hungary.

   C. Napoleon III was forced to empty his troops and be exiled

   D. Serbia and Herzegovina became a nation

   E. Ottoman Empire was unified

71. **What inspired Russia to make its "Great Reforms"?**
(Politics and Diplomacy in the Age of Nationalism, 1850—1914)

   A. Napoleons death

   B. the loss of the Russo-Japanese War

   C. Russian nationalism rebellion

   D. Communism rebellion

   E. the loss of the Crimea War of 1853-1856

72. **What did the Emancipation Reform of 1861 mean for serfs in Russia?**
(Politics and Diplomacy in the Age of Nationalism, 1850—1914)

   A. emancipation (abolition of serfdom)

   B. extensive suppression

   C. emigration

   D. increased debt

   E. decreased food

73. **Otto von Bismarck gave himself the title ____ of Germany.**
(Politics and Diplomacy in the Age of Nationalism, 1850—1914)

   A. fuhrer

   B. konig

   C. herr

   D. chancellor

   E. royal highness

74. **What ended the balance of power which was created in Vienna?**
(Politics and Diplomacy in the Age of Nationalism, 1850—1914)

   A. British imperialism

   B. French industrialization

   C. Russian industrialization

   D. German unification

   E. French imperialism

75. **What war weakened France's industrialization, ended Napoleons III reign, and brought forth a republic?**
    (Politics and Diplomacy in the Age of Nationalism, 1850—1914)

    A. Franco-Prussian War

    B. World War I

    C. The Revolution

    D. British-French War

    E. Austria-Prussian War

76. **What country separated in church and state in 1905?**

    A. Great Britain

    B. France

    C. Germany

    D. Austria

    E. Denmark

77. **In Karl Marx's book, *Capital,* he states, "they wish to prevent the price of labor-power from falling below its value." Who is "they"?**
    (Politics and Diplomacy in the Age of Nationalism, 1850—1914)

    A. government

    B. citizens

    C. unions

    D. enterprises

    E. administrators

78. **What was the first country to legalize labor Unions in 1824?**
    (Politics and Diplomacy in the Age of Nationalism, 1850—1914)

    A. France

    B. England

    C. Germany

    D. Belgium

    E. Russia

79. **What is a social and economic system characterized by social ownership and/or social control of the means of production and co-operative management of the economy?**
    (Politics and Diplomacy in the Age of Nationalism, 1850—1914)

    A. Socialism

    B. Communism

    C. Anarchism

    D. Sysco-Anarchism

    E. Democratic

80. **What was the Paris Commune of 1871?**
    (Politics and Diplomacy in the Age of Nationalism, 1850—1914)

    A. a decree that removed all socialists from Paris and moved them to a nearby commune (St. Felix)

    B. the fist socialist party in France

    C. a radical socialistic group that governed Paris for two months after the Franco-Prussian war.

    D. a radical communist group that governed Paris after the Franco-Prussian war

    E. a radical democratic group that governed Paris after the Franco-Prussian war

81. **Why did most European powers let the Ottoman Empire, no matter how weak, in keep dominion over the Balkan Peninsula in the late 19th century?**
    (Politics and Diplomacy in the Age of Nationalism, 1850—1914)

    A. It was an economic death trap

    B. To keep with the Ottoman-European compact

    C. The land was desolate

    D. to keep the balance of power

    E. They didn't let the Ottoman Empire keep the Balkans.

82. **What did the Three Emperors League consist of?**
    (Politics and Diplomacy in the Age of Nationalism, 1850—1914)

    A. Russia, China, North Korea

    B. Germany, Russia, Austria-Hungary

    C. Germany, France, Britain

    D. Austria-Hungary, Italy, Russia

    E. Germany, Russia, Italy

83. **Which is the best definition of Imperialism?**
(Economy, Culture, and Imperialism, 1850-1914)

A. the term referring only to British dominion in the 18th and 19th century

B. a feeling that people have of being loyal to and proud of their country often with the belief that it is better and more important than other countries

C. when one monarchy takes over another monarchy

D. when one republic takes over another republic

E. the takeover of a country or territory by a stronger nation with the intent of dominating the economic, political and social life of the people of that nation

84. **Between 1700 and 1900, Europe's population increased from about**
(Economy, Culture, and Imperialism, 1850-1914)

A. 10,000-40,000

B. 100,000-400,000

C. 1 million-4 million

D. 10 million- 40 million

E. 100 million- 400 million

85. **What is a world economy?**
(Economy, Culture, and Imperialism, 1850-1914)

A. The amount of global suppression on trade in goods, services, and money worldwide

B. the amount of global revenue

C. the description of the integration of trade in goods, services, and money worldwide

D. European interaction with money

E. none of the above

86. **A group of people who leave their native country to form in a new land a settlement subject to, or connected with, the parent nation is a**
(Economy, Culture, and Imperialism, 1850-1914)

A. colony

B. republic

C. military settlement

D. fort

E. refugee zone

87. What invention allowed Europeans to travel into the interior of Africa in the early 1800's?
(Economy, Culture, and Imperialism, 1850-1914)

   A. muskets

   B. leather based shoes

   C. English saddles

   D. steam boat

   E. machetes

88. From the British victory at the Battle of Plassey who became the leading power in India until 1858?
(Economy, Culture, and Imperialism, 1850-1914)

   A. East India Trading Company

   B. The Virginia Company

   C. West India Trading company

   D. Royal Tees

   E. Great Britain Monarch

89. 80 percent of Europeans, including agricultural works, urban laborers, and skilled artisans, belonged to what class from 1850-1914?
(Economy, Culture, and Imperialism, 1850-1914)

   A. group

   B. the middle class

   C. mass assembly

   D. mass society

   E. civilization

90. Why were departments stores created?
(Economy, Culture, and Imperialism, 1850-1914)

   A. mass leisure

   B. socialism

   C. communism

   D. tyranny

   E. mass education

91. What was the Movement in art and literature called in the mid to late 19th century that rejected the subjective, emotional, exotic characteristics of Romanticism. Instead, artists and writers concentrated on observable, contemporary reality?
    (Economy, Culture, and Imperialism, 1850-1914)

    A. Barbizon School

    B. Cubism

    C. Expressionism

    D. Realism

    E. Pop Art

92. What is the belief that philosophical thinking begins with the human subject—not merely the thinking subject, but the acting, feeling, living human individual?
    (Economy, Culture, and Imperialism, 1850-1914)

    A. Marxism

    B. Phenomenology

    C. Existentialism

    D. Objectivism

    E. German Idealism

93. What were sepoys?
    (Economy, Culture, and Imperialism, 1850-1914)

    A. Indian militants

    B. snakes

    C. African militants

    D. African spheres made from bamboo and rock

    E. English boys raised in India

94. Who fought is the Boer War?
    (Economy, Culture, and Imperialism, 1850-1914)

    A. France and Italy

    B. Germany and Austria-Hungary

    C. Germany and Britain

    D. Britain and Boers

    E. Germany and Boers

95. By 1914 only what two African nations remained free from European control?
    (Economy, Culture, and Imperialism, 1850-1914)

    A. West Africa and Egypt

    B. Libya and Egypt

    C. Congo and Angola

    D. Libya and Ethiopia

    E. There were no countries that were not controlled by European powers

96. What was the initial cause of World War I?
    (The First World War and the Russian Revolution)

    A. the German invasion of Belgium

    B. the assassination of Archduke Franz Ferdinand

    C. the German invasion of Poland

    D. Germany declaration of war on Russia

    E. the assassination of King Alexander I Obrenović

97. What nations did the Triple Entente consist of?
    (The First World War and the Russian Revolution)

    A. Italy, Austria-Hungary, and Germany

    B. Russia, Italy, and Germany

    C. Russia, France, and Britain

    D. United States, France, and Britain

    E. Italy, Germany, and Ottoman Empire

98. What was not a reason for World War I?
    (The First World War and the Russian Revolution)

    A. nationalism across Europe

    B. racism towards Jews

    C. unresolved territory disputes

    D. intricate system of alliances

    E. breakdown of balance of power

99. What treaty ended the war between Germany and allied powers and required Germany to make significant territorial concessions. These were primarily along its eastern and western borders?
    (The First World War and the Russian Revolution)

    A. Treaty of Versailles

    B. Treaties of the Weimar Republic

    C. Arms Trade Treaty

    D. Treaties of the German Empire

    E. Treaty of Paris

100. What western power country's economy was better after World War I had ended?
(The First World War and the Russian Revolution)

   A. Britain

   B. Ottoman Empire

   C. Russia

   D. France

   E. United States

101. Women in World War I:
(The First World War and the Russian Revolution)

   A. drafted into the civilian work force to replace conscripted men or work in greatly expanded munitions factories.

   B. forced to look after their children

   C. saw combat in every country but Russia

   D. took on political offices

   E. none of the above

102. What country was created at the end of WWI?
(The First World War and the Russian Revolution)

   A. Bosnia

   B. Serbia

   C. Finland

   D. France

   E. Russian Empire

103. What country disappeared after WWI?
(The First World War and the Russian Revolution)

   A. Ottoman Empire

   B. Great Britain

   C. United States

   D. Italy

   E. Romania

104. What was the first international organization whose principal mission was to maintain world peace?
(The First World War and the Russian Revolution)

   A. European Union

   B. United Nations

   C. Great Powers

   D. League of Nations

   E. The League of Allies

105. **What dismantled the Tsarist autocracy in Russia?**
(The First World War and the Russian Revolution)

    A. The Hessich Revolt

    B. World War II

    C. The February Revolution

    D. The Russian Civil War

    E. World War I

106. **What was the name of the radical wing of the Russian Social Democratic Labor party, favoring revolutionary tactics to achieve full socialization and, under the leadership of Ulyanov (Lenin)?**
(The First World War and the Russian Revolution)

    A. Revolutionists

    B. Republicans

    C. Bolsheviks

    D. Righties

    E. Stalinist

107. **What dismantled the interim dual government and established the Soviet Union?**
(The First World War and the Russian Revolution)

    A. World War II

    B. The February Revolution

    C. The Bolshevik Revolution

    D. World War I

    E. The Hessich Revolt

108. **Why was the generation after World War I labeled "the lost generation?"**
(Europe between the Wars, the Great Depression)

    A. because of the amount of intellectual elites that became causalities during the war.

    B. because people gave up organized religion

    C. because the amount of rebellions

    D. because industrialization had been destroyed

    E. many felt the world was forever "lost"

109. **What was the difference between the League of Nations and the Westphalian System?**
(Europe between the Wars, the Great Depression)

A. the Westphalian System sought to give support to only Asian countries

B. the League of Nations only allowed elite countries

C. the Westphalian succeeded in keeping Europe in peace for one century

D. the secretive nature of the Westphalian System which had led to petty resentments

E. the League of Nations disabled all the armies in Europe

110. **What nation refused to join the League of Nations?**
(Europe between the Wars, the Great Depression)

A. Italy

B. Britain

C. France

D. Belgium

E. The United States

111. **What event initiated the Great Depression?**
(Europe between the Wars, the Great Depression)

A. the end of World War I

B. stock market crash of October 29, 1929

C. gold standard was lowered

D. the Riots of 1929

E. President Hoover coming to office

112. **What was Stalin's initial five-year plan created to serve?**
(Europe between the Wars, the Great Depression)

A. to increase in military mobilization

B. to increase birth rates in Russia

C. industrialization of Russia

D. expanding Russian lands

E. building up damaged monuments. palaces, and other historical sites

113. **What was the name of the country that replaced the old German Republic?**
(Europe between the Wars, the Great Depression)

A. The Weimar Republic

B. Germany

C. Nazi Germany

D. West Germany

E. Unified Germany

114. **What was one cause of the rise of nationalistic governmental rises in Italy and Germany?**
(Europe between the Wars, the Great Depression)

A. imperialism

B. inherent hatred

C. bad deal after Treaty of Versailles

D. animosity towards all Europeans

E. none of the above

115. **What was the immediate cause of World War II?**
(The Second World War and Contemporary Europe)

A. Killing of the Jews

B. Invasion of the Danzig by the Germans

C. Invasion of Switzerland by the Germans

D. Invasion of Poland by the Germans

E. Russian invasion if Baltic Nations.

116. **What immediate event caused the United States to enter World War II?**
(The Second World War and Contemporary Europe)

A. The Attack on Pearl Harbor

B. German invasion of France

C. The sinking of SS Athenia

D. The breaking of the Treaty of Versailles

E. American nationalism provoked congress to go forward on behalf of the killing of the Jews

117. **What did the United Nations agree on to prevent a third World War?**
(The Second World War and Contemporary Europe)

    A. outlaw on wars of aggression

    B. outlaw German access to military

    C. outlaw radical communism, fascism, and socialism

    D. outlaw nuclear armament

    E. outlaw Germany industrialization

118. **After what war was 70% of all industrial infrastructure destroyed?**
(The Second World War and Contemporary Europe)

    A. World War I

    B. World War II

    C. Revolutionary War

    D. Napoleonic Wars

    E. The Austrian Succession

119. **What art movement was both a reaction against Abstract Expressionism, which was seen as too elitist and non-objective, as well as a celebration of postwar consumer culture?**
(The Second World War and Contemporary Europe)

    A. Expressionism

    B. Cubism

    C. Romanticism

    D. Pop Art

    E. Minimalism

120. **During the Cold War Era the United States and the Soviet Union did not become involved in direct military conflict mainly because of**
(The Second World War and Contemporary Europe)

    A. economic failures

    B. the Soviets military was too small to make a direct attack

    C. fear of nuclear war

    D. there was no conflicts

    E. they were forced allies

WESTERN CIVILIZATION II

ANSWER KEY

Question Number	Correct Answer	Your Answer
1	A	
2	C	
3	E	
4	E	
5	A	
6	A	
7	C	
8	A	
9	B	
10	B	
11	B	
12	E	
13	C	
14	C	
15	A	
16	E	
17	C	
18	A	
19	B	
20	A	
21	E	
22	C	
23	C	
24	D	
25	A	
26	D	
27	A	
28	A	
29	D	
30	D	
31	A	
32	B	
33	A	
34	C	
35	A	
36	B	
37	D	
38	E	
39	A	
40	B	

Question Number	Correct Answer	Your Answer
41	C	
42	D	
43	A	
44	C	
45	A	
46	D	
47	D	
48	D	
49	A	
50	A	
51	D	
52	A	
53	A	
54	D	
55	C	
56	D	
57	A	
58	B	
59	A	
60	E	
61	B	
62	A	
63	E	
64	C	
65	B	
66	A	
67	D	
68	C	
69	B	
70	B	
71	E	
72	A	
73	D	
74	D	
75	A	
76	B	
77	C	
78	B	
79	A	
80	C	

Question Number	Correct Answer	Your Answer
81	D	
82	B	
83	E	
84	E	
85	C	
86	A	
87	D	
88	A	
89	D	
90	A	
91	D	
92	C	
93	A	
94	D	
95	D	
96	B	
97	C	
98	B	
99	A	
100	E	
101	A	
102	C	
103	A	
104	D	
105	C	
106	C	
107	C	
108	A	
109	D	
110	E	
111	B	
112	C	
113	A	
114	C	
115	D	
116	A	
117	A	
118	B	
119	D	
120	C	

WESTERN CIVILIZATION II

RATIONALES

1. **What was the initial reason the Thirty Year War began?**
   (Absolutism and Constitutionalism 1648-1715)

   A. Protestantism opposition to Roman Catholicism domination in the Netherlands and Germany

   B. French imperialism over Nordic European countries

   C. Roman Catholicism opposition to Protestantism domination in the Netherlands and Germany

   D. Spanish imperialism over France

   E. Spanish protestant churches revolted

The answer is A.
The reasons for the war go back to the Reformation. However, at this time the Holy Roman Empire (Catholic) was located in modern day Germany and as far north as the Netherlands. These regions were had large protestant populations. Both sects were very hostile. Though France entered the war it was for other reasons (at this point the war became less about religion). The initial reason for war was an age old conflict between the church. Answers D and E are incorrect because Spain had nothing to do with the war in the beginning.

WESTERN CIVILIZATION II

2. **What principle was the result of the end of the Thirty Year War at the Treaty of Westphalia in 1648?**
   (Absolutism and Constitutionalism 1648-1715)

   A. That religion was more powerful than politics

   B. National dominion was clearly resilient and remained to serve as the basis for the system on imperialism and colonialism

   C. State sovereignty emerged and serves as the basis for the modern system of nation-states

   D. That state sovereignty could not work

   E. That politics were more powerful than religion

The answer is C.
The Netherlands gained independence from Spain, Sweden gained control of the Baltic and France was acknowledged as the preeminent Western power. The power of the Holy Roman Emperor was broken and the German states were again able to determine the religion of their lands. Each nation could practice whatever religion they wanted. Therefore, B and D is wrong. A and E had nothing to with winning the war.

3. **What type monarchical government, such as Louis XIV of France government, has absolute power among his or her people, wielding unrestricted political power over the sovereign state and its people?**
   (Absolutism and Constitutionalism 1648-1715)

   A. Tyrannical Monarchism

   B. Constitutional Monarchism

   C. Monarchism

   D. Aristocracy Monarchism

   E. Absolute Monarchism

The answer is E.
A is wrong because tyrants terrorize the people (tyranny and monarchism are different), B is limited power, C is vague, and D is a combination of constitution, democracy, aristocracy and monarchism.

4. **What is a document outlining the fundamental laws and principles that govern a nation.**
   (Absolutism and Constitutionalism 1648-1715)

   A. Judicial Review

   B. Canon Law

   C. Treaty

   D. Parliament document

   E. Constitution

The answer is E.
A is a system of the court. B is a body of laws. C is an agreement among on other nations. D is not specific.

5. **What is the Glorious Revolution?**
   (Absolutism and Constitutionalism 1648-1715)

   A. Event against King James II (sometimes called the bloodless revolution) that consisted of Whig and Tories forcing him to leave

   B. Religious reformers from Calvinist and Luther sects fight a bloody reformation against Anglicans

   C. French imperialist come to England and displace King James II

   D. French revolutionist come to England and displace King James II

   E. Dutch Republic solidify Catholicism by force.

The answer is A.
The Revolution of 1688 is when the Dutch state holder William successful invaded England. B through E nations had nothing to do with England at the time.

WESTERN CIVILIZATION II

6. What was one outcome of the English Revolution?
(Absolutism and Constitutionalism 1648-1715)

    A. Bill of Rights of 1689 created

    B. English sovereignty over the Dutch Republic

    C. English constitution of 1690 created

    D. Parliament created

    E. King James II remained in power

The answer is A.
Bill of Rights laid down limits on the monarchy. B is not right because the Dutch invaded. C and D were already created. E is not right because King James the II lost the war and forced to leave.

7. What was one outcome of the War of the Austrian Succession?
(Absolutism and Constitutionalism 1648-1715)

    A. Prussia and France became allies

    B. France and Britain became allies

    C. Prussia became a prominent world leader

    D. Austria lost its sovereignty

    E. The war ended all wars

The answer is C.
Prussia won was one of the winners of the war. It gave them a chance to unify German states (German states came to Prussia under the guise of protection). Britain was enemies against France and Prussia, so A and B is wrong. Austria gained its sovereignty. Clearly there have been other wars since then.

WESTERN CIVILIZATION II

8. **Define Boyars:**
   (Absolutism and Constitutionalism 1648-1715)

   A. a member of the old aristocracy in Russia, next in rank to a prince

   B. a member of the Austrian aristocracy

   C. a reformer in the Russian Orthodox church

   D. a member belonging by rank, title, or birth to the aristocracy in the British parliament

   E. an agricultural laborer bound by the feudal system who was tied to working on his lord's estate

The answer is A.
Boyar was part of the aristocracy of Russia, therefore, B and D are wrong because they do not describe Russia. C and E describe the wrong class.

9. **Peter the Great revolutionized Russia by**
   (Absolutism and Constitutionalism 1648-1715)

   A. Introducing communism

   B. Introducing western ideas on education, economy, culture, politics, and military exploits

   C. Allying itself with Nordic countries such as Sweden

   D. Introducing eastern ideas on education, economy, culture, politics, and military exploits

   E. Establishing the Roman Catholic church

The answer is B.
Peter the Great was one of the first of his kind. He tried to tie monarchism and the revolutionary thoughts together. A is wrong because he was a king (therefore, believed in monarchism). C is wrong because he invaded Finland. D represents the Soviet Union. And E is wrong because the majority of Russia was Orthodox.

WESTERN CIVILIZATION II

10. What was one main difference between western European powers economies in the 18th century than in the 17th century?
    (Competition for Empire and Economic Expansion)

    A. Wealth is gold and silver

    B. Free trade will create the best world

    C. There was finite amounts of wealth

    D. Mercantilism ideals

    E. Government should control economy

The answer is B.
Free trade was revolutionary. Countries began creating larger revenue because they could sell and resources that were earlier not possible of acquiring. A is wrong because wealth has always been gold and silver. C through D remained the same.

11. What is the political ideologies, led by Adam Smith and John Locke, called that advocates civil liberties and political freedom with representative democracy under the rule of law and emphasizes economic freedom?
    (Competition for Empire and Economic Expansion)

    A. Liberalism

    B. Classical Liberalism

    C. Modern Liberalism

    D. Democratic Liberalism

    E. Conservative Liberalism

The answer is B.
Those that believed in classical liberalism believed government had been created by individuals to protect themselves from one another, and that the purpose of government should be to minimize conflict between individuals that would otherwise arise in a state of nature. A is to vague. C, D, E are now the opposite.

WESTERN CIVILIZATION II

12. **What was one main difference in France and Britain after the treaty of Utrecht in 1714?**
    (Competition for Empire and Economic Expansion)

    A. Monarchism spread in Britain and Conservatism in France

    B. French became rich while Britain became poor

    C. Britain stopped colonizing, while France increased in colonization

    D. Communism spread in France and socialism in Britain

    E. Absolutism spread in France and Constitutionalism in Britain.

The answer is E.
Louis XIV of France created absolute power while Britain created a constitution. A is wrong because Monarchism powers were weekend in Britain at this time. B is wrong because Britain became powerful. C and D are wrong because they at the wrong times.

13. **What did the Treaty of Utrecht mean for Europe?**
    (Competition for Empire and Economic Expansion)

    A. It kept the Dutch from taking over Europe

    B. It stopped the English from invading Spain

    C. It ended French hegemony and kept the balance of power

    D. It ended the subjugation of Russia and started the empire of Portugal

    E. The union of Versailles was created

The answer is C.
France had more power. After their loss it created the balance of powers. A, B, and D are all wrong them because it would impact the balance of power. And the union of Versailles doesn't exist.

14. **Why did populations in major western nations grow so rapidly in the 18th century?**
    (Competition for Empire and Economic Expansion)

    A. Society began to share wealth amongst poorer classes

    B. Humans had more children at earlier ages

    C. Humans became better at safeguarding food, creation of new advance medicines; ending of the bubonic plague

    D. The death of textile industries

    E. Populations did not grow, however, decreased

The answer is C.
Bubonic plague destroyed large populations. New technological advancements protected livestock and vegetation and required fewer individuals to work. People began working more industrial jobs and making more money while having more time.
A is wrong because though people were making more money it wasn't from destitution of wealth. B and E are in factual. And D is wrong because textile industry just began.

15. **Why did large European inhabits move towards bigger cities by the 1750s?**
    (Competition for Empire and Economic Expansion)

    A. Textile industry

    B. Open-field system

    C. Wartime atrocities does to farms scared the people

    D. mercantilism

    E. Increase in diseases from rural areas

The answer is A.
With less work on farms because of agriculture movement and industrial factories increasing in the cities, people migrated to the city to obtain one of numerous amounts of jobs being offered at factories

WESTERN CIVILIZATION II

16. **Who was the inventor of deductive reasoning which in turn created the idea if Deism?**
    (The Scientific View of the World)

    A. Leonard Fuchs

    B. Albert Einstein

    C. Galileo Galilie

    D. Samuel Hartlib

    E. Rene Descartes

The Answer is E.
Descartes is said to be the father of deism. Fuchs and Hartib were more physicians and botanists. Einstein came way after idea of deism. Galilei was known for Kinematics, Dynamics, telescopic observational, astronomy, and heliocentrism- not deism.

17. **What scientist created the laws of universal gravitation?**
    (The Scientific View of the World)

    A. Rene Descartes

    B. Leonard Fuchs

    C. Isaac Newton

    D. Samuel Hartlib

    E. John Napier

The answer is C.
Universal states that any two bodies in the universe attract each other with a force that is directly proportional to the product of their masses and inversely proportional to the square of the distance between them.

WESTERN CIVILIZATION II

18. **What used observation and experimentation to explain theories on the workings of the universe such as government, environment, religion, society, and culture? This process removed blind adherence to tradition from science Scientific Revolution.**
    (The Scientific View of the World)

    A. The Scientific Method

    B. Natural Rights

    C. Checks and Balances

    D. Religious Thought

    E. Enlightened Despots

The answer is A.
The Scientific method changed the way people thought in the Revolution. Instead of using faith one would use reasoning. A is wrong because it describes the rights of people. C is wrong because it describes a tactic used in government. D is wrong because it the opposite. E is wrong because it describes royalty that supported enlightenment ideas.

19. **John Locke's book, *Two Treatises of Government*, he explains that all men have Natural Rights, which are**
    (The Scientific View of the World)

    A. Sleep, Eat, and Work

    B. Life, Liberty, and Property

    C. Speech, Writing, and Action

    D. Life, Liberty, and the Pursuit of Happiness

    E. Autonomy, Democracy, and Conventionality

The answer is B.
Rights that people supposedly have under natural law. A, C, and D are random. D is close to being right, however, it is slightly different. It comes from the American constitution.

20. Enlightenment thinker Thomas Hobbes created the idea of Social Contract, which stated that human beings were inherently
    (The Scientific View of the World)

    A. greedy, selfish, and cruel

    B. merciful, caring, and agreeable

    C. powerless

    D. religious, dutiful, and ardent

    E. collective

The answer is A.
Social contract questions of the origin of society and the legitimacy of the authority of the state over the individual. Stating that people are "greedy" puts less trust in say one human being and more trust in a system such as a republic.

21. Which belief stated that man was inherently good but society and its unequal distribution of wealth was problematic?
    (Period of Enlightenment)

    A. Checks and Balances

    B. Absolute Monarch

    C. Individualism

    D. Classic Liberalism

    E. The General Will

The answer is E.
In short, it is the will of the people. A and B have to do with governments. C and D values the freedom of individuals.

22. **This work by Montesquieu called for a separation of powers and heavily influenced the formation of American government**
    (Period of Enlightenment)

    A. Democratic Ideals

    B. Republic

    C. The Spirit of Laws

    D. Liberty Bells

    E. Natural Rights

The Answer is C.
A, B, C, and D were influenced or influenced the American government but the Spirit of Laws formulated the how the American republic would eventually work; with three different separate branches of government.

23. **What is the philosophy stressing the recognition of every person as a valuable individual with inalienable, inborn rights.**
    (Period of Enlightenment)

    A. Humanity

    B. Conformity

    C. Individualism

    D. Democracy

    E. Libertarian

The answer is C.
A and B describe a collective. D is a form of government that uses voting and E are political ideologies that upholds liberty as its principal objective; both wrong.

24. **What is the separation of powers?**
    (Period of Enlightenment)

    A. The belief that on country should not have more/less power than another

    B. The concept that all governments should become one universal order

    C. The idea that monarchies have all the power and the people should have none, therefore, separating their powers

    D. The idea that power in government should be divided into separate branches in order to ensure that no one branch of a governing body can gain too much authority

    E. The ideas that no government is the best government

The answer is D.
Separation of powers is the idea the United States has for their government; three branches of government. A, B, C and D are wrong because they describe either the wrong type of system and they don't describe how the government works.

WESTERN CIVILIZATION II

25. **What was the main difference between monarchies prior to the Enlightenment and those during who practiced Enlightened Absolutism**
    (Period of Enlightenment)

    A. Those during the Enlightenment tended to allow religious toleration, freedom of speech and the press, and the right to hold private property. Most fostered the arts, sciences, and education.

    B. Those prior to the Enlightenment tended to allow religious toleration, freedom of speech and the press, and the right to hold private property. Most fostered the arts, sciences, and education

    C. Leaders that practiced ideals of Enlightened Absolutism were extremely intolerable. Any new forms of religion, culture, freedom speech, press, and the ability to hold private property were all banned.

    D. Monarchies prior to the Enlightenment believed more so in rational thinking rather than belief in in an outside divinity.

    E. None of the above, they were absolutely the same. Only thinkers and philosophers ideals were changing during these periods.

The answer is A.
Kings/queens, such as Peter the Great, tied enlightenment ideas together with monarchy. B is wrong because many leaders before the Revolution were intolerable. C is wrong because leaders were comparably tolerable than past leaders. D is wrong because monarchs put their faith usually in divinities. E is wrong because the Revolution influenced everyone.

26. **What is the idea of Devine Right?**
    (Period of Enlightenment)

    A. That lords were allowed to take the newly wife of any of its servants for the first night

    B. That the God had appointed the people to rule

    C. That no one held rights except for the monarch

    D. That monarchs were appointed and held their office by the grace of God

    E. That only leaders of parliament were appointed by God

The answer is D.
The belief that kings/queens are picked by God. This was very popular in the 15-16th century. A, B, C, and D, all actually happened, however none have to do with sovereigns in power.

WESTERN CIVILIZATION II

27. **How was the Polish Enlightenment different than Western countries such as Prussia or France?**
    (Period of Enlightenment)

    A. Those in the west wrote about the need for more checks and balances on their kings, Polish Enlightenment was geared towards fighting the abuses stemming from too many checks and balances

    B. The Polish Enlightenment boasted no real political shifts

    C. Not one enlightened theory came from Poland

    D. There was no bloodshed over the governmental takeover of the libertarian parties. King Stanisław August Poniatowski voluntarily stepped own

    E. Western powers ideals on Enlightenment were based on reasoning while Polish scholars still based ideas on divinity.

The answer is A.
Polish kings were elected and their position was very weak, with most of the powers in the hands of the parliament. Polish reforms desired the elimination of laws that transformed their system into a near-anarchy. B is wrong because the monarchy was dislodged and C is incorrect because writers, such as Franciszek Bohomolec, wrote many theories based on the Revolution enlightenment thought. D is wrong because King Stanisław August Poniatowski was forced out of Poland by war. E is wrong because the enlightenment theories were based on the same as the other revolutionaries.

28. **What proceeded to happen after the third Partition of Poland?**
    (Period of Enlightenment)

    A. Russia took over and became the most powerful portioning power in Poland. Enlightenment supporters were forced to flee the country

    B. France became the most powerful nation in Europe

    C. Poland was revolutionized by Enlightenment thinkers and a true democracy was short lived

    D. Prussia, France, and Russia split Poland

    E. Poland remained a monarchy

The answer is A.
It ended Polish–Lithuanian national sovereignty until 1918. C and E are incorrect because Poland was taken over by Russia. B is incorrect because France loses war to British, Austrians, and Spanish. Time of balance of powers begin. D refers to World War II; therefore, incorrect.

WESTERN CIVILIZATION II

29. What changed during the French Revolution in the political sphere?
(Revolution and Napoleonic Europe)

    A. King Louis XVI's monarchy was empowered

    B. All high ranking members of the French aristocracy became Lords of several pieces of lands

    C. Taxes were raised

    D. It abolished the feudal system and absolute monarchy

    E. Conservative republicanism was implanted

The answer is D.
King Loius XVI got his head chopped off and the French monarchy was destroyed. A, B, and C are incorrect because they refer to a monarchical government. Conservative republicanism was not around at this time.

30. What concepts influenced the French Revolution?
(Revolution and Napoleonic Europe)

    A. Totalitarianism

    B. Romanticism

    C. Socialistic and domesticate rights

    D. Popular sovereignty and inalienable rights.

    E. Classicism

The answer is D.
Poplar sovereignty is the principle that the authority of the government is created and sustained by the consent of its people, through their elected representatives and inalienable rights are rights that cannot be repealed or restrained by human laws. All others are incorrect because they fail to describe the liberalism that influenced so many people in the revolution.

31. Why did the French Revolution begin?
(Revolution and Napoleonic Europe)

    A. Extravagant lifestyles of the monarchy brought France to the verge of bankruptcy

    B. Maria Antoinette statement, "let them eat cake," infused rage in Parisians

    C. King Louis XVI was assonated and had no known heir

    D. German insurgents invaded eastern France

    E. It was a phenomena. No one knows the cause.

The answer is A.
The old regime was brought down, partly by its own rigidity in the face of a changing world, partly by the ambitions of a rising bourgeoisie, allied with aggrieved peasants and wage-earners and with individuals of all classes who were influenced by the ideas of the Enlightenment. The French had aided the Americans in their own revolution, the success of which gave the concept much validity in France. In 1789 France was bankrupt and unable to cope with growing unrest and other aggravating circumstances. D, B, and C are incorrect because they are historically out of place and partially did not happen. And E is incorrect because there are many reasons why the French Revolution took place.

32. What were the three main classes in 18th Century France?
(Revolution and Napoleonic Europe)

    A. Peasant, Serf, and Noble

    B. First Estate, Second Estate and the Third Estate

    C. Upper, Middle, Lower

    D. Lower, Bourgeoisie, and Aristocrat

    E. Lower, Middle, and Gentry

The answer is B.
The first estate was the clergy. The second estate was the nobility. The third estate was everyone else. A is wrong because refers to the Middle Ages. C is to vague. D and E are incorrect because they leave out nobility.

WESTERN CIVILIZATION II

33. Over 50 countries were affected but the Revolution in Europe in the 19th century. However, they had no coordination or cooperation among the revolutionaries in different countries. What were some shared factors involved:
    (Revolution and Napoleonic Europe)

    A. Demands for more participation in government and democracy; demands for freedom of press; the regrouping of the reactionary forces based on the royalty, the aristocracy, the army, the church and the peasants.

    B. Demands for less participation of peasants; demand for stable monarchy.

    C. Every monarch was destroyed and replaced by a democratic republic.

    D. The working (middle) class always led each revolution

    E. The poor (lower) class always led the revolution

The answer is A.
There were no specific leaders of the movement. Those that were quickly became removed or replaced. B is incorrect because the lower class was involved. The demand was for monarchies to be less involved. Obliviously, as in Poland, not all monarchs were destroyed, so C is incorrect. D and E are incorrect because leaders arose and fell from every social class.

34. In the 1840s what did the term "democracy" mean?
    (Revolution and Napoleonic Europe)

    A. Freedom from government

    B. Consent of the governed and the restriction of church and state power, republican government, freedom of the press and the individual

    C. Universal male suffrage

    D. Uniting people bound by (some mix of) common languages, culture, religion, shared history, and of course immediate geography

    E. More power to workers

The answer is C.
Democracy did not mean necessarily more power to workers or freedom from a government. Democracy is a type of government. However, it was not a tyranny. It brought freedom to only white males at the time in many areas.

35. What did the Corn Laws of 1815 enact?
(Revolution and Napoleonic Europe)

   A. imposed restrictions and tariffs on imported grain in Great Britain

   B. restricted farmers from growing only a limited amount of grain products in Great Britain

   C. ratified taxes on grains in United States

   D. decreed every household was allotted one bushel of grain from the government yearly in Germany

   E. restricted grain trade in United States

The answer is A.
The Corn Laws were enforced in the United Kingdom between 1815 and 1846. They imposed restrictions and tariffs on imported grain. They were designed to keep grain prices high to favor domestic producers. Based on this B through E are incorrect.

36. What was the Frankfurt Parliament in 1848?
(Revolution and Napoleonic Europe)

   A. The Assembly of German Aristocrats

   B. The first freely elected parliament in Germany

   C. The Prussian monarchies assembly

   D. The first Belgian freely elected parliament

   E. It was a treaty that sectioned off the southern part of Germany (Bavaria and Saxon) to the Austrians

The answer is B.
The session was held from 18 May 1848 to 31 May 1849. Its existence was both part of and the result of the "March Revolution" in the states of the German Confederation. A is the wrong name. C and D are the wrong nation. And E never happened.

WESTERN CIVILIZATION II

37. Which country did NOT experience a Revolution in 1848?
(Revolution and Napoleonic Europe)

    A. France

    B. Denmark

    C. Poland

    D. Russia

    E. Italy

The answer is D.
The Russian enlightenment was different than the western nations. The revolution was more focused on modernization. However, this was before the French Revolution. The revolution never met Russia.

38. How far east did Napoleon Empire reach in Europe?
(Revolution and Napoleonic Europe)

    A. Russia

    B. Germany

    C. Austria

    D. Denmark

    E. Poland

The answer is E.
Napoleon tried to make his way into Russia but was eventually beat by the immense causalities at the Battle of Borodino, the retreat from Moscow, and the Russian winter. Poland was as far East as he could make it. At its height in 1812, the French Empire had 130 departments, ruled over 70 million subjects, maintained an extensive military presence in Germany, Italy, Spain, and the Duchy of Warsaw, and could count Prussia and Austria as nominal allies.

WESTERN CIVILIZATION II

39. **What was the French civil code established in 1804 that forbade privileges based on birth, allowed freedom of religion, and specified that government jobs should go to the most qualified?**
(Revolution and Napoleonic Europe)

   A. Napoleonic Code

   B. Natural Rights

   C. French Code

   D. Bill of Rights

   E. Rights

The answer is A.
It was established under Napoléon in 1804. The code prohibited privileges based on birth, allowed freedom of religion, and specified that government jobs should go to the most qualified. B, C, and E were not laws. D is incorrect because it is a list of the most important rights to the citizens of a country, most notably in England and the United States.

40. **What were the series of major conflicts (1803-1815) pitting the French Empire led by Emperor Napoleon I against an array of European powers formed into various coalitions?**
(Revolution and Napoleonic Europe)

   A. The Great War

   B. Napoleonic Wars

   C. The Rebellion

   D. The Napoleonic Struggle

   E. The French Wars

The answer is B.
The wars are traditionally seen as a continuation of the Revolutionary Wars, which broke out in 1792 during the French Revolution. Napoleon rose to power. A is incorrect because it refers to World War I. C, D, and E are all made up.

WESTERN CIVILIZATION II

41. Which country was the reason why the first great French Empire collapsed?
(Revolution and Napoleonic Europe)

    A. Great Britain

    B. Austria

    C. Russia

    D. Prussia

    E. Napoleon never lost

The answer is C.
The French dominion collapsed rapidly after the disastrous invasion of Russia in 1812. Though they technically won most of the battles, they could not replenish their military as quick as the Russians. After retreating from Moscow, they went from 400,000 (some say up to 700,000) to a meek 25,000. A, B, and C, are wrong because it is the wrong country. And E is wrong because Napoleon lost 7 times.

42. What was the congress of ambassadors of European States that in 1814 arose because of the French Revolution and the Napoleonic Wars?
(Revolution and Napoleonic Europe)

    A. Europeans Allies

    B. NATO

    C. European Union

    D. Congress of Vienna

    E. Congress of Paris

The answer is D.
A conference of ambassadors of European states held in Vienna from September 1814 to June 1815. B and C were inspired by this congress, however they came later. A is incorrect because that it could be attributed to WWII. E is incorrect because that ended the American Revolution.

WESTERN CIVILIZATION II

43. **What was the Congress of Vienna's main objective?**
    (Revolution and Napoleonic Europe)

    A. Congress was to provide a long-term peace plan

    B. To convict Britain of all its atrocities

    C. To unify Europe and invade Asia provinces

    D. To stop revolutions and support monarchies

    E. To serve the peasants of every European country

The answer is A.
The objective of the Congress was to provide a long-term peace plan for Europe by settling critical issues arising from the French Revolutionary Wars and the Napoleonic Wars. The goal was not simply to restore old boundaries, but to resize the main powers so they could balance each other off and remain at peace. Therefore, B is incorrect because the conference were more so about French atrocities. C and E are not factual. The congress was not necessarily for monarchs or republics.

44. **What treaty ended the Napoleonic Wars between France and the Sixth Coalition in 1814?**
    (Revolution and Napoleonic Europe)

    A. Treaty of Vienna

    B. The Sixth Coalition Agreement

    C. Treaty of Paris

    D. Peace of Paris

    E. Second Treaty of Paris

The answer is C.
A document created to produce peace on 30 May, 1814 between France and the United Kingdom, Russia, Austria, and Prussia, and also Portugal and Sweden and Spain (who all signed later in July). A and E were later. B and D are non-factual.

WESTERN CIVILIZATION II

45. **What treaty ended Napoleons rule as emperor in France?**
    (Revolution and Napoleonic Europe)

    A. Treaty of Fontainebleau

    B. Treaty of Paris

    C. Second Treaty of Paris

    D. Treaty of Vienna

    E. The Sixth Coalition Agreement

The answer is A.
Napoleon I and representatives from the Austrian Empire, Russia, and Prussia. The treaty was signed at Paris on 11 April, by the plenipotentiaries of both sides, and ratified by Napoleon on 13 April.[1] With this treaty, the allies ended Napoleon's rule as emperor of France and sent him into exile on Elba.

46. **What was the Enclosure Act?**
    (The Industrial Revolution)

    A. An act that pushed all British citizens north of England into bigger cities

    B. The creation of industrial zoning areas

    C. Stated that every citizen of Britain had land rights, regardless of gender or ethnicity

    D. It created legal property rights to land that was previously considered common without the request of parliament

    E. None of the above

The answer is D.
The United Kingdom enclosed open fields and common land in the country. A is incorrect because the industrial revolution did this. B is incorrect because it was a law involving agriculture. C is incorrect because it had nothing to do with civil rights.

WESTERN CIVILIZATION II

47. **How did Britain's Agricultural Revolution influence the industrial Revolution?**
    (The Industrial Revolution)

    A. It did not influence the industrial Revolution

    B. It started strife between industrial merchants and agricultural suppliers; often leading to bloody conflicts.

    C. Increased levels of technology produced less jobs.

    D. Increased levels of food increased population. The rise in productivity accelerated the decline of the agricultural share of the labor force, adding to the urban workforce

    E. Decreased levels of technology and increased jobs

The answer is D.
Because there was increased levels of food that required less people to make it, more people had time. Thus it created more time for mass production. Therefore A, D, and E are wrong. B is wrong because merchants and agriculturalists worked hand in hand.

48. **A number of technological advances throughout the 18th century made possible the large-scale production of which of the following?**
    (The Industrial Revolution)

    A. Weaponry

    B. Ships

    C. Money

    D. Textiles

    E. Furniture

The answer is D.
Before the 18th century, the manufacture of cloth was performed by individual workers. Innovations in carding and spinning enabled by advances in cast iron technology resulted in the creation of larger spinning mules and water frames. The machinery was housed in water-powered mills on streams.

49. What was one cause of the Industrial Revolution?
(The Industrial Revolution)

    A. Embargo Act of 1807

    B. Treaty of Tripoli

    C. The Stamp Act

    D. The Revolutionary War

    E. Agricultural decline

The answer is A.
The goal was to force Britain and France to respect American rights during the Napoleonic Wars by outlawing trade with both countries. In turn, Britain and France found that they could produce the same material in their own country for cheaper, sparking the Industrial Revolution.

50. What was one effect of the Industrial Revolution?
(The Industrial Revolution)

    A. The emergence of the middle class

    B. Manufacturing decreased

    C. Trade decreased

    D. Longer transportation times

    E. Population of lower class increased

The answer is A.
Industrial Revolution brought higher pay as well as workers got to work less hours. B, C, and D is incorrect because all increased. E is incorrect because lower class decreased.

WESTERN CIVILIZATION II

51. What two new classes did the Industrial Revolution create?

    A. Republicans and Liberals

    B. merchants, and slaves

    C. bourgeoisie and land owners

    D. capitalists and the workers

    E. lower and middle

The answer is D.
The Industrial Revolution created upper class capitalist and middle class workers. These two classes were composed of people that had wealth and success. Even though most could afford goods anyway, the prices lowered even more, so that those who could not afford them before could now enjoy the comfort and convenience of the new products being made.

52. Industrialization led to the creation of
(The Industrial Revolution)

    A. factories

    B. boats

    C. wooden houses

    D. leather

    E. paper

The answer is A.
Capital and space requirements became too great for cottage industry or workshops. B through E are all things that could be mad in the factories but were already around before the inventions of factories.

WESTERN CIVILIZATION II

53. **What did the Reform Bill of 1832 do for Great Britain society?**
    (Political and Cultural Developments, 1815-1848)

    A. It redistributed the districts to reflect population changes and changed voting qualifications

    B. It made women eligible to work and vote.

    C. Allowed workers to be compensated for work injuries

    D. Abolished child labor

    E. Allowed aristocrats more use of common lands

The answer is A.
It changed to the electoral system of England and Wales. Before this each most members nominally represented boroughs. Each borough could be run by one to 15,000 members. Sometimes one person could run a number of boroughs. B through E are all incorrect because they have nothing to do with representation in parliament.

54. **Republicans in 1815-1840 sought**
    (Political and Cultural Developments, 1815-1848)

    A. economic equality for all

    B. support from monarchies

    C. land in the Middle East

    D. complete political equality in the form of universal suffrage

    E. government control

The answer is D.
Republicans believed in social contract, positive law, and mixed government. They also borrowed from, and distinguished republicanism from, the ideas of liberalism that were developing at the same time. Liberalism and republicanism were frequently conflated during this period, because they were both opposed to absolute monarchy. Modern scholars see them as two distinct streams that both contributed to the democratic ideals of the modern world. An important distinction is that, while republicanism continued to stress the importance of civic virtue and the common good, liberalism was based on economics and individualism.

WESTERN CIVILIZATION II

55. Jeremy Bentham is said to be the founder of?
(Political and Cultural Developments, 1815-1848)

    A. conservatism

    B. socialism

    C. modern utilitarianism

    D. liberalism

    E. economics

The answer is C.
Jeremy Bentham defined utility as the aggregate pleasure after deducting suffering of all involved in any action. A, B, and D are all political ideologies that involve government administration. E is incorrect because it is the study of study of the factors that influence income, wealth and well-being.

56. What two countries did classic liberalism begin in?
(Political and Cultural Developments, 1815-1848)

    A. Britain and France

    B. Germany and France

    C. Prussia and Belgium

    D. Spain and France

    E. Russia and Prussia

The answer is D.
Classical liberalism really began to enlarge in the 1820s. However it included thinkers prior, such as John Locke, Jean-Baptiste Say, Thomas Malthus, and David Ricardo. It drew on the economics of Adam Smith and on a belief in natural law, utilitarianism, and progress.

WESTERN CIVILIZATION II

57. **Classic liberalism consisted of mostly:**
    (Political and Cultural Developments, 1815-1848)

    A. businessman and professionals

    B. the lower class

    C. aristocrats

    D. nobility

    E. slaves

The answer is A.
Because of the idea of free trade and politics without the restriction of a monarch it benefited the profit of business men and professionals most. Therefore, all other answers are incorrect.

58. **What is the definition of Nationalism?**
    (Political and Cultural Developments, 1815-1848)

    A. the idea that one's own nation-state is abysmal

    B. based on the premise that the individual's loyalty and devotion to the nation-state surpass other individual or group interests

    C. complete universal equality

    D. all states are equal

    E. the attitude or policy of placing the interests of the entire world above those of individual nations

The answer is B.
Nationalism is a shared group feeling in the significance of a geographical and sometimes demographic region seeking independence for its culture and/or ethnicity that holds that group together. Because of economic calibration nationalism arose all over the western hemisphere from the mid of the 18th century on.

59. **Conservatism argues**
    (Political and Cultural Developments, 1815-1848)

    A. for prudent and gradual change to be made as slowly as possible.

    B. for no change

    C. for quick social changes

    D. that society should promote distribution of wealth

    E. for the ending of government

The answer is A.
A disposition in politics to preserve what is established (Merriam dictionary). Therefore B and C are incorrect. D and E are incorrect because they are reefing to socialism, Marxism, communism, and anarchism.

60. **What is the definition of socialism?**
    (Political and Cultural Developments, 1815-1848)

    A. small government

    B. complete political equality in the form of universal suffrage

    C. that one person should rule over a large mass

    D. no government

    E. economic equality for all

The answer is E.
Socialism in the Meriam dictionary states, "a way of organizing a society in which major industries are owned and controlled by the government rather than by individual people and companies." In Marxist thought it is a way to distribute money equality through all classes of society. A and B are wrong because it represents Republicanism. C us wrong because Monarchism or tyrannicalism. D is incorrect because it represents more of an Anarchistic government.

WESTERN CIVILIZATION II

61. **What best describes the idea of *Laissez Faire*?**
    (Political and Cultural Developments, 1815-1848)

    A. when all of society is controlled by the government

    B. is an economic system in which transactions between private parties are free from government interference

    C. when government is done away with

    D. the term the men were called when fighting in the French Revolution

    E. is an economic system in which transactions between private parties are dependent on government interference

The answer is B.
Reaching as far back as 1681, it is the idea that an economic system should not be restricted by government. Therefore A and E are incorrect. C is more anarchical and D is not factual.

62. **Charles Fourier created "phalansteries." What were they?**
    (Political and Cultural Developments, 1815-1848)

    A. groups in which everyone would be able to do whatever work they wanted and all be paid the same wages

    B. areas were absolute anarchy was enforced

    C. houses where socialism could be practiced

    D. military forces that would usually invade small nation-sates and set up governments that revolved around socialism

    E. none of the above

The answer is A.
It was a type of building designed for a utopian community and developed in the early 19th century by Charles Fourier. Many utopian communities were rising up at this time because of the rise in socialistic theories.

WESTERN CIVILIZATION II

63. What happened on the "July Days" of 1830?
(Political and Cultural Developments, 1815-1848)

    A. Queen Elizabeth I married into Charles X dynasty

    B. The Belgium rebellion broke out

    C. French stormed Bastille

    D. Napoleon became emperor

    E. the Bourbon King, Charles X, was overthrown and replaced by Louis-Philippe, Duke of Orléans

The answer is E.
King Charles X, the French Bourbon monarch, was routed by his cousin Louis-Philippe, Duke of Orléans. C and D are incorrect because this event came afterwards (thus sometimes called the Second French Revolution). A and B are not factual.

64. What was so significant?
(Political and Cultural Developments, 1815-1848)

    A. King Louis head was taken off

    B. A Belgium constitution was created that protected individual freedom

    C. the substitution of the principle of popular sovereignty for hereditary right

    D. the first English-French royal connection was created

    E. the beginning of the French empire had begun

The answer is C.
Supporters of the Bourbon would be called Legitimists, and supporters of Louis Philippe Orléanists. It proved that there was a change in thought about who could be leader of a country. Those who had divine right or those who were voted in. A, B and E are incorrect because that had to do with the First Revolution. D is incorrect because there were many connections throughout the two nations.

WESTERN CIVILIZATION II

65. What 19th century ideology closely resembles "conservatism" in the United States today?
(Political and Cultural Developments, 1815-1848)

    A. Conservatism

    B. Liberalism

    C. Socialism

    D. Anarchism

    E. Republicanism

The answer is B.
Liberals then believed government should be as small as possible to allow the exercise of individual freedoms. C and D want no government or a large government, therefore, incorrect. A wants slow change, which could be attributed however, the conservatives in the 19th Century were in favor of monarchies. E is incorrect because though its consensus was that liberalism of the 19th century it fails to represent conservative economic values today.

66. What was Karl Marx and Friedrich Engels most notable work in 1848?
(Political and Cultural Developments, 1815-1848)

    A. *The Communist Manifesto*

    B. *The Difference Between the Democritean and Epicurean Philosophy of Nature*

    C. *Atheistic Archives*

    D. "Introduction to a Contribution to the Critique of Hegel's Philosophy of Right"

    E. *Capital*

The answer is A.
The Communist Manifesto was a published work by the Communist League in London right before the 1848 Revolution. It speaks of past history and struggle between classes. All other works except for C and D came at a later dat. D was Marx's doctorate thesis. C is not factual.

WESTERN CIVILIZATION II

67. **What was the first country to implement a government social welfare system?**
    (Politics and Diplomacy in the Age of Nationalism, 1850—1914)

    A. Sweden

    B. England

    C. France

    D. Germany

    E. Russia

The answer is D.
Due to the pressure of the workers' movement in the late 19th century, Otto von Bismarck introduced the state social insurance scheme in the 1880s which included Sick Insurance Law, Accident Insurance Law, and Old age and Disability Insurance Law.

68. **What two European countries (one having over 310 nation-states) was unified in 1871?**
    (Politics and Diplomacy in the Age of Nationalism, 1850—1914)

    A. Italy and France

    B. Poland and Prussia

    C. Germany and Italy

    D. Serbia and Bosnia

    E. Austria and Ottoman Empire

The answer is C.
In 1848 both countries became unified. After this the balance of powers was shifted. A and E are wrong because some of these nations were already countries. B and D are wrong because these nations did not become nations until after WW1 and II.

WESTERN CIVILIZATION II

69. **What type of government did Austria-Hungary have?**
    (Politics and Diplomacy in the Age of Nationalism, 1850—1914)

    A. Dictatorship

    B. Dual monarchy

    C. Republic

    D. Democracy

    E. Socialist

The answer is B.
Austria-Hungary was a constitutional union of the Empire of Austria and the Kingdom of Hungary that existed from 1867 to 1918. It was a dual monarchy from the Compromise of 1867. All other answers are wrong because they are not made up of two different governmental authorities in dominion of one nation.

70. **What was the Compromise of 1867?**
    (Politics and Diplomacy in the Age of Nationalism, 1850—1914)

    A. established Prussia as a nation east of Leipzig

    B. established the dual monarchy of Austria-Hungary.

    C. Napoleon III was forced to empty his troops and be exiled

    D. Serbia and Herzegovina became a nation

    E. Ottoman Empire was unified

The answer is B.
The Compromise re-established partially the sovereignty of the Kingdom of Hungary, separate from, and no longer subject to the Austrian Empire. All other answers are wrong because they deal with the wrong countries.

WESTERN CIVILIZATION II

71. **What inspired Russia to make its "Great Reforms"?**
    (Politics and Diplomacy in the Age of Nationalism, 1850—1914)

    A. Napoleons death

    B. the loss of the Russo-Japanese War

    C. Russian nationalism rebellion

    D. Communism rebellion

    E. the loss of the Crimea War of 1853-1856

The answer is E.
While Russia commanded the largest army in Europe (in numbers), poor roads, antiquated weapons, and low morale prohibited the effective use of that awesome potential power. The defeat proved to the autocracy in charge that Russia had fallen dangerously behind its Western neighbors. A through D all reflect different time periods.

72. **What did the Emancipation Reform of 1861 mean for serfs in Russia?**
    (Politics and Diplomacy in the Age of Nationalism, 1850—1914)

    A. emancipation (abolition of serfdom)

    B. extensive suppression

    C. emigration

    D. increased debt

    E. decreased food

The answer is A.
The reform effectively abolished serfdom throughout the Russian Empire. Therefore B and C are incorrect. The emancipation had nothing to do with D and E.

73. Otto von Bismarck gave himself the title ____ of Germany.
    (Politics and Diplomacy in the Age of Nationalism, 1850—1914)

    A. fuhrer

    B. konig

    C. herr

    D. chancellor

    E. royal highness

The answer is D.
In 1871 he formed the German Empire with himself as Chancellor, while retaining control of Prussia.

74. What ended the balance of power which was created in Vienna?
    (Politics and Diplomacy in the Age of Nationalism, 1850—1914)

    A. British imperialism

    B. French industrialization

    C. Russian industrialization

    D. German unification

    E. French imperialism

The answer is D.
German unification made the new nation the industrial powerhouse of Europe that had enormous military strength. Thus making a uneven balance of power. A and E did not alternate the balance of power (first). B and C did not because every country was going through an industrial revolution.

WESTERN CIVILIZATION II

75. What war weakened France's industrialization, ended Napoleons III reign, and brought forth a republic?
    (Politics and Diplomacy in the Age of Nationalism, 1850—1914)

    A. Franco-Prussian War

    B. World War I

    C. The Revolution

    D. British-French War

    E. Austria-Prussian War

The answer is A.
Prussian and German victories in eastern France saw the French army decisively defeated; Napoleon III was captured at Sedan on 2 September. A Government of National Defense declared the Third Republic in Paris on 4 September and continued the war. For the next five months the German forces fought and defeated new French armies in northern France. Following the Siege of Paris, the capital fell on 28 January 1871. The German states proclaimed their union as the German Empire under the Prussian king, Wilhelm I, uniting Germany as a nation-state. B is incorrect because it was too late. C is incorrect because it was too early. D and E had nothing to do with it.

76. What country separated in church and state in 1905?

    A. Great Britain

    B. France

    C. Germany

    D. Austria

    E. Denmark

The answer is B.
The 1905 French law on the Separation of the Churches and State was passed by the Chamber of Deputies. It established state secularism in France. All other options did so much later.

WESTERN CIVILIZATION II

77. In Karl Marx's book, *Capital,* he states, "they wish to prevent the price of labor-power from falling below its value." Who is "they"?
    (Politics and Diplomacy in the Age of Nationalism, 1850—1914)

    A. government

    B. citizens

    C. unions

    D. enterprises

    E. administrators

The answer is C.
Trade Unions are traced back to the 18th century but became extremely popular in the late 19th century (one cause is because the rise in socialism). Obviously A (sometimes), D (always), and, E (always) want labor prices to fall so that firms make more revenue. A and B are ambiguous, therefore incorrect.

78. What was the first country to legalize labor Unions in 1824?
    (Politics and Diplomacy in the Age of Nationalism, 1850—1914)

    A. France

    B. England

    C. Germany

    D. Belgium

    E. Russia

The answer is B.
Labor unions were widespread in the United Kingdom in the 18th century but harsh laws prohibited them. Combination of Workmen Act 1824 legalized unions. However I 1825 they were outlawed. It was not until the Trade Union Act of 1871 when unions were legalized again.

WESTERN CIVILIZATION II

79. **What is a social and economic system characterized by social ownership and/or social control of the means of production and co-operative management of the economy?**
    (Politics and Diplomacy in the Age of Nationalism, 1850—1914)

    A. Socialism

    B. Communism

    C. Anarchism

    D. Sysco-Anarchism

    E. Democratic

The answer is A.
Socialism is a theory or system of social organization that advocates the vesting of the ownership and control of the means of production and distribution, of capital, land, etc., in the community as a whole. C and d refer to no government and E refers to a republic where government is not so big. B could fit into the answer, however, it is not based on the public good rather what the government thinks is good.

80. **What was the Paris Commune of 1871?**
    (Politics and Diplomacy in the Age of Nationalism, 1850—1914)

    A. a decree that removed all socialists from Paris and moved them to a nearby commune (St. Felix)

    B. the fist socialist party in France

    C. a radical socialistic group that governed Paris for two months after the Franco-Prussian war.

    D. a radical communist group that governed Paris after the Franco-Prussian war

    E. a radical democratic group that governed Paris after the Franco-Prussian war

The answer is C.
The Paris commune ruled Paris for three month in 1871. They created laws mainly for the working class, such as no work for bakeries on Sunday.

WESTERN CIVILIZATION II

81. **Why did most European powers let the Ottoman Empire, no matter how weak, in keep dominion over the Balkan Peninsula in the late 19th century?**
    (Politics and Diplomacy in the Age of Nationalism, 1850—1914)

    A. It was an economic death trap

    B. To keep with the Ottoman-European compact

    C. The land was desolate

    D. to keep the balance of power

    E. They didn't let the Ottoman Empire keep the Balkans.

The answer is D.
If one country invaded this area it would offset the balance of power, this creating conflict, i.e. war. All other answer are not factual.

82. **What did the Three Emperors League consist of?**
    (Politics and Diplomacy in the Age of Nationalism, 1850—1914)

    A. Russia, China, North Korea

    B. Germany, Russia, Austria-Hungary

    C. Germany, France, Britain

    D. Austria-Hungary, Italy, Russia

    E. Germany, Russia, Italy

The answer is B.
An alliance drafted by Otto Bismarck from 1873 to 1887. Germany was afraid that France, Austria, and Russia my make an alliance and destroy Germany as a unified nation. So Bismarck acted first. A and C are incorrect because it refers to today. D and E are incorrect because they refer to WWI and II.

WESTERN CIVILIZATION II

83. **Which is the best definition of Imperialism?**
    (Economy, Culture, and Imperialism, 1850-1914)

    A. the term referring only to British dominion in the 18th and 19th century

    B. a feeling that people have of being loyal to and proud of their country often with the belief that it is better and more important than other countries

    C. when one monarchy takes over another monarchy

    D. when one republic takes over another republic

    E. the takeover of a country or territory by a stronger nation with the intent of dominating the economic, political and social life of the people of that nation

The answer is E.
Imperialism is the policy of extending the rule or authority of an empire or nation over foreign countries, or of acquiring and holding colonies and dependencies. A, C, D is incorrect because it is an absolute, one dimensional, and incomplete. B is the definition for nationalism.

84. **Between 1700 and 1900, Europe's population increased from about**
    (Economy, Culture, and Imperialism, 1850-1914)

    A. 10,000-40,000

    B. 100,000-400,000

    C. 1 million-4 million

    D. 10 million- 40 million

    E. 100 million- 400 million

The answer is E.
Industrial Revolution and Agricultural Revolution caused huge growth spurts in population.

WESTERN CIVILIZATION II

85. **What is a world economy?**
    (Economy, Culture, and Imperialism, 1850-1914)

    A. The amount of global suppression on trade in goods, services, and money worldwide

    B. the amount of global revenue

    C. the description of the integration of trade in goods, services, and money worldwide

    D. European interaction with money

    E. none of the above

The answer is C.
Global economy is the international spread of capitalism across national boundaries and with minimal restrictions by governments. A, B, D are all incomplete.

86. **A group of people who leave their native country to form in a new land a settlement subject to, or connected with, the parent nation is a**
    (Economy, Culture, and Imperialism, 1850-1914)

    A. colony

    B. republic

    C. military settlement

    D. fort

    E. refugee zone

The answer is A.
A colony is a group of people who leave their native country to form in a new land a settlement subject to, or connected with, the parent nation. B is a form of government. C and D refer to the military. E is an area for refugees.

87. **What invention allowed Europeans to travel into the interior of Africa in the early 1800's?**
    (Economy, Culture, and Imperialism, 1850-1914)

    A. muskets

    B. leather based shoes

    C. English saddles

    D. steam boat

    E. machetes

The answer is D.
The era of steamboats came in 1787. Prior to that sail boats were used which were not as consistent and fast. All other answers were made before the steam boat.

88. **From the British victory at the Battle of Plassey who became the leading power in India until 1858?**
    (Economy, Culture, and Imperialism, 1850-1914)

    A. East India Trading Company

    B. The Virginia Company

    C. West India Trading company

    D. Royal Tees

    E. Great Britain Monarch

The answer is A.
Answer (A) was a British joint stock company. At one point the company accounted for one half of world trading. Due to the Indian Rebellion of 1857 The British crown took direct control creating the Government of India Act 1858. All other answers are nonfactual.

89. **80 percent of Europeans, including agricultural works, urban laborers, and skilled artisans, belonged to what class from 1850-1914?**
    (Economy, Culture, and Imperialism, 1850-1914)

    A. group

    B. the middle class

    C. mass assembly

    D. mass society

    E. civilization

The answer is D.
Mass society is any society of the modern era that possesses a mass culture and large-scale, impersonal, social institutions. Therefore all other answers are not correct.

90. **Why were departments stores created?**
    (Economy, Culture, and Imperialism, 1850-1914)

    A. mass leisure

    B. socialism

    C. communism

    D. tyranny

    E. mass education

The answer is A.
Mass leisure is the idea that people can pursue leisure in the middle classes, as opposed to the past, where only the rich and noble could afford entertainment. Mass leisure arose during the time of the Industrial Revolution, which spanned from the 18th to 20th centuries. Therefore all other answers are incorrect.

WESTERN CIVILIZATION II

91. What was the Movement in art and literature called in the mid to late 19th century that rejected the subjective, emotional, exotic characteristics of Romanticism. Instead, artists and writers concentrated on observable, contemporary reality?
(Economy, Culture, and Imperialism, 1850-1914)

   A. Barbizon School

   B. Cubism

   C. Expressionism

   D. Realism

   E. Pop Art

The answer is D.
Barbizon school was from the 1830 through 1870s. Cubism depicts the subject from a multitude of viewpoints to represent the subject in a greater context. Expressionism sought to express meaning or emotional experience rather than physical reality. Pop art revolves around late twentieth pop culture. All of which are wrong. Realism represent subject matter truthfully, without artificiality and avoiding artistic conventions, implausible, exotic and supernatural elements.

92. What is the belief that philosophical thinking begins with the human subject—not merely the thinking subject, but the acting, feeling, living human individual?
(Economy, Culture, and Imperialism, 1850-1914)

   A. Marxism

   B. Phenomenology

   C. Existentialism

   D. Objectivism

   E. German Idealism

The answer is C.
Existentialism is a term applied to the work of certain late 19th- and 20th-century European philosophers who shared the belief that philosophical thinking begins with the human subject— not merely the thinking subject, but the acting, feeling, living human individual. A, B, and E are incorrect because they are not related. D is incorrect because t is the opposite.

93. **What were sepoys?**
    (Economy, Culture, and Imperialism, 1850-1914)

    A. Indian militants

    B. snakes

    C. African militants

    D. African spheres made from bamboo and rock

    E. English boys raised in India

The answer is A.
Sepoys were Indian soldiers. After the rebellion of 1857 the title represented a rank below the rank of lance-naik, except in cavalry where the equivalent ranks were sowar. All other answers are false.

94. **Who fought is the Boer War?**
    (Economy, Culture, and Imperialism, 1850-1914)

    A. France and Italy

    B. Germany and Austria-Hungary

    C. Germany and Britain

    D. Britain and Boers

    E. Germany and Boers

The answer is D.
The First Boer War was fought from December 16, 1880 until March 23, 1881 and was the first clash between the British and the Boers (Dutch colonists).

WESTERN CIVILIZATION II

95. **By 1914 only what two African nations remained free from European control?**
    (Economy, Culture, and Imperialism, 1850-1914)

    A. West Africa and Egypt

    B. Libya and Egypt

    C. Congo and Angola

    D. Libya and Ethiopia

    E. There were no countries that were not controlled by European powers

The answer is D.
European colonization encompassed mostly all of Africa. Only Libya and Ethiopia remained. Italy tried to colonize Ethiopia but the Ethiopians fought back and defeated them twice (the second time Great Britain allied with Ethopia), the last time at the Battle of Adwa. Therefore A, B, C, and E are all incorrect.

96. **What was the initial cause of World War I?**
    (The First World War and the Russian Revolution)

    A. the German invasion of Belgium

    B. the assassination of Archduke Franz Ferdinand

    C. the German invasion of Poland

    D. Germany declaration of war on Russia

    E. the assassination of King Alexander I Obrenović

The answer is B.
Though the cause of war was really from prior years of animosity, the initial reason was because Austria-Hungary competed with Serbia and Russia for territory and influence in the region and they pulled the rest of the Great Powers into the conflict through their various alliances and treaties. The assignation of Franz Ferdinand only sparked the flame.

WESTERN CIVILIZATION II

97. **What nations did the Triple Entente consist of?**
    (The First World War and the Russian Revolution)

    A. Italy, Austria-Hungary, and Germany

    B. Russia, Italy, and Germany

    C. Russia, France, and Britain

    D. United States, France, and Britain

    E. Italy, Germany, and Ottoman Empire

The answer is C.
Italy, Germany, Austria Hungary, and Ottoman Empire were all part of the triple alliance. Therefore, A, B, and E are all wrong. The United States came in later, thus D is wrong.

98. **What was not a reason for World War I?**
    (The First World War and the Russian Revolution)

    A. nationalism across Europe

    B. racism towards Jews

    C. unresolved territory disputes

    D. intricate system of alliances

    E. breakdown of balance of power

The answer is B.
Racism towards Jews was not a factor. A, c, D, and E all influenced why WWI began, therefore incorrect.

WESTERN CIVILIZATION II

99. **What treaty ended the war between Germany and allied powers and required Germany to make significant territorial concessions. These were primarily along its eastern and western borders?**
    (The First World War and the Russian Revolution)

    A. Treaty of Versailles

    B. Treaties of the Weimar Republic

    C. Arms Trade Treaty

    D. Treaties of the German Empire

    E. Treaty of Paris

    The answer is A.
    Treaty of Versailles ended the state of war between Germany and the Allied Powers. It was signed on 28 June 1919. B, C, and D are not factual. Treaty of Paris was another time period.

100. **What western power country's economy was better after World War I had ended?**
     (The First World War and the Russian Revolution)

     A. Britain

     B. Ottoman Empire

     C. Russia

     D. France

     E. United States

     The answer is E.
     All nations that were involved in the war, especially earlier on, produced debt trying to keep up with the war. The United States sold many goods to other militaries at the beginning of the war. They raised inflation to make revenue. Furthermore, their placement in the war allowed for less causalities as well as none of the fighting was done on American soil, therefore, industrialization never came to a halt as in other nations.

WESTERN CIVILIZATION II

101. Women in World War I:
(The First World War and the Russian Revolution)

    A. drafted into the civilian work force to replace conscripted men or work in greatly expanded munitions factories.

    B. forced to look after their children

    C. saw combat in every country but Russia

    D. took on political offices

    E. none of the above

The answer is A.
Unlike any other war, women had to fill the roles of men in the workplace because of a lack of workers. It was the highest any large amount of women had been paid in the history of modern western civilization. They were paid two to three times more than their usual amounts. B and E are then false. Women did see combat in Russia and basically only in Russia. C is incorrect. D is also incorrect.

102. What country was created at the end of WWI?
(The First World War and the Russian Revolution)

    A. Bosnia

    B. Serbia

    C. Finland

    D. France

    E. Russian Empire

The answer is C.
France was already a country. Russian Empire fell. Serbia and Bosnia did not become countries until after WWII. After fall of Russian Empire, Finland demanded independence because it differed with the communist regime. It gained independence on December 6, 1917 (it wasn't recognized by the Soviets until December 22, 1917).

103. **What country disappeared after WWI?**
    (The First World War and the Russian Revolution)

    A. Ottoman Empire

    B. Great Britain

    C. United States

    D. Italy

    E. Romania

The answer is A.
Greatly weakened by WWI, the Ottoman Empire was taken over by the Turkish national party after Turkish War of indpendence in 1922.

104. **What was the first international organization whose principal mission was to maintain world peace?**
    (The First World War and the Russian Revolution)

    A. European Union

    B. United Nations

    C. Great Powers

    D. League of Nations

    E. The League of Allies

The answer is D.
A and B came later. C and D are nonfactual. League of Nations was formed on January 10, 1920 after WWI to prevent another war.

WESTERN CIVILIZATION II

105. What dismantled the Tsarist autocracy in Russia?
(The First World War and the Russian Revolution)

    A. The Hessich Revolt

    B. World War II

    C. The February Revolution

    D. The Russian Civil War

    E. World War I

The answer is C.
The February Revolution was the first of two Russian Revolutions. It ended the Tsarist government and replaced it with the momentary Russian Provisional Government (dual liberal and socialist government). A is nonfactual. B, D, and E all are incorrect because they come after the Russian monarch was dismantled.

106. What was the name of the radical wing of the Russian Social Democratic Labor party, favoring revolutionary tactics to achieve full socialization and, under the leadership of Ulyanov (Lenin)?
(The First World War and the Russian Revolution)

    A. Revolutionists

    B. Republicans

    C. Bolsheviks

    D. Righties

    E. Stalinist

The answer is C.
Bolsheviks were a faction of the Marxist Russian Social Democratic Labor Party. A is to vague. B and D were not socialists. Stalinists were more Trotskyists than Bolsheviks.

WESTERN CIVILIZATION II

107. What dismantled the interim dual government and established the Soviet Union?
(The First World War and the Russian Revolution)

    A. World War II

    B. The February Revolution

    C. The Bolshevik Revolution

    D. World War I

    E. The Hessich Revolt

The answer is C.
Bolshevik Revolution was the second phase of the Russian Revolution. Bolsheviks seized of state power instrumental in the larger Russian Revolution of 1917.

108. Why was the generation after World War I labeled "the lost generation?"
(Europe between the Wars, the Great Depression)

    A. because of the amount of intellectual elites that became causalities during the war.

    B. because people gave up organized religion

    C. because the amount of rebellions

    D. because industrialization had been destroyed

    E. many felt the world was forever "lost"

The answer is A.
Starting in Europe (Britain) it referred to the upper class of intellectuals lost during the war. Therefore, B through e is nonfactual.

WESTERN CIVILIZATION II

109. **What was the difference between the League of Nations and the Westphalian System?**
(Europe between the Wars, the Great Depression)

A. the Westphalian System sought to give support to only Asian countries

B. the League of Nations only allowed elite countries

C. the Westphalian succeeded in keeping Europe in peace for one century

D. the secretive nature of the Westphalian System which had led to petty resentments

E. the League of Nations disabled all the armies in Europe

The answer is D.
The Westphalia System was a secretive order that only allowed aristocrats in European nations. It was created to keep the peace after the Thirty Years War. Therefore, B and C are inaccurate. A and E are also inaccurate.

110. **What nation refused to join the League of Nations?**
(Europe between the Wars, the Great Depression)

A. Italy

B. Britain

C. France

D. Belgium

E. The United States

The answer is E.
The United States did not join because it was afraid of being entangled in another war.

WESTERN CIVILIZATION II

111. **What event initiated the Great Depression?**
    (Europe between the Wars, the Great Depression)

    A. the end of World War I

    B. stock market crash of October 29, 1929

    C. gold standard was lowered

    D. the Riots of 1929

    E. President Hoover coming to office

The answer is B.
On October 24, 1929 the Stock Market crashed. There numerous reasons and theories why it did so (such as lack of agrarian economy, unstable oversees stocks, etc.). A and C was well before the crash, therefore incorrect. D happened afterwards. E is vague (President Hoover could not prevent the inevitable).

112. **What was Stalin's initial five-year plan created to serve?**
    (Europe between the Wars, the Great Depression)

    A. to increase in military mobilization

    B. to increase birth rates in Russia

    C. industrialization of Russia

    D. expanding Russian lands

    E. building up damaged monuments. palaces, and other historical sites

The answer is C.
The first of thirteen, the idea was to get the nation to produce mass amounts of what the country was in need of. Soviets based it on the theory of productive forces. A, B, D, E are all incorrect. Although the Soviets did try some of these, they were not in the "five year plans".

WESTERN CIVILIZATION II

113. **What was the name of the country that replaced the old German Republic?**
    (Europe between the Wars, the Great Depression)

    A. The Weimar Republic

    B. Germany

    C. Nazi Germany

    D. West Germany

    E. Unified Germany

The answer is A.
The Weimer Republic immerged after the German Revolution and WWI. The country itself lasted for 14 year. B through E all came later.

114. **What was one cause of the rise of nationalistic governmental rises in Italy and Germany?**
    (Europe between the Wars, the Great Depression)

    A. imperialism

    B. inherent hatred

    C. bad deal after Treaty of Versailles

    D. animosity towards all Europeans

    E. none of the above

The answer is C.
The Treaty of Versailles left nations like Germany and Italy in extreme debt. Hyper-inflation and political upheaval only heightened the tension in Italy and Germany. These nations had to0 much debt to be imperial, therefore, A is false. These individuals that practiced nationalism were not naturally more hateful then the next person. Their circumstances were different. A and D are then incorrect.

WESTERN CIVILIZATION II

115. **What was the immediate cause of World War II?**
    (The Second World War and Contemporary Europe)

    A. Killing of the Jews

    B. Invasion of the Danzig by the Germans

    C. Invasion of Switzerland by the Germans

    D. Invasion of Poland by the Germans

    E. Russian invasion if Baltic Nations.

The answer is D.
Beside the problems that came with the Treaty of Versailles, the invasion of Poland was the initial cause of WWII. Poland was allied with Britain and France. Germany with Russia. The invasion set off a number of events. A was not found out until later, so incorrect. B, C, and E all happened before the invasion of Poland.

116. **What immediate event caused the United States to enter World War II?**
    (The Second World War and Contemporary Europe)

    A. The Attack on Pearl Harbor

    B. German invasion of France

    C. The sinking of SS Athenia

    D. The breaking of the Treaty of Versailles

    E. American nationalism provoked congress to go forward on behalf of the killing of the Jews

The answer is A.
B, C, D, and E all are incorrect. Although all these events happened they did not get enough reaction from the United States as the bombing of Pearl Harbor.

WESTERN CIVILIZATION II

117. What did the United Nations agree on to prevent a third World War?
(The Second World War and Contemporary Europe)

    A. outlaw on wars of aggression

    B. outlaw German access to military

    C. outlaw radical communism, fascism, and socialism

    D. outlaw nuclear armament

    E. outlaw Germany industrialization

The answer is A.
War aggression is a military conflict waged without the justification of self-defense, usually for territorial gain and subjugation. This was one of the first thing the UN outlawed. B through E are all nonfactual.

118. After what war was 70% of all industrial infrastructure destroyed?
(The Second World War and Contemporary Europe)

    A. World War I

    B. World War II

    C. Revolutionary War

    D. Napoleonic Wars

    E. The Austrian Succession

The answer is B.
Although all four of the other answers had large amounts of death and damage, none saw as much dame as WWII on infrastructure due to the use of advances military technology.

119. **What art movement was both a reaction against Abstract Expressionism, which was seen as too elitist and non-objective, as well as a celebration of postwar consumer culture?**
(The Second World War and Contemporary Europe)

   A. Expressionism

   B. Cubism

   C. Romanticism

   D. Pop Art

   E. Minimalism

The answer is D.
Pop Art celebrated pop culture in the late twentieth century. Expressionism expressed emotional feeling, Cubism takes an object and reassemble it in an abstract form. Romanticism conveys a quixotic outlook. Minimalism portrays the art as it is with primal design elements. All of which fail to meet the definition.

120. **During the Cold War Era the United States and the Soviet Union did not become involved in direct military conflict mainly because of**
(The Second World War and Contemporary Europe)

   A. economic failures

   B. the Soviets military was too small to make a direct attack

   C. fear of nuclear war

   D. there was no conflicts

   E. they were forced allies

The answer is C.
Both nations became super powers prior World War Two. They never fought each other outright for fear of total war; thus, leaving global catastrophic issues. A is incorrect because both countries were economic giants and competed all the way up to the Soviet collapse in 1991. B is incorrect because Soviet military was very large. D and E are both wrong because there were several conflicts between the two nations.

XAMonline
The CLEP Specialist
Individual Sample Tests in ebook format with full explanations

eBooks

All 33 CLEP sample tests are available as ebook downloads from retail websites such as **Amazon.com** and **Barnesandnoble.com**

American Government	9781607875130
American Literature	9781607875079
Analyzing and Interpreting Literature	9781607875086
Biology	9781607875222
Calculus	9781607875376
Chemistry	9781607875239
College Algebra	9781607875215
College Composition	9781607875109
College Composition Modular	9781607875437
College Mathematics	9781607875246
English Literature	9781607875093
Financial Accounting	9781607875383
French	9781607875123
German	9781607875369
History of the United States I	9781607875178
History of the United States II	9781607875185
Human Growth and Development	9781607875444
Humanities	9781607875147
Information Systems	9781607875390
Introduction to Educational Psychology	9781607875451
Introductory Business Law	9781607875420
Introductory Psychology	9781607875154
Introductory Sociology	9781607875352
Natural Sciences	9781607875253
Precalculus	9781607875345
Principles of Macroeconomics	9781607875406
Principles of Microeconomics	9781607875468
Principles of Marketing	9781607875475
Principles of Management	9781607875468
Social Sciences and History	9781607875161
Spanish	9781607875116
Western Civilization I	9781607875192
Western Civilization II	9781607875208

TO ORDER XAMonline.com or amazon or BARNES & NOBLE BOOKSELLERS

XAMonline
CLEP
Full Study Guides

CLEP College Algebra
ISBN: 9781607875598
Price: $34.95

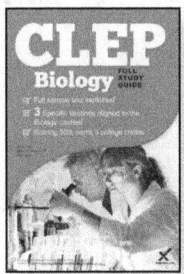
CLEP Biology
ISBN: 9781607875314
Price: $34.95

CLEP Analyzing and Interpreting Literature
ISBN: 9781607875260
Price: $34.95

CLEP College Composition and Modular
ISBN: 9781607875277
Price: $19.99

CLEP College Mathematics
ISBN: 9781607875321
Price: $34.95

CLEP Psychology
ISBN: 9781607875291
Price: $34.95

CLEP Spanish
ISBN: 9781607875284
Price: $34.95

 TO ORDER    XAMonline.com   or    amazon   or    BARNES & NOBLE BOOKSELLERS

XAMonline
CLEP Subject Series
Collection by Topic
Sample Test Approach

CLEP Literature
ISBN: 9781607875833
Price: $34.95

CLEP Foreign Language
ISBN: 9781607875772
Price: $34.95

CLEP History
ISBN: 9781607875789
Price: $34.95

CLEP Sociology
ISBN: 9781607875796
Price: $34.95

CLEP Science
ISBN: 9781607875802
Price: $34.95

CLEP Mathematics
ISBN: 9781607875819
Price: $34.95

CLEP Business
ISBN: 9781607875826
Price: $34.95

TO ORDER XAMonline.com or amazon or BARNES & NOBLE BOOKSELLERS

XAMonline

CLEP Favorites

Collection by Topic
Sample Test Approach

CLEP Five Favorites
ISBN: 9781607875765
Price: $24.95

CLEP Military Favorites
ISBN: 9781607875512
Price: $24.95

TO ORDER → XAMonline.com or amazon or BARNES & NOBLE BOOKSELLERS

www.ingramcontent.com/pod-product-compliance
Lightning Source LLC
Chambersburg PA
CBHW080722230426
43665CB00020B/2583